Vessel of Peace

The Voyage Towards Spiritual Freedom

By Doug Shadel and Ellen Stephen

Ellen Stephen

Foreword by M. Scott Peck, M. D.
Author of *The Road Less Traveled*

Three Tree
Press

Seattle, Washington
2000

Copyright © 1999 by Doug Shadel and Ellen Stephen. All rights reserved. No part of this book may be reproduced in any form without the express written consent of the publisher, except by a reviewer, who may quote brief passages in connection with a review.

ISBN: 0-9703020-0-2

First Edition August, 2000
10 9 8 7 6 5 4 3 2 1
Printed in the United States of America

All Biblical quotations are from the New Revised Standard Version (NRSV) unless otherwise specified.

Contributing Editor - Ann Prentice, O.S.H.
Cover Photo of Two Medicine Lake, Montana
Will Brewster, Brewster Photography (406) 587-5619
Cover Design by W. Kas Kaseguma
Kas Design (206) 633-3539

Much of the wisdom in this book was given to us
by generous human spirits, some by Holy Spirit.
Now it is yours.

Ad Majorem Dei Gloriam

Vessel of Peace
The Voyage Towards Spiritual Freedom

By Doug Shadel and Ellen Stephen

Foreword

There is but one Secret, and its name is God.

A few years ago I attempted to sum up my work in *The Road Less Traveled and Beyond*. It was a most prosaic attempt, save for the final chapter, entitled "The Poetry of God." Following a chapter on "The Science of God," it seemed to me appropriate to end with a format that did greater emotional justice to the subject. So I concluded the book with a twenty page love poem to God. The last words of the poem were:

> In the meantime
> Thank you for letting me know
> That it is you
> Who are the name of the game.

There are a million translations for the name of God. Some thousands of them are subsumed under the statement: "You are a part of God." The proclamation is often subject to mistranslation. In this book, however, it is spoken truthfully in the concept that we are "co-creators" with God.

We cannot create ourselves any more than we can create an iris or a simple rose petal. We are creatures—meaning that God is our original and ongoing creator. What we can do, however, is to cooperate with God in the process of our ongoing creation. Sometimes in our youth this cooperation is unconscious. But for its fullest extent, it is required that we become conscious: conscious of God; conscious of our personal relationship with Him or Her; conscious of our souls; conscious of how we may interfere with God's deepest desire for our unique destinies. Such consciousness comes only with adulthood.

If it comes at all. Most largely ignore God. Many others run away from Him. This is understandable. As the author of the Epistle to the Hebrews said, "It is a fearful thing to fall into the hands of the living God."

Still, it must be done if we are to become whole. We must become prayerful creatures to be fully effective co-creators. Indeed, we must have a burning thirst for glory. Yet at the very same time we must empty ourselves of any notion that glory is ours to achieve. All glory belongs to God; as co-creators the most we can hope for is to participate in it.

But that's the name of the game. In this wise book, Doug Shadel and Ellen Stephen have a great deal to teach us about how to play that game.

M. Scott Peck, M.D.

Introduction
The Vessel Metaphor

"The point of the spiritual journey is freedom."

This was the very first bit of wisdom I received five years ago from Ellen Stephen, an Anglican nun who prefers to be known as "ES." It was an appropriate opening to what has become a long, fruitful learning relationship between a teacher and a student that ultimately has culminated in the writing of this book. ES and I met in 1993 at what is known as a "community building workshop." She was and still is a facilitator for the Foundation for Community Encouragement which sponsors workshops that give people the opportunity to empty themselves of that which is getting in the way of finding their true purpose, and to explore their relationships with others and with God.

I had never been to anything like a community building workshop before and it basically blew me away. It blew me away so much that I co-authored a whole book about the effects it can have on the individual, particularly from the standpoint of gaining more meaningful relationships with others (*The Power of Acceptance*, with Bill Thatcher.)

In addition, ES became a kind of spiritual mentor for me. She was living in Seattle at the time in a branch house of the Order of St. Helena. We met periodically for spiritual direction and after a couple of years, she moved back to the Order's convent in New York. In 1995, I had an opportunity to travel to the east coast and ES, who is now on the Leadership Council of the Order, graciously offered me the opportunity to spend a week at the convent. I took her up on it.

This beautiful 50 acre site is noted not only for its tranquillity and majestic oak trees overlooking the mighty Hudson River, but it also has one of the most comprehensive private libraries of books about spirituality I had ever come across. For nearly a week, I resided in a small hermitage on the grounds of the convent, taking time out only to eat and pray with the sisters who worship many times per day: morning Matins, Diurnum at noon, Vespers at 5 p.m. and evening Compline. The rest of the time I was checking out some of the 12,000 books that embrace all the religious traditions in order to start to try to make sense of my own growing sense of the transcendent. I did not realize it fully then, but I was in the midst of a spiritual conversion or awakening that had been emerging ever since I had been told eight years before by my parents that I was adopted at birth.

I knew I wanted to write about this growing sense of God within me, but I had no clue where to look. Mine had been a strictly secular upbringing in which religion was viewed as something for the weak, for those who somehow couldn't make it in the real world.

My openness to talking about spirituality with ES was due to the fact that she too had not been baptized until she was about twenty-eight, and up until that time had had similar qualms about this thing called "religion." My conversations with ES seemed unthreatening even though I knew she was an Anglican nun. She had a way of conversing with me that made it okay to not be sure about my belief. And furthermore, she was so well-acquainted with literature that I respected her intellect, something that socialization had taught me to disrespect in the religious, those "needy people who believed in some invisible God."

I was someone who had a million questions and ES had "an" answer for all of them. She would preface her remarks with things like "Here is *an* answer, not necessarily *the* answer," and she would always encourage me to keep thinking about things and "hold the mystery." This approach gave me the choice whether to accept or not accept her response. She would also say things like "well, if there isn't a God, then I don't know. But if there is a God... "

At the convent, I decided to do a mini-literature review of all the religious traditions to see what they had in common. In community building circles, there had been a lot of talk about this concept of "emptiness" and I still wasn't clear about that. I was at the beginning of my explorations, so I checked out books on Buddhism, Hinduism, Shamanism, Christianity, Quakerism, etc. You name the religious tradition, the convent had a book on it. I would later come to appreciate the fact that Anglicans were often characterized as being intellectuals who explored all viewpoints and were willing to live in ambiguity, to lean into and even embrace the mystery of the divine rather than oversimplifying it in order to package it more neatly for congregants. Perhaps they saw the difficulty of finite minds seeking to grasp that which is infinite.

I left the convent that cold December in 1995 with about 100 pages of a rough literature review on what the major religious traditions have as common themes. While this was no brilliant work of scholarship and I knew that many hundreds of religious scholars had written major works on the same topic, it nevertheless struck me that there were four major themes which kept reappearing in all the traditions:

*Love:	The idea of forgiveness and compassion;
*Emptiness:	The idea of emptiness or non-attachment;
*Spirit Within:	The idea of a divine spirit within;
*Connectednesss:	The idea that lying beneath the field of duality is a unity or oneness of all beings.

These four themes are important to keep firmly in mind as you read *Vessel of Peace*. For in one way or another, you will see them emerge and reemerge as we embark on our discussion of the basic question: "How should I live my life?"

This is the question, with numerous sub-components and permutations, with which I initially came to ES some five years ago. I was moved to ask her if she would consider writing this book with me because she was so instrumental in my transition from a non-religious person who was extremely ambitious in the secular world but also very unhappy, to a fairly serious believer who has found a peaceful way to live. It occurred to me that her insights and spiritual genius was the door in for me and it could be for others.

Another theme that runs through this book draws from what we know in the literature and from our intuition about the mechanics of these things we call human beings. How does one leave the stress and strain of our materialistic world and return to the simpler, more fundamental origins from which we came? Paul Tillich makes a distinction between the "essential" and the "existential" self. Our essential self is born into this world of divine spirit connected to all creation. In our essential state, we were free from the need to please others, from self-doubt and self-blame and were free to be ourselves without qualification or reservation. Over time, says Tillich, our "existential self" takes over—filled with attachments and worry and noise. The existential or social self builds up layer upon layer of defenses and social masks as a means of surviving, but is quite distanced from the simpler and more peaceful origins from whence we came. These layers of defense become a barrier to spiritual growth.

The "vessel of peace" is a metaphor for how to make the journey from the existential back to the essential self. Or as one person we interviewed for this book said, "I spent the first half of my life learning what to do and I am spending the second half of my life unlearning it all."

Part of the inspiration for the use of the vessel metaphor came from M. Scott Peck in a letter he wrote to *Theology Today* in 1985. He was responding to some criticism about a section in his best-selling book *The Road Less Traveled* which said, "We are growing towards Godhood. God is the goal of evolution." Several theologians took exception to this, believing that it would encourage narcissism if not idolatry. He responded by saying:

> Were I to rewrite *The Road Less Traveled*, I would add something like "we cannot ourselves become God except by bumping ourselves off." The process is one that real theologians refer to as "kenosis"— the process of self-emptying. The goal is imaged as that of the empty vessel, in which there is still enough ego left to comprise the walls of the vessel, but which is otherwise sufficiently empty to be able to become spirit-filled.

Thus, the goal is to empty oneself of cultural baggage in order to become spirit- or peace-filled. We outline three primary sources of psychological "fullness" that are the ground out of which our stress and restlessness grows: beliefs from our family systems, beliefs from our peer groups (friends and acquaintances) and beliefs from our culture and the culture's messenger, the media.

The point of discussing these sources of stress is to surface them and their origins into awareness. This can help one realize that the beliefs that we embody and which in many cases drive our behavior can be selected and deselected, but only if we are *aware* of them. It will also be pointed out that beliefs we hold about the world are not necessarily the same as fundamental truths or natural principles which are at work whether we realize it or not. If we had to summarize the central message of this book, it would be as follows:

People are stressed out and most have no idea why. The roots of this stress can be found in excessive attachment to beliefs which are out of alignment with natural laws and spiritual truths. Learning to identify and empty oneself of such attachments and align oneself with truth can relieve stress and help one live a more peaceful and fulfilling life.

This is a book about the myths that human beings can carry around that stress us out and get in the way of spiritual growth. For example, I realize that most, if not all, of the stress I experience has to do with attachments to beliefs that I hold closely. I am attached to money and so paying bills at the end of the month is stressful; I am attached to the opinions others have of me and so I get stressed out by social functions where I feel people are judging me; I am attached to the belief of individualism and so it is stressful for me to work in teams; I am attached to the belief that I need to appear to have it all together and be happy even though I clearly don't have it all together and there are many days when I am profoundly unhappy and in pain. We hope to get you thinking about which of these cultural attachments impact you in your life.

We will also be describing some very basic spiritual principles which sages from across all religious traditions have agreed are essential and timeless truths. Most of these truths are whispered in books or in monastic communities or in an occasional Sunday church sermon. You will be getting these insights from someone I consider to a spiritual master, someone who has devoted her entire life to pursuing the truth, someone who had to be dragged into writing about such truths in such a public way. The insights that come from ES contained in this book have never been published before and if they impact you the way they did me, it will be like finding a bright red ruby under a pile of rocks.

Some of the questions we address are: How does one practice detachment and emptiness in a world so dedicated to materialism and fullness? And what happens if I do empty myself of stressful beliefs? What then? Do I just walk around as an empty shell seeking to connect with an invisible, transcendent God? And whose definition of God do I use? My own? My church's? My parents'? The televangelist's? These are not easy questions and not all of our answers are easy to digest. But they are our best, most authentic attempt to see the greater context in which we live our lives, a context often hidden by the roar of culture. We seek to provide some rationale for reconnecting with truth in an age of myth and lie.

The idea of reconnecting is at the root of most religions. In fact, the word "religion" means to reconnect. The principle barrier to reconnecting with our true selves is the sense of psychological fullness which stresses us out and fills us up. By de-emphasizing (not discarding) our individual selves and our well-developed egos, we begin to reconnect to ourselves as well as to others.

In a study of participants who attended community building workshops that were mentioned earlier, we asked individuals to report their feeling of connectedness to others in their lives before and after the workshop. Since the point of the community building workshop is to empty oneself of that which is getting in the way of connecting both with one's authentic self and with others, it was important to quantify this.

Our research clearly showed that people did experience a significant improvement in their sense of connectedness to others from before to after the workshop (*The Power of Acceptance*, 1997). They also showed dramatic improvement in their sense of connectedness to God. As one participant put it: "When you empty yourself of everything else, worries about relationships, money, the need to be accepted, what is left?"

One could argue that a key message of the Hebrew Scriptures is about the importance of emptiness: in effect, God is saying, "When you were in the desert and had nothing, you believed. Once you arrived into civilization and gained comfort, your faith weakened." Is that what is going in the modern world? Have we become so consumed by our own ability to live independently that we have forgotten about God? Is our current sense of restlessness and stress a manifestation of what has been lost by this preoccupation with consumption and materialism? In the process of running as far and as fast as we can down the road most traveled, have we lost sight of what created us in the first place? And has this distance from creation made us more vulnerable to becoming filled with unhealthy cultural attachments? These are some of the questions we address in *Vessel of Peace*, questions we should all be asking at the beginning of the 21st century.

Practicing emptiness to obtain peace is not about giving up all of one's worldly possessions and sitting under a Bo tree, nor is it about running off to a monastery and praying eight hours a day. Becoming a vessel of peace is, for us, very much about making the world your own monastery and walking through it with a true sense of connection to oneself, to others and to God.

It is a paradox. Philosophers throughout the ages have said that in order to fill up with life, one must die. To experience that which is new, one must remove that which is old. If you want a more peaceful life, you can have it. But you must be intentional about making room for that new life by giving up the things that prevent you from experiencing it.

St. Ireneus said, "The glory of God is a human being fully alive." We hope that by exploring the concept of emptiness and peace in great detail, this book can help you begin to understand how to find peace amidst an ocean of stress and become more fully alive.

> If thou could'st empty all thyself of self,
> Like to a shell dishabited,
> Then might He find thee on the ocean shelf,
> And say, This is not dead,"
> And fill thee with Himself instead.
> But thou art replete with very thou
> And hast such shrewd activity,
> That when He comes He says, "This is enow
> Unto itself—'twere better let it be,
> It is so small and full there is not room for me."
> —Sir Thomas Browne
> (Quoted from *A Wrinkle in Time*,
> Madeline L'Engle)

Preface
On Myth, Beliefs and Attachment

There are several key terms we use throughout this book which we feel need some clarification before moving forward. They are: myth, belief and attachment.

Myth—Of the classical myths it has been said, "History is the vehicle for fact; myth is the vehicle for truth." While classical myths like the Myth of Sisyphus are vehicles for truth, there are many "cultural" myths that are, in effect, vehicles for untruth or lie. It is these "cultural lies" that we address as myths. They are cultural phenomena which are true to the extent they exist and are present in the culture, but false in terms of what they point towards: namely a reality which brings meaning and fulfillment to one's life. In consumer protection terms, we would call these myths a kind of "bait and switch" in which we are led to believe that if we do "A", "B" will follow: if you just follow the myth of perfection, you will find satisfaction; if you buy into the myth that you can control your environment totally, then you will feel fulfilled; if you accumulate enough material possessions, you will be happy, etc.

Belief—Webster defines "belief" as "a state or habit of mind in which trust or confidence is placed in some person or thing." We are using the word to mean the "habits of mind" that get installed into our consciousness by family, peer groups and the culture and, when taken together, comprise the myth discussed. Beliefs are the sort of psychological software which, consciously or unconsciously, drive our thinking and behavior. Some of these beliefs can "fill up" our psyche and cause enormous stress. For example, I might internalize the belief that I can some day write the perfect book and so this belief becomes a component part of the overall cultural myth of perfection described in Chapter One.

Attachment—Another important word we use and want to define is "attachment." Attachment is the psychological glue that connects us to beliefs and myths. The literal definition comes from the French *"attache"* meaning to "nail to." Thus to attach oneself to something is to literally become nailed to it. Attachment is a primary source of stress and anxiety when we become "nailed to" cultural lies.

A central idea in the Zen tradition is to practice watching one's thoughts and then let them go by. The thoughts are driven by beliefs which are part of an overall mythology to which we so often attach ourselves. The process of emptying out is the process of detaching from these myths and beliefs: paying attention to them, observing them, even feeling them, but then letting them go along their way to make room for the next thing.

A key message in *Vessel of Peace* is that to get the most out of life, one must accept things the way they are, experience them fully, but then let them go on their way. We are creatures who tend to either run away from things or attach ourselves to them and consequently get stuck. In many ways, this book is about how to run full steam into life without getting stuck.

Section One

Emptying the Vessel:

Seven Cultural Myths to Leave Behind

1

The Myth of Perfection

Myth: The goal of human life is to continuously improve oneself in an ongoing attempt to become the best in one's field of chosen endeavor and, ultimately, achieve perfection.

Truth: The goal of life is not to become perfect as in flawless. It is to become ripe as in complete in every detail. To this end, we must try to empty ourselves of anything that stands in the way of accepting ourselves *as we are* and becoming aware of what God is calling us to do with our lives.

> **When people start to work with any kind of spiritual discipline, they often think that somehow they're going to improve, which is a sort of subtle aggression against who they really are. It's a bit like saying, "If I jog, I'll be a much better person, if I could meditate and calm down I'd be a better person." The point is not to try to change ourselves. It isn't about trying to throw ourselves away and become something better. It's about befriending who we are already. The ground of practice is you or me or whoever we are right now, just as we are. That's the ground, that's what we study, that's what we come to know with tremendous curiosity and interest.**
>
> **—Pema Chodron, *Entering the Stream***

Imagine for a moment that when you were born, you were like a bowl that was completely empty. No one had yet told you how to have good table manners or how noisy or quiet to be around adults or what kind of jeans were cool and which kind were dorky or that it was impolite to burp in public. In your inner-most being, free from all social inputs at the beginning of life, all behavior was acceptable because it was all a natural and authentic reflection of who you were as a human.

Then one day, you are minding your own business at the dinner table and you spill your milk. All of a sudden the giant humans in the room come practically unglued and start to yell at you for creating such a mess. Your mom might even say something like "Good little girls don't spill their milk." In response to this interaction, you not only stop the action that is unacceptable to others, but you make a record of the transaction in your mind.

We are continually "filled" with notions about how we should or should not be or how perfect or imperfect we are. We are also filled with the agendas of others. The people who provide you with this input have their own beliefs and values which have been formed by their upbringing and consequently they are passing on to you their view of the world: how much money constitutes success; how many kids constitute the perfect-sized family; how much education is enough; what kind of school your kids should go to, on and on. It is the nature of the belief systems of others and how much of those systems we allow into our "vessel" that determines our sense of self. In this chapter, we will discuss the myth that there is such a thing as "perfection" and that human beings are capable of achieving it.

Family Systems and The Myth of Perfection

The family is a primary source of data about how we should live in the world. The most important thing we learn about the myth of perfection from our family is that such a thing exists. Every moment of my life up until about age thirty-five, I believed that the goal of life was to continually improve, to get better, to hone my skills and my personality so that eventually I was at maximum effectiveness in my personal and professional life.

This belief was reinforced at almost every turn. When I was a child and I would come home with a "B" on my report card, Mom would say, "That's good honey, but if you try harder, I'm sure you can get an "A" next time." In high school, when I would score 10 points in the basketball game, my coach would say to me the next day, "That's great, but if you practice harder, I'm sure you can score 20 points per game some day." Once I became an adult and got a job that paid $20,000 per year, my boss would say, "If you work harder and hone your skills, some day you'll make $40,000 to $50,000."

The assumption underlying this kind of thinking is "You are not good enough where you are right now." I have gotten into arguments with people in my church about kids in the youth group to which I minister. It will start by someone saying, "Johnny isn't doing as good a job as he is capable of." My response is, "Of course he is doing as good as he can. If he could do better, he would do better!!" And the other person will say, "No, you don't understand what I mean. I think Johnny has much more potential than he is showing. He can do better." To which I would respond by saying, "He may have the *potential* to do better, but the way he is *right now* is as good as he can do or he would be doing better right now."

People are doing the best they can right now. But from the beginning of one's existence, most family systems encourage the child to "develop skills" or "improve." We are taught how to set goals and are encouraged to find role models and mentors whom we can use as a standard for our own growth and development.

And while there is nothing inherently wrong with wanting to improve or setting goals or relying on family members for input, the struggle is that some families' input is healthier than others. There are many healthy families that accept and support their members, and others that use the myth of perfection as a weapon against each other. And once the perfection myth is installed, the individual can and often does use it against himself, engaging in brutal self-blame and self-judgment.

Alice Miller writes about this phenomenon in *For Your Own Good*, a book which chronicles 200 years of German child-rearing manuals that teach parents to "break the will of the child" as a central strategy for child-rearing. Miller suggests that this technique leads to an ensuing generation of parents so full of self-loathing and devoid of self-confidence that they seek to recoup their sense of self-worth which was taken from them by their parents by breaking the will of *their* children. And so it becomes a vicious cycle. The same cycle can exist with parents who carry the perfection myth into the relationship with their children; they seek fulfillment of their imperfection by projecting impossible-to-achieve perfection standards onto their offspring. Thus we see the 40-year-old, balding, overweight basketball coach who, cut from his own high school team, demands impossible feats of athletic accomplishment from his equally-average 12 year old son on the court.

A lot of this judging and demand for perfection is more about the pathology of the judger than it is a clear objective statement about the person being judged. As Wayne Dyer has said, "When you squeeze an orange, what you always get is orange juice." What comes out of the orange is what is in it. What comes out of a human being is what is in that human being. In the movie *Mother* starring Albert Brooks and Debbie Reynolds, Brooks plays a 40-year-old, newly-divorced science-fiction writer who is going through a midlife crisis. In his search for answers, he decides to move in with his mother to reflect on his life. The more he interacts with her, the more he is reminded of the fact that his mother is highly critical of everything he does, but especially about his being a writer.

As the son moves back into his old room, he discovers one night some old hat boxes in his closet which contain dusty manuscripts. He begins to look through them and finds that they are over forty years old and were written by his mother before he was born. In the end, both he and his mother realize that the reason she was so critical of him and of his writing is that she had started out on her own career as a writer, but had to abandon such dreams once she got pregnant. She spent the ensuing 40 years unconsciously blaming her son for having to give up the one thing she felt truly passionate about. Her blame of him had nothing to do with him and everything to do with her, but because she hid (or was herself unaware of) this underlying motivation, her son grew up thinking he was inherently flawed. As Carl Jung said, "Nothing affects the environment of a child as much as the unlived life of a parent."

This realization about the root cause of her judging him set them both free. The son realized it was her issue that caused her to judge him, not anything he had done and the mother realized a painful reality she had been carrying around unconsciously for decades. Once surfaced, they both were freed from it.

This is an example of the power of awareness, of becoming conscious of the forces at work within our lives. As you will hear throughout this book, awareness carries with it the potential to free us from beliefs that hold us back. For it is only possible to empty damaging beliefs if one is first able to surface them into awareness.

For many of us, such insights do not come quickly or easily and sometimes they never surface at all. As children, we were highly influenced by our role models and many times found it difficult not to internalize such criticism. Once internalized, we begin to believe that we are not good enough and we need to improve.

In my own experience, I find that when I am feeling particularly imperfect, that is, when I compare myself to others and feel like I am nowhere near as good at something, I tend to respond to others with judgment and hostility. I pull others down to build myself up. Conversely, when I am feeling good about myself, usually when I have done something I am proud of, I tend to be more forgiving or accepting of others.

Over the years numerous studies have been conducted of patients in group therapy sessions. Some of the earliest studies were conducted by Carl Rogers and his associates at the Chicago Institute for Mental Health. One of the questions they sought an answer to was this: what kind of a therapeutic environment is most conducive to improving the self-esteem of the patient? Rogers and others hypothesized that the optimal therapeutic environment was one which had three characteristics: unconditional positive regard, empathy and congruence (alignment between feelings and actions).

The idea was that therapy groups with these characteristics allowed people to drop their social masks and begin to see and accept their authentic selves. Rogers found consistently that when exposed to such an environment, a significant number of participants reported dramatic improvement in their self-image. The implication was that by allowing the patient to empty out negative programming like the idea that perfection is achievable, patients began to accept themselves *as they are.*

This suggests that the stimuli which we are exposed to in our normal environment, such as perfection images, cause us to be much harder on ourselves than is justified by reality. Once people experience an environment of unconditional acceptance and authentic sharing, they begin to see that others have problems just like they do but rarely if ever share those problems. In light of such authentic sharing, they realize they are not as bad as they had thought.

Peer Groups and The Myth of Perfection

If family systems plant the perfection myth seed into us as individuals, peer groups often throw fertilizer and water on that seed. We have discussed the idea that the extent to which one carries the perfection myth around is the result of how judgmental or accepting one's family of origin system was to them. Perfection is a subjective concept which is more or less in play depending on the upbringing of the parents. Parents cannot give what they do not have, and if their upbringing was characterized by continuous judgment and scrutiny, they will typically pass that behavior on to the child. The result is often greatly diminished self-esteem for the child.

In peer group settings, the myth of perfection is in full play, especially among teenagers, and often to the detriment of all concerned. Numerous studies have shown that when kids enter first grade, a majority of them have a positive self-image. By the time they are juniors in high school, the statistics are reversed, with a majority of teenagers having a negative self-image. Why?

One reason is the complicated interplay among kids whose family systems have filled them up with harsh judgment and a sense that who they are deep inside isn't good enough. These kids, filled with judgment and anger, are going to go to school and that harsh judgment will spill over onto other kids. Even kids whose parents have themselves come from accepting homes will be vulnerable to such criticism since peer influence is so powerful that even the strongest, most secure child finds it difficult not to be impacted.

Another dynamic in the quest for perfection is competition. I measure my progress towards perfection on a kind of social bell curve in which I am constantly assessing who is ahead of me and who is behind me. Both groups are a threat to my sense of self-acceptance. Only those who are far behind me pose no threat. It is around such people that I can feel a sense of acceptance and peace.

I took a field trip a couple of years ago with my son Nick's fifth grade class. We went to a cabin on Hood Canal on a beautiful sunny spring day. There were about 50 kids on this field trip and, as a chaperon, I felt a particular responsibility to watch out for the kids assigned to my group. As it happened, I was hooked up with the mother of one of the students, Kevin, who was a quadriplegic. While I did not have to watch out for Kevin since his mother was there, I did get first hand experience of just how time-consuming it is to care for someone who, since birth, had no use of either his arms or legs. He was completely dependent on others to live.

As the other kids played football and volleyball on the beach, I noticed that they would engage in the normal back and forth about "I'm faster than you" or "You can't throw a football half as far as me." But when the kids interacted with Kevin, they were different. He was so totally nonthreatening to them that many kids gravitated towards him. It was almost as though he was surrounded by an invisible field of unconditional love and acceptance. Kids would joke and play with him, volunteer to help him eat lunch, but always with a kind of respect they rarely showed for one another. Their behavior changed when they were around Kevin.

As I sat there observing this completely helpless human being squirming around on the deck, I felt deep compassion for Kevin and wondered what in the world was God's purpose for him. He was never going to be able to care for himself or have any kind of independence. He'd never play sports and he may never even have a job. And yet the feeling I got around him was that he was completely happy and he caused kids to forget their quest for perfection, their need to compete. It was as though Kevin's purpose was to help kids empty themselves of their limiting beliefs about perfection and competition and find their compassionate center. He did this by modeling what it would be like to be empty of expectations. He was not a threat to anyone, he was not someone who would tease others, he couldn't beat anyone in a race—heck—he couldn't even walk. His total vulnerability made him unconditionally accepting of anyone whom he encountered. And the kids responded in kind with unconditional acceptance of him. In a very real sense, Kevin was a living vessel of peace.

Culture and the Myth of Perfection

The ultimate force which teaches us the myth of perfection is the culture itself and the culture's messenger, the media. As we mentioned earlier, one of the key aspects of American culture is the idea of continuous improvement. The assumption underlying this idea is that who you are right now is not good enough. If who you are was good enough, you wouldn't need to improve, right?

The marketplace is filled with messages that reinforce this idea. Sports heroes and business tycoons as well as movie stars and models are all held up on a pedestal by the media because they are uniquely "good" at something and ostensibly because they have maximized their potential.

Other perfection images abound: the ultimate in baseball is to pitch a "perfect" game; it is possible to bowl a "perfect" game; some opera singers are said to have "perfect" pitch; the most expensive diamonds are the ones that are nearly "flawless"; it is possible to get a "perfect" score of 1600 on your college entrance exams, something for which thousands of students strive each year.

Self-improvement books and tapes which are designed to help you "maximize your boundless potential" or "double your income" fill bookstores. We live in a kind of self-improvement, self-help Mecca where the land of opportunity has become the land of, "You're doing okay, but if you buy my product, you'll do even better."

Thus, we see the best basketball player in the world, Michael Jordan, endorsing basketball shoes and convincing everyone from poor inner-city youth to wealthy suburbanites to pay $150 for them. The genius of Phil Knight and Nike was to see that while there are only a handful of top athletes who come close to so-called "perfection," there are literally millions who want to attain it. Since they have not been given these kinds of gifts, they buy Michael Jordan shoes in order to become, in effect, vicariously perfect. The logic is "If I can't be in the NBA, I can at least buy shoes from someone who is."

The female image of perfection in modern culture is embodied by the super model and/or actress. Body image, in particular, characterizes the concept of perfection and it is once again driven by advertisers who understand that sex appeal and beauty sells. The effect on individuals' beliefs and values, beyond convincing us to buy stuff, is that we also must look like these models of perfection. Since most of us do not look like these models and never will, we are *playing a game we cannot possibly win*. How many stories have we heard of young girls, who in a desperate attempt to gain approval from others, enter the dark world of bulimia or anorexia in order to obtain the perfect figure as modeled by Madison Avenue?

There is a multi-billion dollar plastic surgery and cosmetics industry and, for men, a burgeoning industry in hair transplants and hair-growing products, all designed to inch us closer to becoming perfect-looking human beings.

And woe to the person who chooses to remain satisfied with the way they are. We have come to equate standing pat with losing, and losing in our culture is the ultimate source of self-judgment and self-blame. My former boss had a saying that reinforced this idea of constantly having to move up. He said, "There is no such thing as standing still: you are either falling behind or moving ahead." And we wonder why the most common time during the week to have a heart attack is first thing Monday morning!

But the myth of perfection is not limited to appearance. Because of the pervasiveness of advertising imagery and the focus on success, Americans hold specific beliefs, conscious or unconscious, about the whole of their lives. We are constantly assessing where we are in relationship to others, all the while using images we see on television as the barometer of our career success *and* our core identity.

I have been aware for years now that every time I watch a television program profiling some highly successful entrepreneur, I immediately want to know the person's age, where he came from, what advantages or disadvantages he had growing up, in order to compare myself to him. In addition, I am constantly comparing myself to people I work with, to those men I see on television commercials, to movie stars, asking, "How do I stack up against these guys? Am I closer to perfection than he is? Am I a slacker? Am I successful? "

This brings us back to the phenomenon we discussed earlier: the idea of self-judgment, the uniquely human tendency to relentlessly compare oneself to others or to some impossibly high standard and, upon concluding that one falls short, beat oneself up. What is wrong with this strategy of self-assessment? Why shouldn't we rely upon external reinforcement for determining our self-worth? Deepak Chopra, M.D. was asked this question while doing a book promotion recently. He was asked "Dr. Chopra, you are big on saying that we should not rely on the opinions of others for our self-worth. But does that mean if I were to tell you, 'Dr. Chopra, I think you are a brilliant writer and physician,' that you would reject that comment, that you wouldn't be flattered?"

Chopra responded "My ego would be flattered by such a comment. But what happens when I write a book that you do not like and you criticize me for it? Whether I am listening to your flattery or your criticism, I am giving you all the power."

If we rely on the opinions of others and their standards of perfection, we are giving away our power. And as we have already discussed, so often what a person thinks about you is more about what they think of themselves *in relation to you* than an objective assessment of who you are in reality.

So how do we move from being an externally-motivated person who judges our own self-worth based on the unreliable and subjective opinions of others, to a more inner-directed self-accepting person who feels it is okay to be just the way we are?

Concepts like perfection, conditional love and judgment are simply beliefs which fill our mind and make us less free to be who we really are. This psychological baggage or what ES calls "negative programming" also creates barriers for our interacting freely with others. To empty ourselves of attachment to concepts like perfection and constant improvement is to move closer to acceptance and, ultimately, closer to God:

> In Zen, there is a wonderful statement: "Spring comes and the grass grows all by itself"... To let go of control is to enter into creation in the act of becoming. We discover who we have always been when we stop attempting to become better than who we really are. The very desire to be better than who we are is to have forgotten God.
> —Steven Levine, *For The Love of God*

Ernest Kurst and Katherine Ketchum, in their book *The Spirituality of Imperfection*, suggest that the quest for perfection is in itself evidence of the human predicament:

> ...spirituality is founded in the recognition and acceptance of one's creatureliness and finitude. There is, of course, "something wrong" with us: finite beings, we thirst for the infinite. "Man is the creature who wants to be God," as Sartre sadly observed. But we are not God, and given our human nature, spirituality suggests not "I'm okay, you're okay," but "I'm not okay, and you're not okay, but that's all right."

Could this be the source of our infatuation with perfection? Are we finite creatures yearning for the infinite? If such yearning is indeed a fundamental characteristic of the human animal, it would go a long way towards explaining why we spend so much time attempting and inevitably failing to obtain the unobtainable. The wisdom of the Twelve-Step movement is contained in the first step: "Give up." This step, points out Kurtz, is a particularly healing notion for the alcoholic who tends to be an all or nothing personality. By "punting" or "kicking it upstairs," as some call it, they are relinquishing the obsession with perfection which drives them to drink in the first place. So it is that Kurst wrote a comprehensive history of Alcoholics Anonymous and called it *Not God*.

If we are clearly "not God" but are creatures who inherently yearn to become God or to move towards perfection, how are we to live? And if it is really okay to be "not okay" or not perfect, then why does even the Bible call for us to seek perfection? Matthew 5, verse 48 says, "Be perfect therefore as your Father in Heaven is perfect." This is one of many questions I had for ES.

Dialogue on The Myth of Perfection

Doug: Are we unconditionally accepted by God?

ES: God made us as we are. Or even from the evolutionist point of view, we evolved the way we did to *be* as we are. It doesn't make sense, then, that God, the creative force, would only accept us if we fulfilled *conditions* that made us different from the beings we are, e.g. you will only be an acceptable creature *if...*

However, being accepted without conditions still means being accepted as a member of *Homo sapiens:* a creature who is supposed to have wisdom, will and choice. Part of how we are at this moment is the potential to become, to grow and mature. This potential is called forth not by a cosmic imperative, but by a cosmic invitation. And, if we believe God is Love, then one might say we are *wooed* into becoming. Becoming what? If we are made in the image of the Creator, that means becoming more and more loving, free, and further along the continuum from compulsion to choice.

Doug: What about this business of perfection as it is mentioned in the Bible. Are we really called to become perfect as in flawless?

ES: Have you ever thought what our culture means by perfection? Do we *mean* the unattainable? Heaven help us! Striving for the unattainable is surely the most stressful thing on earth. Fortunately, in the bible, the Greek word for "perfect," *teleios*, means "complete in all its parts," or "full grown." You might say then, that a perfect human being was a complete human being, or a mature one. The point is not to be rigorous, but to be ripe.

Doug: But wait. When you say the word *teleios* in Greek means "complete in all its parts," does that mean the Bible is saying we don't have to continually improve, but merely become complete by growing old? I always thought this passage meant we were supposed to be perfect as in flawless?

ES: I think there are two issues here. The first is to consider *in what* are we to be perfect? As you've brought up the scriptural reference, it's important to look at the context in which Jesus says these words. As you noted, the passage is found in Matthew's gospel, chapter 5, verse 48. If we look back ten verses or so, we find that Jesus is at this time urging his friends to move beyond vengeance—"an eye for an eye and a tooth for a tooth"—and to go the extra mile. In verse 43 Jesus says that shocking thing "love your enemies," not just those who love you. So you see, in context, being perfect is most probably referring to being perfect in *love*. To grow beyond self-serving and self-aggrandizement.

Doug: To learn to accept people unconditionally?

ES: Exactly. The second issue is to explore how quickly one must do this. It would be wonderful if we could wave a wand and be perfect in love instantly—or at least tomorrow! But being human, that's as impossible as a little yellow tomato blossom becoming a luscious ripe tomato tomorrow, or an Olympic runner breaking the record without long training. We should be able to mature at our own pace, which need not be either instantaneous or lazy. The turtle in the old fable went at his own pace, which ordinarily was a lot slower than the hare's, but the turtle won the race.

What is referred to, of course, is not an actual race towards either material or even moral perfection. Saint Paul picks up on this when he uses the analogy of the Olympic runner. (It is thought that Paul, being brought up in the Helenized culture of Tarsus, would himself have been trained in the Greek games.) It's not a perishable crown of laurel, he says, that we are running for, but an imperishable, that is, a spiritual one; it is a spiritual "race" toward full humanity and mature love. So it's not how fast we run; it is not our pace that matters in "the long run" so to speak, but our purpose. We are not to be in the rat race, but the human race.

Doug: But my upbringing has filled me with the belief that I am supposed to "excel" to become the best, and consequently I am filled with a belief structure that says if I am not moving towards being the best (perfection being the ultimate manifestation of such movement), then I am not working hard enough. Are you saying that to become complete is enough? Does that mean I can just sit around and do nothing, becoming complete just by breathing? Why do anything?"

ES: We will get *old* just by breathing, but we may not necessarily get *ripe*. A green tomato left in a cupboard can eventually shrivel up and rot instead of getting succulently ripe. To stretch the image: for a tomato's ripeness, there needs to be ample moisture, soil nutrients, and sun; for human ripeness, there needs to be sufficient nurture, learning, and consciousness. A ripe human being is a conscious human being. Consciousness enables what Plato referred to as the examined life, the only life worth living.

The way you asked your last question, it sounded as if you saw only two alternatives: to stress yourself out by striving to be perfect, or to sit around and "do nothing." Either of these courses of action by itself is admittedly fruitless.

There is a story about an old holy man. One day a hunter came and asked him to teach him how to pray. The old man said "First teach me how to use your bow." The hunter was delighted that such a venerable person should ask to be taught by such a humble hunter as he. "Well," he said brightly, "the real trick is how you string your bow. If you string it too tight it will break; if you string it too loose it will not shoot the arrow." The holy man said, "Thank you. That is also how you should pray."

Major stress comes from feeling trapped between two unacceptable extremes. Constantly striving for the unattainable is of course super-stress. Just sitting around and "doing nothing" is stressful and frustrating too, because one is not living one's life: one is being lived by it. Bearing the tension between extremes can be a creative and liberating effort opening the way for other alternatives to be seen.

To keep the effective tension on the bow and shoot at our target takes awareness and practice. When to work your tail off and when to sit around. There is a time to "just sit around." As the director said to the actress: "Stop doing something and just sit there." That might also have been said by a Zen master. The need for discernment recalls the prayer of the Twelve-Step programs: to change what we can, to accept what we cannot change and to keep increasing our wisdom so that we may know the difference.

Of course, if you feel compelled to strive for perfection in the super-ego-driven misuse of the word, then to think of stopping the scramble and just sitting—being conscious of where and who you really are—may at first have disturbing implications; new kinds of anxiety and guilt. Questions such as "Where am I" and "Who am I?" may arise. Anxiety and guilt are parents of stress, and they are demanding and constricting parents. It is helpful to remember that questions are not demands, they are invitations.

As you quote me in the Introduction, the point to our human existence is ultimately freedom. Freedom to respond to our life's opportunities and not feel victimized by them. Such freedom is born of a maturity of consciousness that is not ours at birth. To be fully human, we must tend the ripening of consciousness.

Doug: Does God accept me just the way I am if all I do is become ripe as opposed to the president of a company? Because all of this talk about not needing to perform is not my experience in the real world; people do move up (and down). Where is God when all I am doing is becoming ripe?

ES: That brings up an important point. Performance is not a condition of God's love and acceptance, and should not be a criterion for our self-worth.

However, human beings need work that both fulfills and challenges them. People need scope to exercise their gifts. Those who have the gifts of management or leadership should learn how to use them in the way that best serves those whom they manage or lead. True leadership is not about prestige or control, but about responsibility and discernment. In this context performance does matter. I like to see where words come from. *Performance* comes through Old French from the Latin, and has, among its definitions, "to furnish, complete, form thoroughly," and "carry through." My dictionary doesn't say anything about looking good or measuring up to some abstract standard. The danger in performing or winning success, is when we invest our worthiness or loveable-ness in them, as in: "I will only be loved, admired, affirmed, respected, be okay, *if...*" Climbing the ladder of success does not affect a person's true worth. But on the other hand, care and efficiency in our work are good, and appropriately lead to promotion. Jesus said, "You have been trustworthy in a few things, I will put you in charge of many things." (Matthew 25:21). It's an issue of trust that advancement will happen naturally, and not through our wheeling and dealing.

Also, challenging and creative work does not always need to be the same as a person's salaried job. An avocation, hobby or volunteer work can provide scope for one's creative energies. But whether paid or unpaid, the unfolding of one's gifts, and the maturing of one's personal power play a significant part in an individual's "ripening."

Let me say a little more about human "ripeness" and how it evolves. There are many theories about human development and its stages. One model that has particularly informed my thinking was taught by Herbert Holt, M.D. As I have adapted it, I call it "The Three Levels of Love."

A mature human being is created to "ripen" in several ways: in consciousness, in the capacity to choose well, and in how to love well. Ripening in love is of paramount importance because it affects our ability to relate to ourselves, to others and to God.

Scott Peck has written: "I define love thus: The will to extend one's self for the purpose of nurturing one's own or another's spiritual growth" (*The Road Less Traveled*). Later in the same book, Peck elaborates: "Although the act of nurturing another's spiritual growth has the effect of nurturing one's own, a major characteristic of genuine love is that the distinction between oneself and the other is always maintained and preserved. The genuine lover always perceives the beloved as someone who has a totally separate identity....In its most extreme form the failure to perceive the separateness of the other is called narcissism."

Level One Love - Narcissism

The human infant is like a kernel or seed which *may* ripen into a mature human person. As an infant, however, the human animal is an utter narcissist. The baby is the center of its universe—in fact it cannot even distinguish the other from itself. The other is only a means to its end, and exists only to fill its needs. The infant's cry demands, "Feed me! Pick me up! Change me! Burp me! Cuddle me!" Of course we think this is cute in a baby—and rightly so—it's a baby's appropriate way of relating. But do you know any people who are chronologically adult to whom any other person and the universe exist only to fill their needs? Not so cute anymore. And if you give them power, watch out—you may have a Hitler or a Machiavelli. Love which is fixated on this first level of development is attachment; attachment to self-survival and self-aggrandizement. Ernest Becker writes, "This is the price of our animal narcissism: very few of us, if pressed, would be unwilling to sacrifice someone else in our place" (*Escape from Evil*). Every human being, including you and me, has these instincts in common with the animals.

Level Two Love - Justice

If the infant is treated as a human being and not as an object, if it receives sufficient nurture and encouragement, the seed of narcissism breaks open and begins to send out roots and shoots. Somewhere around puberty, the child will recognize himself or herself as an individual, separate from others, and therefore can begin to perceive others as persons in their own right. If I am a person in my own right, then you are a person in your own right. At this second level of development, the concept and practice of justice is possible. If I am I, and you are you, we can negotiate. Loving at this stage means fairness and equity.

The downside of this second growth level between puberty and ripe adulthood is the tendency to need a lot of rules and laws. "This is my side of the room, and that is your side! Woe unto you if you leave your junk on my side!" "If you scratch my back, I'll scratch yours." "If you invite me to dinner, I will invite you back." Teen-age gangs are characterized by rules and the breaking of rules, rewards and punishments, rigid identification with "my kind of person" and rebellion or violence against others who are different. Many chronologically "adult" conclaves in our society are fixated in and foster this "Us and Them" mentality. At best this stage of human development can bring about covenant; at worst, vendetta. The adverse side of negotiation, justice and contract is vengeance: an eye for an eye, a tooth for a tooth; the *Lex talionis*—the "Law of the Claw." But the human being has the capacity for being "full grown," for true maturity. True maturity is not only freedom to choose; it is freedom from attachment to what other human beings think.

There is a kind of conventional thinking which individuals and groups of individuals pass down through the ages. It is lazy thinking. It is a patchwork of generalizations, old wives' tales, prejudices, group-think, gossip, tribal taboos, half-truths and comforting lies. It is a hotbed for the nurture of "shoulds" and "oughts" and the attachment to hopeless perfectionism. It advertises itself as traditional wisdom and common sense but it is closer to traditional tyranny and common intolerance. In fact, it is what we are calling the cultural myths. I remember having lived in fear of its implicit or explicit censure, and I have heard many others report the same. "If I do this, or if I don't do that, *they* will say..."

To react against this oppressive group-think may not yet be freedom, though it may be the first step toward freedom. A fierce reaction to anything usually implies a strong residual attachment to that thing. Freedom lies not in rebellion, but in what psychologists called "individuation." That's a fancy word meaning something like becoming your own person.

Level Three Love - Gift

If a human being evolves beyond the stage of "tit-for-tat" negotiation, she or he no longer needs to be ruled by tribal loyalties, peer pressure or the conventional "should" system. Discernment has developed to the point where the person can see what *is*, instead of what is generally *supposed to be*, and act out of choice rather than ignorance or compulsion. There is no longer the need for certainty—that if I scratch your back you will scratch mine; that if I am good I will be rewarded. If certainty and reciprocity, and even "fairness," are no longer demanded, one can live by possibilities in a dynamic structure of change. It means that risk is possible. A person can choose a course of action in any circumstance, not because of any external stress or pressure, but because he or she chooses to live that way. Of course this way of living implies taking a certain responsibility for one's life, and that means there is no one "out there" to blame. But it also means freedom. The freedom to be one's own self, and to let others be themselves. To love on this third level has ceased to be attachment, or even fairness, and has become mature intimacy.

No one is ever perfectly ripe. *Nobody lives on Level Three all the time.* We are all constantly making a mess of things, doing things we regret, "blowing it." To say nothing of regression. I don't know anybody—especially myself—who feels or acts mature all the time. There are moments, if not days, when I still feel and want to act like a narcissistic two year old. But every moment of the process can be used to learn from. And the truth will lead us to freedom, and wisdom.

Doug: Okay, I think I get the thing about becoming ripe as opposed to perfect as in flawless. That's a big relief. But is there nevertheless something I can do to move towards becoming ripe?

ES: Rather than *doing*, let's say *cooperate with*. Becoming a full human being is a cooperative project. An atheist might call it a combination of the luck of the draw—gene pool, early environment, educational advantages—and the individual's commitment to seek the truth about things. A Christian might call it the interaction of God's grace and a person's free will. A partnership. Or better, a friendship: "I do not call you servants any longer...but I have called you friends" (John 15:15). So, first, a word about mutuality before we get into *what can I do*?

Have you ever been in a relationship where the other person did everything important and wouldn't trust you to do anything? Or, conversely, when the other person wouldn't do anything; you had to do whatever it took to keep the alliance going? I have, and both instances caused me stress and grief. The way of love, human or divine, is neither doing it all yourself, nor having it all done for you.

Pelagius was a much maligned Irish monk of the fifth century who got an entire heresy named for him. In a capsule, the heresy called Pelagianism teaches that "getting somewhere" spiritually is all up to us. Webster defines Pelagianism as follows: "...each person's freedom of the will includes the unassisted initiating power to move toward salvation and to appropriate the divine grace necessary thereto." A pretty good description of the spiritual "ladder of success." Of course, there was the *opposite* extreme. Jansenism, the heresy named after Cornelis Jansen (1585-1638), taught among other things that freedom of the will was non-existent. More or less the "Why do anything?" approach to spirituality. So you see this dilemma has been around causing people stress for a long time. I think it might have been St. Augustine who said, "We must pray as if it were all up to God, and work as if it were all up to us."

Doug: What can a person do to cooperate in this ripening process?

ES: I'd begin by mentioning three things: trying to stay awake, trying to see things clearly, and trying to grapple with the question of how to accept the unacceptable.

First, staying awake. I had a wake-up experience when I was eight years old that was so stunning that I remember it vividly today. I was at a friend's house, and we were in her room, sitting on her bed. I looked down at the bedspread which was a faded pink cotton chenille, and focused on one of the little pink tufts. Then a strange thing happened. I said to myself, "I am aware of myself noticing this little tuft, and I am aware of being aware of myself noticing this little tuft—and I wonder how far this being aware of being aware can stretch." Then I told myself this was crazy, and I quit thinking and went on playing whatever game we were playing. But I never forgot the stunning excitement of that moment which felt like waking up to my own potential to be aware. I never told anybody, though, for fear they would think I was weird or different.

Doug: And being different means not being like others. I felt this same way growing up. I was routinely teased for "thinking too much" or taking life too seriously.

ES: Being different runs the risk of not being what your culture, your school-teacher, your father, your boss, your mother think you should be. Do you remember the Hans Christian Anderson fairy tale of "The Ugly Duckling"? It's a wonderful parable about the frustration and stress of perfectionism and the joyful freedom of awakening to reality. The little cygnet did his best to be a perfect duck like all his supposed siblings, but inside himself he knew he had failed. The ducks did *their* level best to make him out to be a duck too, but they also must have known on some level that they had failed. Even his mother, *who loved him,* failed to see his true nature; she simply did not have the scope. So they all called him "Ugly." And he accepted the name.

The breakthrough only happened many moons later, when he became aware of some other swans in their grace and beauty, and looked down to see his own similar reflection in the water. Even then, I imagine, it was very scary for that little creature to realize that his true beauty lay in renouncing his duck-ness, because he had spent his whole life up to that point trying to pass for an acceptable, if not perfect, duckling; to be seen as one of the crowd. What a challenge it must have been to claim his hitherto unacceptable swan-hood! But in the end, what relief from all that stress and frustration; what joy, what freedom! In my own experience it felt like waking out of a nightmare. I once wrote a poem about it.

> My mother had another female child
> with my own name and years, of whom I heard
> by implication; and this undefiled
> socialized creature was, of course, preferred.
> She was, and was not, I. I tried to be
> and not to be this hovering presence—wrought
> out of expectation and anxiety—
> like a small bird in winds' cross-currents caught.
> Then once, while walking to the park, I saw
> the corpse of a gray pigeon moldering
> between two buildings; a symbolic flaw
> of April's and my own tumultuous spring.
> In that defiled and absolute wing and claw
> the real child broke into awakening.
> It was I. I would die. But I began to see
> I would not live my mother's fantasy.

Doug: Is the point then to wake up and see yourself the way you really are—not the way other people expect you to be—and settle for that?

ES: That's the beginning. If we stopped there, though, it would be pretty lonely and narcissistic. What about seeing others the way *they* really are? Maturity implies the capacity for intimacy: for your most true self to risk opening appropriately to the other, and to receive the other in the same spirit. The first thing that means is to get beyond the conventional stereotypes and judgments.

Of course people never see themselves or others the way they *really* are. In the first place, the point is not to be *transparent*. Some things are nobody's business except yours and the God "to whom all hearts are open and all desires known." The point is rather to be *congruent*; which can mean when your inward being matches your outward manifestation. That is, if you are angry you won't have a smile on your face; if you secretly envy somebody you won't criticize them; if you dislike something you won't gratuitously say it's fine.

In the second place, nobody actually has the ability to be certain of what really *is*, or who they and others really *are*. The quantum physicists have taught us that. They can never be *certain* of seeing and accurately measuring one sub-atomic particle, or tell what it will do. If they know its location they cannot at the same time know its velocity. If the hard sciences have humbled their certainties to probabilities, how can we be so arrogant as to say we humans understand our own or another's being and actions? But it is possible to stay open to reality, to approach it with respect and even awe, somewhat in the manner of the new physicists, and not to categorize it for our own ease. To be willing and even desirous to see *what is* tends to be risky and not as easy as it might sound. A friend recently shared with me a wonderful quotation: "There is only one heroism in the world: to see the world as it is and to love it." (Rolland, Romain 1866-1944.)

I have thought there are three kinds of people who best see things and people the way they "really are": children before they go to school, great artists, and contemplatives. Before children go to school they will color a sky green, red, purple, orange or black. Most children I have known, including myself, when they go to school, are taught to paint skies *blue*. And trees green. And mountains purple. And, up until very recently, to use pink as "flesh color." But in fact, skies are at one time or another many different colors, and human flesh comes in a rich variety of hues. Great artists know this: Van Gogh looked in the mirror and saw green and painted green on the face of his self-portrait. El Greco painted the sky above Toledo green.

By real, I don't mean realistic. Abstract artists see a different kind or dimension of being in shape and color. Henry Moore saw and sculpted the human form and its being in space far beyond its realistic details. Both children in their rich fantasies, and contemplatives in their openness to mystery, also see beyond surface appearance to essence and potential. Whether they are contemplating a lotus, a mandala, or the convolutions of the human heart, their stance is one of openness and awe. Contemplatives must check their prejudices and stereotypes at the door. Young children haven't developed them yet. Artists often wage a life-long battle against them.

One good thing about not having to keep striving to be perfect, or at the top, or Somebody, is that then we don't need other people to be perfect either. We can, heroically, see other people as they are and love them. I like Romain's word "heroic." The exercise of loving the unlovely is not as easy as it might sound.

Once, many years ago, I was staying at a convent with the idea of discerning whether this might be a life-context for me. One evening shortly after my arrival, the monks from the neighboring monastery joined us for a celebration. There were thirty or so monks and nuns in the large common room and spilling out onto the patios. I felt very much the outsider, the non-member, the Ugly Duckling. I stood in a corner of the room watching the proceedings. It happened that the monks' and the nuns' Superior arrived a little late. He was called Father Taylor, and he was known to be a very wise and charismatic man. When he came into the room he looked around, and walked easily, but directly over to Sister Mary Teresa. Mary Teresa was in her eighties, and because her hearing was impaired and her attention tended to wander, it was not easy to converse with her. This evening, as was often the case, she had been sitting alone. As I watched, I noticed that when Father Taylor leaned over to talk to her, her face lit up—she had a radiant smile—as if she were transformed from an apparently sour old woman to one as young in heart as a girl. I marveled.

Then, with a jolt, I realized that when *I* walked into a room, I habitually made a bee-line for the person I saw as most attractive and popular, the one who had the most to offer me on my path to achievement and "perfection." Being "on the make" in that way, seemed a normal, though very stressful, way to relate. I then wondered if it was the case that Father Taylor had disciplined himself to do this act of charity, or if he simply did it without thinking? I looked at his face—it was lit up too! He was obviously having a fine time talking to Sr. Mary Teresa. Long ago, it may have been a discipline of his to pay attention to the disenfranchised, but it clearly was not the case now. His evident delight transcended discipline.

Just about the time that I had concluded these observations, he came over and introduced himself to me! Father Taylor had checked his stereotypes at the door. He did not see in Mary Teresa an old woman, used up and difficult. He did not see in me the newest and least significant member of community. He saw in each of us rich potential for delight in mutual exchange. He was the living embodiment of a vessel of peace.

Doug: What about the Greek idea that it is possible to obtain perfection through self-knowledge? Is this partly where we get our ideas about improvement—that if we just had enough self-knowledge, we would see perfect form and be able to obtain it?

ES: The great spiritual traditions of the world do put a lot of emphasis on self-knowledge. I have heard that the inscription over the entrance to the Delphic Oracle read: "Know yourself." And I think you're right that the ancient Greeks thought that progress in self-knowledge would advance one's growth up the ladder of perfection which, for instance, began with the appreciation of a beautiful body and moved on up to an appreciation of spiritual or ideal beauty.

In the Christian tradition, there is an alternative to getting somewhere in that poignant prayer of St. Augustine's: "Lord, that I may know myself, that I may know You!" And Eastern spirituality gives us the concept of *kensho*—the moments of insight, of self-awareness, which are the heralds of enlightenment. But in any tradition, self-knowledge is never "perfect." Paradoxically, the height of self-knowledge is to accept its limitation, to be able to say, "I don't know everything, and probably never will." We have noted that quantum physicists have called it "the uncertainty principle," and moved from certainties to probabilities. It is very interesting to note that after presumably living the "examined life," Socrates summed it up in the paradox: "I only know that I know nothing." Zen Buddhism speaks as much about no-mind and not-knowing as about knowing. And in the words of the Sufi poet Rumi:

> writing about love
> my pen splinters
> expounding love
> the ass of intellect
> lays down in the mire.

Jesus urges us to love ourselves. To love our true selves we must know our true selves. He also charges us "to leave self behind." Self-knowledge may well be our best tool, but being mortal and finite, it "splinters" and must be left behind before the complete self-gift of love.

Eastern spirituality has more images of "being there" rather than "getting there," of growing into a deeper awareness of where one actually is. The Eastern images of "being there", of awareness and interconnectedness, might be seen as complements to the quest and attainment images of most Western spirituality as conceived by men. Some women in our Western tradition have given us less linear and more relational images. These include Catherine of Sienna's *Dialogues*, Julian of Norwich's *Revelations*, and Hildegard of Bingen's visions and illuminations. (It is tempting to point out that when Dante achieves the end of his climb through Hell and Purgatory to Paradise, he finds a woman, Beatrice, just being there!)

Doug: Is it true that we are attached to perfection because we are finite beings seeking the infinite?

ES: I would say yes, *if* we can get our heads beyond the common, oppressive use of the word "perfection." Divine perfection has to do with love, compassion, mercy and justice, not with what grade we get or how much money we make, or how famous we are. My favorite definition of the human soul was conceived by a man named Edward Leen: "The soul is the capacity for divine reality to be held finitely." As we mature in wisdom and love, we co-operate in forming and re-forming that capacity.

2

The Myth of Control

Myth: It is not only possible to completely control one's own destiny, it is our responsibility.

Truth: The process of living in the world is about interacting in harmony with others and with the rest of creation. Working hard to discern when to hold on and when to let go is the only thing over which we have control.

> **One begins to realize that it is not possible to belong to the universe, to participate in its vital flow, if one is either being controlled by it or trying to control it.**
> **—Gerald May, *Will and Spirit***

If one of the pervasive beliefs we internalize is the idea of moving towards perfection, a concept right next to that idea is the myth of control: the idea that if we pay enough attention to details, have clear goals, strong will and a relentless drive, we can, indeed become master of our own fate. After all, civilizations throughout history were established based on human beings' ability to conquer, organize and control their natural environments. Our history is filled with stories of the hero overcoming impossible odds to climb a mountain, or cross an ocean, or discover a cure for a deadly disease or overcome an oppressive regime to bring freedom to the land.

In this chapter, we are going to look at how the belief of control gets installed into our consciousness, how it can lead to enormous stress and ultimately, how we can begin to look at the issue of control as a kind of give and take or dance between ourselves as individual vessels and the creative force we call spirit.

Family Systems and The Myth of Control

It should not come as a great shock that the myth of control has been installed into our belief system since childhood. After all, if we really are, as Sartre noted, "individuals who want to become God" and "finite beings who yearn for the infinite," then a logical strategy would be to begin the long road towards the infinite by gaining control of one's immediate environment.

Parents and children embark on an epic battle of control, especially during the teenage years, as the child attempts to gain a separate identity from his or her parents, while the parents try, often in the best interest of the child, to teach the rules of society so they will conform enough to survive. These struggles mirror the overall struggle humans face in wanting freedom on the one hand and approval on the other. The consequence often is the attempt to control each other to preserve individual freedom. It appears to become a sort of zero-sum game in which freedom for me depends on the denial of freedom for you.

I have noticed in my own relationship with my son Nick that we have frequent battles with control, especially as Nick has become a teenager. On the one hand, I encourage Nick to take more and more responsibility for his life and operate independently of me, yet I have many household rules with which he must conform as a member of the family. So it is a constant negotiation between us as to who has control in any given situation.

I began to worry about what I am teaching Nick about the myth of control when I noticed our collective behavior at home relating to something as seemingly trivial as television viewing. Both Nick and I are channel surfers. We have one channel changer and when we are both watching television, we are constantly battling over who gets control of the "controller." It goes from the comical to the absurd. When Nick has the channel changer, I am always complaining that he is staying on one channel too long or flipping through channels too quickly. When I have it, the reverse is true. Where it gets to be absurd is when we actually agree on what to watch, but still fight over who gets to hold the channel changer!

This little annoying battle we have is symbolic of our desire to secure mastery over our environment and a part of that environment is what information comes into our home over the air waves. The battle for control is exacerbated by the fact that we live in a "zero-sum" society, a place where we learn we have only two choices: winning and losing. Or to follow the line of reasoning in this chapter, the options are to control or be controlled.

As I was growing up, I was taught that there was only so much success in the world and I had to hustle to get my piece of it. This is consistent with the zero-sum idea. I began to look at others not in terms of how I could engage in a meaningful and mutually supportive relationship, but rather as threats to my success. If there was only so much success to go around, then it would be stupid of me to think of sharing with others or offering to help others, unless of course there was a clear quid pro quo: I do this for you, you do that for me. To view others as objects to control is not exactly something which nurtures human relationship nor is it, I now believe, what God wants for us in this life.

But it is a reality of modern life which has created barriers to individual growth as well as to the growth of human relationships. For if each individual feels compelled to get the upper hand and control the other, mature relationships are almost impossible to achieve. Our attachment to control gets in the way of pursuing our God-given right to freedom and love. As ES and I will discuss, the antidote to this myth of control may lie in discerning when to hold on and when to let go: when to lead the dance and when to let the other lead. More on that later.

Peer Groups and The Myth of Control

The first encounter with control one had outside the family was in school, where elaborate systems with bells and lines and report cards and rules about talking and raising one's hand predominated. The goal of such school yard rules was on one level to more efficiently deliver educational services to children. On a more reflective level, it was to teach us the importance of control.

The games we played as kids further demonstrated the payoff that was available to those who could gain the upper hand and control others. The game of Monopoly was all about systematically buying up all the property on the board so that when other players landed on the piece of real estate you controlled, you could charge them rent. Ultimately, by owning all the real estate, you gained a monopoly and won the game by obtaining total control. "Risk" was another game that had control as a central theme, only there the stakes were even higher: win the game and take control of the entire world! Even simpler games like "keep-away" taught the concept of control. Two kids play catch with some object, usually a ball of some

kind, and a third child tries to intercept it. The object of the game for
the two with the ball is to keep control of it. The object of the game
for the third person is to intercept the ball and "gain control."

We become filled with the notion that we are to take
responsibility for our lives and it is a central tenet of the American
Dream that, like Horatio Alger, we can become successful by the
sweat of our brow. But the path to success is not very clear nor is it
necessarily easy. Hence you see fast-track baby boomers now sitting
in restaurants or in their cars during a traffic jam or in line at the
grocery store talking on their cell phones with a beeper on their belt.
If one ever hopes to gain control in this chaotic world, the logic goes,
one must at least stay connected to the people and organizations that
will take them to this fictitious place.

One of the biggest selling points used by cellular phone
companies is that their product will ensure that you will *never be out
of touch* with clients. One cell phone ad showed two guys in the
dugout of a professional baseball farm team sitting on the bench with
cell phones. They switch to the big league dugout where the star
pitcher has just gotten injured and they call one of the two guys to tell
him he is being called up to the majors: the big break he has been
waiting for. But the batteries in his cell phone have died, so they go
back to the big league manager who says, "No answer? Call the next
guy on the list," who of course has the ad sponsor's cell phone which
never runs out of batteries.

This kind of aggressive approach to control and success is not
lost on kids who are watching and imitating their parents (and
television commercials) at every turn. Hence it is not unusual to see
15-year-old kids with beepers and cell phones trying to keep up with
parents who are running as fast as they can, trying to keep a handle
on their lives. The most annoying thing about cell phones to me are
those individuals who have them on an answer them during the
middle of a conversation. I have been eating lunch with friends of
mine, having a great conversation and a break from the fast pace of
modern life, only to have their beeper go off or cell phone ring right
in the middle of a conversation. And rather than ignore it, they reach
instantly for the device, anxious to hear who it might be.

The message this sends to the person they are with is this:
anyone who might be calling me, even if I don't know them, is more
important than you are. And this logic extends to the rest of one's
life. In order to stay competitive, there is a constant searching for new

opportunity, new markets, new business contacts, which renders any one encounter with another human being less meaningful.

Where the myth of control can have dire consequences for people is when they lose any sense of balance and become obsessed. Addiction is the ultimate manifestation of such obsession and it is a common affliction among those with chemical dependency issues. Unable to strike a balance between holding on and letting go, the addict tends to anesthetize himself or herself seemingly as the only escape from striving to control the uncontrollable. Once again, this is why the AA people have "letting go" as the first step to recovery.

We are even told that our relationship with God is something over which we can and should have control. If I am not experiencing the kind of rich prayer life that I am encouraged to believe is possible, then I must try that much harder by spending two or three hours a day in meditation or prayer or until I break through.

Gerald May in his book *Will and Spirit* describes the dynamic between obsessing over wanting to control a situation and losing ground versus letting go. He says even when a person increases the extent to which they engage in spiritual practices like meditation or prayer, they can become victimized by doing it too willfully:

> The more one willfully sets up activities that threaten self-image, the more self-image will rebel. The more specific and direct the attack, the more emphatic and resolute will be the resistance. Setting up a specific hard-line regimen of spiritual practice gives self-image something very substantial to fight against, and at the same time enables ego to take possession of spiritual responsibility.

May's idea that the self-image or ego sets up resistance in proportion to the threat it faces resonates with me. It seems that whenever I have set a goal for myself and am experiencing frustration in moving towards it, the moment I give up on it or let go or empty myself of the need to achieve that goal, a breakthrough occurs and progress is made. But if I continue to obsess over the goal and just increase my resolve to break through on it despite huge resistance, the resistance tends to increase. May's discussion of the difference between willfulness and willingness is instructive in beginning to clarify the contrast between holding on and letting go. He writes:

Willingness implies a surrendering of one's self-separateness, an entering into, an immersion in the deepest processes of life itself. It is a realization that one already is a part of some ultimate cosmic process and it is a commitment to participation in that process. In contrast, willfulness is the setting of oneself apart from the fundamental essence of life in an attempt to master, direct, control or otherwise manipulate existence.

For me, knowing when to hold on and when to let go is the single biggest challenge I face. Having grown up in the school of rugged individualism, I used to believe that everything I did and everything that happened to me was my responsibility and my fault. It was like I was the screenplay writer and everyone around me was an actor in my play. But the idea of controlling the world was not limited to fixing societal problems. I had to control my household as well. I had to call the shots in my marriage, deciding where to go for vacation, where to live, which friends to socialize with, etc. Ultimately, when I realized I could not be in total control, my response was to flee rather than to accept the differences.

In retrospect, I realize what a narcissistic, self-involved kind of world view this represented. I was intent on changing the world, convinced that I could single-handedly end all crime and poverty and rebuild the world to conform to my vision of the ideal reality. For years I toiled under this system of beliefs, carrying the burdens of the world on my shoulders. During this time, many people accused me of having a big ego. I realize in retrospect that the problem was my ego was too small. As Ken Wilbur has said:

> Narcissists are simply people whose egos are not yet big enough to embrace the entire Cosmos, and so they try to be central to the Cosmos instead. (*Tikkun*, September, 1998).

It is about moving from the position of saying "Why doesn't the world meet my demands?" to "How can I meet the world's demands?"

Culture and The Myth of Control

Just as marketers seek to attract our consumer dollars by claiming their product will move us closer to perfection, so too will they claim we can regain control of our lives through the products we buy. Whether it is regaining control of your weight problem, regaining control of your cigarette habit, eliminating drug and alcohol abuse, regaining control of your relationships with a spouse or a teenager—for every aspect of your out-of-control life, the marketplace has a product that will put you back in control.

Convinced that I have to be thin, rich, powerful, happily married, successful and that all of it is in my control, I place enormous pressure on myself every single day to perform in such a way as to make all of it happen. And I look to the marketplace to provide me with the tools I need to get there: a faster computer, a beeper to be available at all times to control emergencies that occur at work, E-mail to communicate with everyone I need to rise to the top, a fancy car, books promising the "seven ways to control your financial future" or the "10 immutable laws to help you win."

Not all aspects of our culture emphasize control as the key to success. I recall my son and I watching the movie *Meatballs* starring Bill Murray while ES and I were finishing this book. This rather crude comedy about teenagers at summer camp seems the least likely place to find spiritual wisdom. Yet once one starts looking for wisdom, it seems to emerge everywhere. At the end of this movie, two rival camps are participating in a kind of summer Olympiad. Bill Murray's camp, Camp Northstar, has a bunch of average, middle-income kids with not much talent. The opponents are from camp Mohawk, a private, expensive camp where all the kids are rich and talented and—well—above average.

Going into the competition, the Camp Northstar kids believed they had very little chance of winning. After the first day of competition, Camp Mohawk had indeed won every event and had a seemingly insurmountable lead. That evening, the kids at Camp Northstar were on the verge of giving up. Bill Murray then stood up and provided what amounted to a pep talk using emptiness or detachment as the central message:

That's just the kind of attitude we don't need. Sure, Mohawk has beaten us 12 years in a row. Sure, they're terrific athletes, who have the best equipment money can buy. Hell, every team they're sending over here has their own personal masseuse...but it doesn't matter.

Did you know that every Mohawk competitor has an electrocardiogram, blood and urine tests every 48 hours to see if there is any change in their physical condition? But it doesn't matter, it just doesn't matter, it just doesn't matter, I said it just doesn't matter, it just doesn't matter, it just doesn't matter [group repeats with him] it just doesn't matter, it just doesn't matter. . .

And eeeeevvvvveenn if we win, even if we win, and play so far over our heads that our noses bleed for a week to ten days, even if God in heaven above looks down and points his hand towards our side of the field, even if every man, woman and child holds their hands together and prays for us to win, it just doesn't matter because Camp Mohawk will still get all the girls cause they got all the money. It just doesn't matter if we win or if we lose, it just doesn't matter, it just doesn't matter, [group starts chanting] it just doesn't matter, it just doesn't matter...

Following this "pep rally" which one could argue was intended to get the campers to empty themselves of the need to win, Camp Northstar went out the following day and, to the amazement of everyone, won every event and took the championship away from the much more talented rich kids. This is a somewhat light-hearted but nevertheless profound example of giving up the need to control an outcome, which paradoxically leads to that outcome occurring.

Have you ever tried as hard as you could to do something and the harder you worked at it, the further it slipped away? And then, when you gave up and said, "I'll try my hardest, but it's not up to me what happens," there was a breakthrough? This is what happened to Camp Northstar. They didn't stop trying to compete, they merely gave up attachment to the outcome and in effect said "The outcome is up to the Universe." They moved from willfulness (we can impose our will) to willingness (we will try hard, but the outcome "just doesn't matter").

How are we to know when and with how much vigor we should engage in life and when we should let go and let the forces over which we have no control prevail? How do I empty myself of the myth that I have to control everything in my environment and yet know when it is appropriate to act?

I asked ES about this issue of holding on and letting go. Of all the areas she has counseled me in, this is the area where I have at once had the most trouble and experienced the most benefit from her input.

Dialogue on The Myth of Control

Doug: I guess the first question on this topic of control is why doesn't it work to try to control everything in my world?

ES: Because when you try to control everything, you are playing God, and the truth is that you are not God. Another way of putting it is that the Universe does not like to be told what to do (although I don't think it minds being *asked*). The thing is, it doesn't work to try to control *everything*, though it does work for us to control *some* things. If it didn't work at all, the desire for control wouldn't be so compelling. You might call control the junk food of the soul. It tastes great going down, but it isn't so great for us in the long run.

Once I knew a young woman who was under a lot of stress. She had come to try her vocation in our community and was struggling with new geography, new climate, new relationships, new customs and new authority structures. One morning I asked how she was doing. To my pleasant surprise she said, "I feel a lot better this morning, thanks." I asked her if she knew why she felt so much better today, and she replied, "Well, this morning I organized my underwear drawer." That was the one thing in her environment she felt she had complete control over.

It seems to me that cosmic chaos (either on the macro or on the micro level) is too scary for most human beings. We want to carve it up into bite-size or human-size chunks. And before we go into why that doesn't *ultimately* work, I think it's fair to say the inclination isn't all bad. (Maybe that's part of what the Incarnation is about: God knowing that we long for, and in fact need, a human-sized chunk of God.) As with alcohol or any other thing, some uses of control may be good and God-given. A fine wine is good when sipped with appreciation and not guzzled in an addictive manner. In the same way, it is the misuse of control or addiction to it that "doesn't work."

Art is an example of our desire for control that does "work." We cannot get our heads around the seemingly terrible randomness of life, so we put a frame around it, or, as Aristotle said of drama, we give it a beginning, a middle and an end. Whether it is a happy ending or a tragic ending, the effect is that wild chaos is corralled and things are under control again. King Oedipus suffers for his tragic mistakes and order is restored to the land.

Unfortunately there are many ways in which control is misused in a frantic attempt to keep us from the acceptance of reality. Some of the most poignant and distressing examples are those I have noticed in people who are terminally ill.

I went one day to visit my Sister who was dying of cancer. One of her household jobs had been to bundle and tie up the old newspapers and magazines for recycling. On the day of my visit, she asked me and the hospice aide to do this job. The aide was tying the string around a bundle of magazines and I had my finger on the knot. My Sister cried out, "Tighter, tighter!" We pulled the string tighter, but before we knew it, she was out of bed and limping toward the table where we were working, still saying, "Tighter, tighter!" If you can't be in control of your life span, you can at least be in control of *something*. Often it comes down to how you will take your medications, or how you will manage your visitors and care-givers.

As I said, control isn't all bad, but there are a number of reasons why excessive attempts at control—"trying to control everything in my world"—don't work. Desire for inordinate control stems from fear or insecurity. It is a vain attempt at sticking your finger in the dike against the raging flood of reality.

Doug: I have found over and over again that when I have tried to do something with all my will and have not achieved it, that when I just sort of surrender and say, "It's up to the universe now," invariably it happens. Why does surrender work when all my willpower will not?

ES: The concept of surrender needs some thinking about, some "unpacking." Suppose the dike of attempted control I was just talking about breaks and the raging flood of reality sweeps over us. Just suppose that, to our amazement, we find the waters we feared would be death-dealing are in fact life-giving if we "go with the flow"? I think that is what Elizabeth Kubler-Ross indicates in her work on the stages of dying: from denial through rage, bargaining (a kind of last-ditch attempt at control), and depression to acceptance.

There is a crucial distinction between wise acceptance, the surrender to reality, and cowardly "cop out." Not long ago I was visiting someone I had known as very intuitive and courageous, who also was facing death. The big question my friend was wrestling with she put like this: "People talk about acceptance, emptying, letting go. Why should I accept this—it's the pits! Why should I stop fighting? I've always been a fighter and proud of it. Why 'go gentle' into that good night? Why *not* 'Rage, rage against the dying of the light'? What is surrender but a cowardly cop-out?"

I guess the first answer that springs to mind is "If you can't beat 'em, join 'em." But this answer isn't enough. It sounds defeatist and fatalistic. True surrender or emptying isn't giving up. It is an act of doing, not of being done to. If I am *forced* to give up or surrender something—my property, my rights, my life—that puts me in the victim position, and my response is submission or conciliation.

Being a victim is very bad news. It is not only bad for the victim, it is bad for the oppressor. The victim stance is an adversarial one; the victim feels "It's them against me" just as much as any warring party. Victimization breeds rage which may prove to be impotent, but which creates a hostile atmosphere. It may result in hatred, which has been described as "drinking poison and hoping the other person will get sick."

The key to true, life-giving emptiness or surrender is *choice*. The minute you feel other people or external sources are forcing you to surrender, you become a victim. Surrender is a kind of giving, and all true gifts must be freely made.

Surrender must be freely chosen and it must be realistic. It is critical to remember that *you cannot give what you do not have.* You can't pour milk out of a pitcher that doesn't have any milk in it. I think that concept may lie behind what many women theologians are saying. They don't want any more of this "surrender, die to self" theology; they want a theology of fulfillment and celebration. I think the *kind* of surrender and ego-death which they don't want, nobody should want. If you don't have a full pitcher of respected person-hood, what can you pour out? The people of the First Covenant knew that if you wanted to surrender something, to make a sacrifice to God, it must be the *best* you had, full, perfect, unblemished. In true sacrifice, oblation must come before immolation (thank offering before the sacrificial death).

People I talk to have a lot of trouble with the concept of surrender. Many women say they have for so long been made to surrender, by which they mean "to comply, to capitulate, to give in," that they will not, in conscience, do it any longer. They want to feel what it's like to hold on, to be in control of their lives. On the other hand, many men say that surrender is really hard for *them*, because they've been brought up in the culture you describe, where men especially are pressured into always holding on, winning, being top dog, and being in control. In that mindset, no kind of surrender is seen as an option. These women and men need to experience more fullness before they are ready to empty. Both groups may need, for example, to come to a desire for the fullness of justice, and a sense of self-worth, for a fullness of emotional range and a ripened compassion. Again, you can't give away what you don't have. You can't make a real choice until you have real alternatives.

So, "Why does surrender work when all my willpower will not?" As you indicated in the opening of this chapter, one of the most cogent answers of our time is to be found in the wisdom of the Twelve-Step programs. "We admitted we were powerless...we made a decision to turn our will and our lives over..." The only real point of surrender, of letting go of control, is to move closer to truth; the truth is we are never in control of the Cosmos. To pretend to be is to move away from truth towards lie.

Doug: You have described the experience of spirituality or relationship with God as a kind of dance. What do you mean by that?

ES: I like the dance image because it suggests mutuality. Neither over-control nor unwilling surrender is respectful of the other. Let me tell you a story. When I was a child I was sent to dancing school to learn ballroom dancing. We were a class of awkward twelve- and thirteen- year olds trying to learn the steps and treading on each others' toes. The better I learned the steps, the more I tried to push and pull my partner around. Naturally he was trying to do the same thing. I knew that, being the boy, he was supposed to "lead," but he was doing it all wrong! Consequently we kept trying to go in different directions, holding on to each other tightly in order to push or nudge the other the way we thought the dance ought to go. It was a vain attempt to control and it was not a fulfilling experience!

Fortunately, with time and long practice, I became quite a good ballroom dancer. One evening when I was in my mid-twenties, I was in a famous nightclub in New York with some friends, one of whom was a ballet dancer with the Sadlers Wells Ballet. He was also a marvelous ballroom dancer. It was one of those magical evenings and we danced very well together. I began to notice that as I followed his lead, he hardly had to "lead" at all; I could barely feel his hand on my shoulder or his fingers touching mine. After a while it was as if I knew instinctively which way we would move or turn—we were so at one with each other and with the music.

And finally it seemed as if it were no longer clear who was leading; sometimes he would initiate the direction, and other times I would make the slightest of movements that would become, say, a change of direction or a turn. Yet, you see, he was still formally "leading." It was as if by some sort of mystical delegation I could indicate "What if we went this way?" and we would.

That experience has seemed to me the very best analogy for the way our human spirit "dances" with Holy Spirit, or if you like, with the Cosmic Energy or the Great Unknown. We never formally take the lead, but when we have lived enough and practiced to the point where practice is transcended, then it can seem that our own will is truly one with divine reality. This may be what is special about the prayers of people who are full enough to choose to be empty. Perhaps their "What if we went this way?" touches God, and Infinite Love responds out of its abundance, "Why not; let's do." This is the very opposite of trying to control the Universe or God's will by "telling it what to do." There is a wonderful saying (in an old book called *Triumphant in Suffering: A Study in Reparation,* by W. F. Adams, S.S.J.E. and Gilbert Shaw): "The power of prayer can never be exaggerated. It does not change the will of God, but it releases it."

Doug: Why do you think that so many people get caught up in the trap of needing to control their environment?

ES: A major cause of stress is when we think we need to live up to some ideal of perfection. Many people feel impelled to be the greatest, or produce the greatest, or be the most admired. The repressed feeling that they in fact are not perfect, and that they *may never be*, causes anxiety, strain or depression. I remember when I was young I felt I must live in that rarefied atmosphere of superlatives. At the same time I had a nagging feeling I was *less* than acceptable in looks, in achievement, in intelligence and in physical and social graces. Hence much stress.

It seemed, when I was a child, that no matter what I did I was always disappointing to my mother. Luckily for me this feeling of not being perfect became conscious. And as it became conscious I could start to deal with it. I began to see the "trap." When I was about eight years old I was in the school playground at recess. I was standing on the sidelines feeling left out of the play and anxious about that. Then I started noticing what the other kids were doing. They were either trying to control the play or the other children, to get someone to admire them because they "won," to play the game their way, or to be their special buddy. I didn't put it into words at that age, but there was definitely the insight that those kids were all "on the make" and that came from the same need to be the one in control or most popular that I had. It also came from the fear that maybe we weren't as much as we "should be." We weren't quite up to the expectations of our parents, teachers, culture, so we had to try harder. The freeing part of the insight that day on the playground was that the only difference between the other kids and me in trying to control our environment was that I began to see what was going on and they didn't.

The control trap starts very early in life. Learning to control some things, like our sphincters and certain expressions of our rage in the "terrible twos," is very useful in the process of becoming civilized and mature. But there is an aspect that is counter-productive and dangerous. When an individual feels "caught in a trap," as you put it, the emotions usually aroused are not only anxiety but desperation and rage. (If one is trapped or caged up too long, of course, the emotions can change into misery and despair.) If people get trapped in the conviction that they should or must control their environment, or, as you also have put it, be the screen-play writer for their own lives, they may come to the point that if they are *not* in control, they don't know what they are worth; some simply may not know that they *are,* that they exist.

When an animal—even the human animal—is trapped, it may become dangerous not only to itself, but to others. Stress and fear easily lead into rage and hostility. The cornered rat bares its teeth and gets ready to fight to the death. Watch out when a person driven to control feels threatened or trapped!

Doug: Have you personally struggled with the issue of control and if so how have you coped with it? What steps did you take to address your own control issues?

ES: I've told you about my awareness of the drive to control from my early childhood. I continued to struggle with issues of control as I grew older. I can try to tell you "the steps" I took, but—like my story about dancing—the steps I took were only half the reality. The other half had a lot to do with the leading of the Spirit.

First, I tried to control people, to get them to pay attention to me and love me. I remember trying so hard to get certain boys in high school to do that. I tried various things like carrying around books that would make me look intellectual, playing the clown, even sometimes picking a fight. It took a long, long time before I noticed that the boys I ran after ran away as fast as they could, whereas the ones I didn't try for were clamoring at my door.

A couple of decades after high school graduation, something happened to make me realize what this was all about. I was at a friend's house and the cat jumped into my lap. (I am not really a pet person—I have never had a pet of my own except a goat that I found abandoned as a new-born in the woods.) My friend said, "That's odd, the cat hardly ever pays attention to visitors. They do say, though, that a cat will jump up on the person who least likes them, or even one who is allergic."

What clicked for me is that neither boys nor cats like to be wooed or made a fuss over *because of someone else's control need.* The way to love and receive love is not to try to control a person, animal or thing, not to entice or manipulate it into relationship, but to let it remain its separate, unique self. That kind of distance and respect can foster mutual delight and invitation. Remember what we discussed in Chapter I about ripeness and mature love? Emptying myself of the need to coerce or wheedle others into paying attention to me took conscious effort, time and grace. I had to, like most of us do, ripen into the capacity for real intimacy.

Secondly, I not only had an issue with trying to control people, I had an issue with trying to control the supernatural. (My long struggle to surrender to God is a story for another place.) I'll give you one small example. In my late twenties I read a book by Charles Williams called *The Greater Trumps*. It had fascinating references to the Tarot cards, and I went and bought myself a deck and a "how to" book on telling fortunes with the cards. I was enchanted by the quasi-mystical aspect of using the Tarot deck, and I soon mastered the mechanics of laying them out, etc. I began trying the process on my family and friends. I was very successful; people were amazed at what I told them. They said I had a real, almost uncanny talent for it. One day the cards "said" that someone very close to the person I was reading them for would die unexpectedly. It happened. The part that was terrifying to me was not so much that this dreadful thing had happened and that I had "foreseen" it, but the exultant feeling of power and control that surged unbidden within me. The minute that feeling passed I felt contaminated, somehow, and sick. The incident scared the daylights out of me, and I got rid of the cards and I have never touched anything like them again. I knew that kind of control could be for me addictive and dangerous.

Another big control issue in my life has been in relation to art. Since I was twelve years old I have known that I am called to be a writer. Over the years I have written poems, stories and plays. I obtained an undergraduate degree in English Literature and a Master of Arts in Creative Writing at Stanford. All this was a great blessing, but there was a fatal flaw in it. I had come to identify not only my worth, but my identity with my writing. If I was not "Ellen-the-Writer," I didn't know who I was. Consequently my writing was driven by anxiety. Through a series of events, many of which seemed incomprehensible at best and devastating at worst, I came in my mid-thirties to give up writing, and perforce to give up my self-image as "The Writer." It was traumatic—an identity crisis. I didn't know who I was. I was nothing; I felt totally out of control of my life. It was an existential "bottoming out."

Ram Dass said once in a lecture something like: "We are born into the world little nobodies, but pretty soon we begin to get 'Somebody-training.' It takes a lifetime to undo that, and come once again to be 'nobody in particular.'" In my mid-thirties, then, I realized that my Writing-Somebody had been crafted in defiance of the Somebody that my parents had tried to train me to be. Both were masks; neither was me. Masks and self-images were just another way of trying to control my sense of myself.

After that mid-thirties crisis I worked for twenty years on identifying my self-images and then sitting loose to them, emptying myself of them. In psychotherapy this process became more and more conscious. One Christmas I painted a Christmas card for my therapist. There were my self-images gathered around the tree—the Little Orphan Waif, the independent Queen of Sheba, the Writer, the Mystic, the Holy Nun, the Ravening Wolf. A banner over their heads read: "Merry Christmas from all of us!" A sense of humor about them meant I had perspective on them—I could let them go.

During those twenty years, I found I didn't *have* to write in order to exist, so I didn't write. Two decades later, in my mid-fifties, I awoke one morning and a story was in my head. It was as if I had been given a present. I began writing then every early morning and haven't stopped since. The difference in the two periods of writing, before and after the long dry period, is incalculable; it is the difference between compulsion and gift. Not long ago I found myself one morning asking God about the writing, "Are you doing this for me—or am I doing this for you?" And then a moment later, "Or are we doing this for them?"

This transformation of my writing has been one of the most profound lessons in my life: that letting go of demand and control leads to freedom and mutual gift. Telling my truth in words was given back to me, beyond my expectations and beyond my control, and like a grain of wheat that falls into the earth and dies, it bears much fruit.

Doug: What would you say to the person who has been given enormous gifts of administration or business and who consequently has a lot of control? Like a CEO who has been very successful in his or her life by virtue of being able to control a certain business or whatever. Do highly effective people need to look at their walk in the world as a dance also? Or are some people fully capable and even called to control things?

ES: Some people are called to leadership. Leadership by definition implies working well in community. No one walks in the world totally alone—captain of their fate and master of their soul—although often it feels like that. So yes, I would say that highly effective people are also, and maybe especially, called to be aware of what we're calling the dance. John Donne wrote, "No [person] is an island"; St. Paul said, "We who are many are one body." And I am not sure who the scientist was who said that if a butterfly in Beijing flaps its wing, the repercussions will travel out to affect the furthest star. C. S. Lewis has the most wonderful description of this cosmic interconnectedness in the last pages of his novel *Perelandra*. He calls it the Great Dance. The nice thing about the dance image is that it implies invitation, not coercion. As Lewis Carroll's Whiting said to the Snail, "Will you, won't you, will you, won't you come and join the dance?"

As I have said, control isn't all bad; we need control in some areas, and some people do have a calling and a gift for controlling or ordering situations in a most effective way. I would rather call the proper use of such a gift *authority* rather than control. The word "authority" can be traced back to Latin *augere*, meaning "to increase, produce." Authority, rightly exercised, increases responsibility in others; self-serving control diminishes it. A great CEO encourages and increases creative effort and responsibility in those around her or him. True authority comes out of personal fullness and the will to make order out of chaos. Driven control comes out of insecurity and hidden self-doubt and the need to adjust the environment for one's own self-aggrandizement. Control by force or manipulation might be called the junk food of power; it may satisfy the moment's ambition, but it won't effect any lasting good.

A shepherd may be said to control a flock. If the shepherd is a true shepherd and not a hired hand, the flock will be led out of care for its welfare and not out of the control needs of the shepherd. It is good to remember that the ability to order things well is a gift, and not necessarily a better gift than others. Peter S. Beagle has a wonderful paragraph illustrating this in his book *The Last Unicorn*. You can substitute "administrator" or "leader" for "hero."

"My Lady," he said, "I am a hero. It is a trade, no more, like weaving or brewing, and like them it has its own tricks and knacks and small arts. There are ways of perceiving witches, and of knowing poison streams; there are certain weak spots that all dragons have, and certain riddles that hooded strangers tend to set you. But the true secret of being a hero lies in knowing the order of things. The swineherd cannot already be wed to the princess when he embarks on his adventures...Things must happen when it is time for them to happen...The happy ending cannot come in the middle of the story....Heroes know about order, about happy endings—heroes know that some things are better than others. Carpenters know grains and shingles, and straight lines."

Doug: Why do people become addicted to control?

ES: Like any addiction, control *seems* to fill a need. The bottle, the cigarette, the needle, the Tarot pack, or the ability to put down or fire a threatening subordinate makes one feel temporarily less lonely, less ineffective or less vulnerable. The idea of letting go involves risk and fear. People ask, "What if I let go and don't make it to the top of my profession, lose people's admiration, lose my own sense of myself, completely fall apart? Is there any guarantee that I will not fall into the pit of despair—of no-self?" One faces a crisis of trust. I once asked a wise person, "How many battles can you lose and still win the war?" He answered, "All of them."

Sometimes when a person begins the hard transition from attempted control over his or her environment towards the freedom of "the dance" there is fear, or at least an uncomfortable insecurity. For a closer look at this adventure beyond the seeming guarantee of control, see Chapter Eight on transition. Suffice it to say here that in the end, risking without being *certain*, breaking the addiction to control, most often ushers in good news. You have written a whole book about how emptiness, letting go of control, though risky, "pays off," and may even go so far as to actually improve the bottom line! (*The Power of Acceptance*)

It is not hard to see why a human being becomes or stays addicted. It is *hard* to quit, to surrender. What must be given up is the lie that this substance or this behavior will do away with, or at least dull, the existential pain. Ultimately lies don't work. "The truth will make you free." Yes, but first it will make you miserable! The crucial point is trust that it will indeed and finally make us free.

Doug: Is it important to empty oneself of the need to control things in order to make room for grace? A related question, which may seem silly, is "do we experience less grace when we are "filled" with control or other issues?

ES: A word about grace: "Grace is God acting on the soul of [a human being]" (Mackenzie, K.D., *The Faith of the Church*). Another way to think about grace is that it is the way divine love is manifested and becomes effective in our lives. Classically there are two kinds of grace. The first is called "prevenient," and suggests the idea and wish to do what is good; the second is "cooperating," and gives the power to do it. If we see grace in this way, as the active power of Love's divine energy in our lives, then it's not too hard to see why our attempts to control things on our own might thwart or not leave room for that power. The attachment to personal control, the use of power for self-aggrandizement—these leave no room for grace, for the spirit. And it takes two to tango.

3

The Myth of Accumulation

Myth: The person with the most stuff wins.

Truth: The accumulation of wealth is only a tiny fraction of what it means to lead a fulfilling life. There are many different levels of desire and happiness, of which accumulation is only one.

> **If you live for having it all, what you have is never enough. In an environment of more is better, enough is like the horizon, always receding. The "more" that was supposed to make life better can never be enough.**
> **—Vicki Robin/Joe Dominguez**

The first order of business is to define what we mean by the word "accumulation." In general, it means "to gather, collect or pile up" according to Webster. It derives from the Latin *cumulare*, "to heap." What we mean by it is that there is a strong current in our culture that suggests that anything worth striving for in the material world is worth accumulating in large quantities. In America, and increasingly in other industrialized countries, "more is better."

This concept of more is better is not limited just to material wealth or material possessions but can also mean the accumulation of all kinds of things: honors, public adulation, children, romantic conquests or, as Thorstein Veblen put it, anything that facilitates "conspicuous consumption" (*The Theory of the Leisure Class*). We are a society that likes to hoard and collect material possessions in quantities that would boggle the minds of our forebears. And we do so because, ever since we were little, we were taught that fulfillment comes from such accumulation. This chapter will look at how we come to believe such things and how counter-productive such beliefs are in terms of helping us achieve a fulfilling life.

Family Systems and The Myth of Accumulation

Lest there be any doubt about how Americans have come to view the importance of wealth accumulation in the last 25 years or so, consider this statistic: a 1990 study asked, "If you could change one thing about your life, what would it be?" An astounding 64% or almost two out of three said, "More wealth" (Meyers, *The Pursuit of Happiness*). Numerous other studies have asked Americans what "quality of life" means to them and the most frequent response has referred to some kind of income security. A recent poll of baby-boomer-aged school teachers asked whether or not their students were significantly different than they had been as kids. The results of this poll confirm other research regarding the increase in materialism among youth. The poll found that 76% of the teachers felt their students were more materialistic than they were as kids (*The Power of Acceptance*).

These kinds of polls should come as no surprise to anyone who has been paying attention to the messages we have been digesting from our families, friends and from society. According to Martha Rogers, author of *The One to One Future*, American businesses produce between 2,000 to 3,000 commercial messages *every day* for every man, woman and child in the United States. We are literally bombarded with the notion that having and spending money will greatly improve our lives.

The way accumulation became important to me growing up was that it was all my family ever seemed to occupy themselves with. Every time I turned around, we were either thinking about buying something, shopping for it or actually picking it up. My parents were rather normal in this way and it was equally normal for my brother and me to be rewarded for doing well in school or doing chores around the house by receiving some material possession. It did not take long for us to figure out that in a market economy, stuff mattered—a lot.

Another way we received the message that money mattered was that our circle of friends was always talking about people who had a lot of money and holding them up on a pedestal—it was as though money was equated with ultimate power and success. Wealth accumulation was also the way we showed love for each other through the acquisition and transfer of material possessions. Thus at Christmas time, we would exchange a ridiculous number of gifts, in a genuine effort to show love for each other, but through the means of purchasing stuff. Since this system of showing love is pervasive in the United States, one can only imagine how heart-wrenching it is for the growing number of people in poverty to live through a holiday season with a limited ability to show their children and each other love in this way. This may partially explain the unprecedented credit card debt Americans have accumulated during the past ten years. Many people teeter on the brink of financial ruin as a result.

Since the predominant thing a majority of Americans would change about their life is more wealth, this suggests they have been socialized to spend most of their time striving to accumulate money. And as David Meyers has suggested, they pursue wealth because it carries with it the promise of happiness. Unfortunately, there is a significant body of research which suggests wealth accumulation alone does not lead to more happiness. Meyers points out that between 1957 and 1990, real per capita income in the United States, controlled for inflation, doubled from about $7,500 to about $15,000. Yet by many different measures of fulfillment or happiness, we have not become significantly happier as a society. According to data from the National Opinion Research Center, during this same period when per capita wealth was doubling, the number of people reporting they were "very happy" actually declined slightly from 34% to 29%. Thus, we have doubled our per capita wealth, but the number of those "very happy" has gone down.

Further, researcher Martin Seligman has suggested that Americans born after 1946 are *ten times* more likely to experience depression in their lives than those born prior to 1946. And when juxtaposed with the data about wealth increases, it raises serious questions about the value of wealth in contributing to mental health. As Seligman points out in his book *What You Can Change and What You Can't,* "It is shocking that Americans, on average, may be victims of unprecedented psychological misery in a nation with unprecedented prosperity, world power, and material well-being."

Peer Groups and The Myth of Accumulation

The primary way that accumulation manifests itself in the context of peer influences is in the comparison game. Kids at the teenage level are so concerned with the way their peers view them that they become obsessed with wearing the right clothes, the right shoes, make-up, etc. As I look back on my childhood, I was by no means the only child whose family played this game. My friends and I would compete for who had the coolest stuff and the most stuff after a birthday or a holiday season of gift exchanges had taken place. I can remember opening presents faster and faster, ultimately not even paying much attention to what was being unwrapped since I had my eyes on opening the next thing. Some people argue that rather than being too materialistic in the 1990s, we may actually not be materialistic enough in the sense of really valuing things. There is so much of everything in and around us that any one item becomes devalued.

There is something more insidious about this myth as it relates to peer influence. Since material possessions seem to be the preeminent path to esteem and acceptance, money becomes the magic elixir without which one will suffer. Individual relationships in this kind of environment become characterized by conditional love, the quid pro quo, you scratch my back and I'll scratch yours. Genuine, accepting, unconditional relationships become a measure of one's naiveté. As a youth group leader, I have often been shocked at the level of cynicism and cold-heartedness that kids demonstrate towards one another. And these are church youth group kids!

Many of them say that life for them is really just about surviving high school so they can go out and get a job and survive a little bit longer. Despite the booming economy we are experiencing at the time of this writing, many of the kids I encounter are not happy. Why? Part of the reason is that what they really need the most is a loving adult to guide them through the crucial teen years. But even in so-called nuclear families (those that haven't exploded), both mom and dad are working all the time in order to afford the stuff we have become convinced we need. As the pace of society quickens and shrinking time forces families to make hard choices about how to spend their time, the quest for material possessions has left human relationships in the dust for many Americans. It has led to what Michael Lerner has called "shrinking circles of concern" (*The Politics of Meaning*).

But it doesn't need to be this way. We don't need to make the accumulation of wealth the only measure of worth. I remember a time about five years ago when I was still reeling from a series of life-events that had caused me to be depressed and on the brink of financial disaster. The two true joys I had were spending time with my son Nicholas and reading books. I remember Nick and I having a profound conversation. One day, totally out of the blue, he asked me if we were rich. After picking myself up off the floor from laughing, I told him, "No, Nick, we aren't rich. In fact, I am quite poor right now by American society's standard measurement of wealth."

Then I recall having an insight which I shared with Nick. "You know, Nick, who ever decided that the dollar bill was the only measure of one's wealth? I don't remember voting on that one, do you? So from now on, what if we declared that the standard measure of one's wealth can be whatever we say. How about it?" I then went on to say that I thought the printed word should be the measure of wealth in our household because we both loved words and knowledge so much. We then went through every book we had and estimated the number of words in each book. Since the one thing I did have a lot of back then was books, the total came out to some 35 million printed words and we spent the rest of the weekend declaring ourselves filthy rich millionaires!!

I later thought about what a clever reframing of reality that had represented, but, on further reflection, I realized that I was still caught up in and completely brainwashed by the myth of accumulation, by continuing to define our worth in terms of the *quantity* of printed words we had accumulated.

Culture and The Myth of Accumulation

It is an old and almost worn-out idea that the media and specifically advertisers are the culprits for our over-consumption and over-accumulation. And while it is true that Americans in effect brainwash themselves by choosing to watch four or five hours of commercial-laden television per day, our desire to accumulate may have deeper roots. Television advertising and the retail-driven consumer society are really just symptoms of a deep yearning we all have for love and acceptance. And because we are either unable or unwilling to think more reflectively about why we do things like run up large balances on our credit cards and purchase huge quantities of unnecessary stuff, accumulation becomes the only apparent avenue to getting what we want on a deep level. Hence we get the phrase "retail therapy" as a way of describing the root of many consumers' motivation in the malls.

I have a number of friends who say they go shopping just because it is an activity they enjoy. Others are more direct about its palliative effects. "I had a bad day yesterday and so I am going to go do some damage to my Nordstrom card," one such friend has said. Another common phrase is, "No one else is going to be nice to me today, so I am going to go do something nice for myself and buy a new dress."

The problem with accumulation as a means of satisfying deeper types of yearnings is that it simply doesn't work or, if it does work, it doesn't work for long. It may be what ES would call another example of "junk food for the soul." Joe Dominquez and Vicki Robin, in their book *Your Money or Your Life*, described a concept called "The Fulfillment Curve." The idea is that when one starts out in life, one assumes that each additional material possession will result in a corresponding rise in one's fulfillment or happiness. And

The Fulfillment Curve

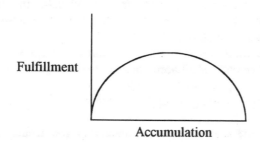

Fulfillment

Accumulation

for quite a while, this is what happens. But as Dominquez and Robin point out, as we continue to acquire material possessions, the curve begins to flatten and pretty soon we are buying more and more stuff and it is not producing more fulfillment. At some critical level, each additional purchase results not only in the absence of an increase in fulfillment, but a decline. This is because we are spending so much time working to pay for and maintain things that it is reducing our happiness.

When I first read this book about five years ago, I instinctively agreed with Dominquez and Robin. It seemed to make sense that there would be, in effect, a law of diminishing returns with regard to consumption and accumulation. But because there was no real data behind it, it was an easy thing to dismiss. As we have pointed out, however, there is data which suggests that accumulation of wealth alone will not result in limitless increases in fulfillment and happiness.

If we were to graph the research cited earlier about the doubling of per capita wealth versus polls which gauge individual happiness, it would look almost exactly the same as the Dominquez/Robin's Fulfillment Curve. From 1957 to 1990, wealth increased but those reporting they were very happy flattened and started to decline slightly. Factor in the huge increases in those reporting bouts with depression and you have a strong indication that declines in happiness may continue despite increases in wealth.

So how do we make sense of all of this? Why is it that we start out so thoroughly convinced that we are going to become happy by accumulating wealth, only to find that there is a limit to the extent to which it will get us there? One of the most remarkable educational experiences I have had was in the second year of the doctoral program at Seattle University in 1995. It was a Saturday morning and we had an instructor from the Philosophy Department, Bob Spitzer, come and talk to us. Spitzer taught undergraduate-level philosophy courses on the classics: Aristotle, Plato, St. Augustine, and so, being somewhat snobbish doctoral-level students, some of us began the morning with a bit of an attitude about what an undergraduate professor was doing teaching at this level.

Spitzer, however, was no normal undergraduate professor. He had been an accountant, then a Jesuit priest who earned a doctorate in philosophy. In addition, at the time of this writing, Bob Spitzer had just been appointed President of Gonzaga University. Not bad for a 45-year-old former accountant. He began in the following manner: "If I could describe for you a theory of human happiness upon which every philosopher, theologian, historian and poet during the last 2,400 years would agree, would you be interested?"

Needless to say, this statement piqued the curiosity of every student in the room. We were listening. Bob went on to describe the four main desires of human beings or, as some call it, the four levels of happiness. I describe here what he had to say because I think it is an effective way to put into context the reasons why accumulation of stuff alone does not get us where we want to be on the "fulfillment curve" of life. Spitzer diagrammed the four levels of human desire or happiness:

Level Four   -   Ultimate Reality
Level Three -   Good Beyond Self
Level Two   -   Ego Satisfaction
Level One   -   Physical Pleasure

The way to view these levels of happiness is in terms of how deep, wide and long the happiness pay-off is for each. In general, Level One and Two activities offer more immediate gratification which wears off more quickly. Levels Three and Four tend to have a slower payoff, but the rewards are deeper and more long-lasting.

Level One is the pleasure produced by an external stimulus like the sensory stimulation of drinking a latte or the satisfaction derived from owning a fancy car. This level is where we would put most of the accumulated possessions that we have been discussing, although some things are purchased for other reasons. Certainly buying and owning things like new furniture, fancy foods, a bigger or better house, computers, etc. would be purchased pursuant to this desire.

Level Two of happiness is about ego gratification, such as achievements or recognition, or power and control. We would accumulate impressive awards, fancy job titles, impressive-sounding degrees in order to address this type of desire. Accumulating expensive things might also serve to satisfy this level. It is also the stimulus behind the wearing of social masks and trying to lose weight and stay in shape in order to compare favorably to others and gain their approval.

Level Three of happiness is the pleasure derived from serving others beyond oneself; it is making a contribution to society. Spitzer says that in terms of how we live our lives, Level Three activities are likely to generate more lasting fulfillment and happiness than levels one or two, but that each level represents legitimate human needs. By extending oneself beyond one's immediate needs, wants and ego, one is beginning to participate in the broader context of life. It is also Level Three that cultivates our relationships with others and helps build social networks of community. There is much research which shows that people who interact with others regularly are more fulfilled or happy than those who do not. Extroverts always score higher on happiness survey instruments than introverts. Speaking as an introvert, I have always found this statistic annoying.

Level Four of happiness is the pleasure to be derived from being associated with the infinite, something which is transcendent and of

The Four Levels of Human Happiness

Level Four — Ultimate or Infinite Reality

The focus is on understanding the broader context
in which one exists. Some have called this level
"Spirit."

Level Three — Good Beyond Self

The focus is on connection to something other
than one's own needs and expectations. As it
relates to relationship, ES calls this level "Gift."

Level Two — Ego Satisfaction

The focus is on competition, winning and on
re-enforcement from others. As it relates to
relationship, ES calls this level "Justice."

Level One — Physical Pleasure

The focus is on physical pleasure and satisfaction.
As it relates to relationship, ES calls this
level "Narcissism."

ultimate significance. It is moving into the realm of higher
consciousness, where the broader context is glimpsed, however
fleetingly. Level Four is about recognizing that there is a bigger
universe which we often cannot fully grasp but to which we are
nevertheless connected.

These four levels of happiness are useful as a way of putting into
context one of the reasons accumulation is in fact a myth. Spitzer's
point is that while material wealth is indeed a legitimate source of
pleasure and happiness, it is only one level of happiness and the
bottom level at that.

The trick to operating within these four realms, says Spitzer, is
to stand on the ground of one level, with a vigilant eye on the
horizon of the next level. Understanding the limited nature of
materialism and its accumulation is the key to not getting stuck in it.
Likewise, realizing that one's ego needs are important but not the
sole point of human existence is crucial to increasing the extent to
which life can be fulfilling. Too often we get stuck by asking
materialism (Level One) to do something for us it was not designed
to do (provide ultimate happiness and meaning.)

In order to avoid becoming stuck in any of the levels of one's
desire, we must understand the context, the infinite horizon against
which we live and breathe. As Frederick Buechner has said, idolatry
is "ascribing absolute value to something of relative worth" (*Wishful
Thinking: A Seeker's ABC*). Part of what ails us may be that we are
filled with beliefs that do precisely that: place ultimate value on
things of relative value. The mistake is to believe "things" to have
absolute value. Too many of us are stuck going back and forth
between Levels One and Two, not understanding the importance of
Levels Three and Four, because our culture places so little emphasis
on them. I asked ES to begin to help us explore these ideas in a
series of questions on the subject of accumulation.

Dialogue on The Myth of Accumulation

**Doug: First of all, there seems to be a lot of evidence and
research to prove that money can't buy happiness. Why do you
think we continually clamor for more stuff when it clearly is not
making us happier?**

ES: "More stuff" is very attractive. You might say it is irresistible. Evidence of the attraction goes back to Adam and Eve. They had a whole garden of fruit trees to eat from. Why did they want *one more*? When Eve "saw that the tree was good for food, and that it was a delight to the eyes and that the tree was to be desired to make one wise, she took of its fruit and ate." "More stuff" always shows itself as good and delightful and something we need to make us better, greater, happier, richer, or wiser. The desired object sets up in us a mental static that drowns out any rational knowledge. We can't or won't hear that in the *long run* inordinate amassing of things will make us not more fulfilled, but diminished.

King Midas, for instance, wanted more gold. Gold is by nature good and delightful. It's both very attractive and very useful. The gods granted Midas's wish that everything he touched would turn to gold. His delight lasted only one day. That evening when he sat down to dinner he realized with a shock that his food and drink also turned to gold. Dying of hunger and thirst, he had to go back to the gods begging them to take their gift away, which they mercifully did.

I once met a King Midas in real life who was not so fortunate. Shortly before I entered the convent, I was visiting my parents. I went with them to a party at a prestigious club in New York City given in honor of my stepfather's birthday. I was sitting at the edge of a large room and had a feeling similar to the one I had in the school playground which I described in Chapter Two. Here, there were not children but men and women in their late middle age. They seemed to have everything—success, money, education, culture—in some cases, fame and public honor. And yet as I watched and listened to them socializing, they still seemed to be restless, "wheeling and dealing," still "on the make." They still wanted *more*; more stuff, more recognition. They "had arrived," but they did not seem content. Then one of my stepfather's colleagues came and sat next to me. He was curious about the vocational decision I had made, by which I would disenfranchise myself from my inheritance. For some reason, in the course of our conversation he shared with me the sorrow of his life. He had an only daughter to whom he and his wife had given everything, and of whom they had had high hopes. She was endowed with beauty, talent, connections, and wealth. She was a Golden Girl. She had been killed by throwing herself out of her college dorm window. Having everything she could want was, in the long run, not enough.

Human beings have a built-in desire for what is good. One problem comes in discerning between short-term good and long-term good (or intrinsic and extrinsic values). For instance, a young person is faced with the choice of studying or going to the movies. Going to the movies has intrinsic value; it is seen as good in itself. The young person may, however, choose to stay home and study because of the extrinsic values of a better job and a fuller life in the future.

It's hard for us to discern between immediate and lasting goods, particularly in the heat of the moment. Maybe it's even harder to choose between goods appropriate to our immaturity and those we are called to choose out of our "ripeness." The goods or stuff we clamor for out of infant narcissism are very different from those of ripened wisdom when we have learned how to delay gratification. Your citation of Spitzer's four levels of human desire is very helpful here. One reason we "continually clamor for more stuff when it clearly is not making us happier," is that we either get stuck in, or regress back to, Spitzer's levels one or two. Getting stuck often has to do with personal and cultural unawareness; we are just going along with the flow. Regression often happens when we are under stress. I wish everybody could have a glimpse of levels three and four. Then when people, like that young woman who "had everything," come to the stark realization that, in the long run, levels one and two are not going to be enough to make them happy, there would not be so many instances of tragic despair.

Doug: You and I have previously discussed your idea that people may strive for accumulation because we really think in terms of scarcity: the fear that some day we will run out of stuff, so we should hoard it. Is that a factor in this rush to consume?

ES: I think so. Perhaps the fear, and in many cases the experience, of deprivation, of having everything one prizes taken away from one, underlies the scarcity syndrome. I know several people who as children lived in fear that anything they really wanted, or wanted to do, would be denied them. They grew up feeling deprived. As adults they find it very difficult to throw anything away, or to sit lightly to honors and recognition. It seems that because they did not have enough in the past, nothing is enough now.

The "Pack-rat" is one type of accumulator. Another type is the Collector. Perhaps the difference is that the Collector doesn't accumulate everything, just selected things. My mother was a Collector. She was a brilliant woman (Phi Beta Kappa, an M.A. in Philosophy from Columbia), who, because of the cultural norms of her youth, had been deprived of the means to the appropriate expression of her gifts which would have been available to her today. She said to me just before she died, that what she really would have liked to have been in life was not a wife and mother, but editor of *The New York Times*. Possibly it was because she had been deprived of what would have been for her a fulfilling career, that she put so much energy into collecting. I am not suggesting that being a collector is a bad thing in itself. One thing Mother collected was pre-Columbian gold. She left her gold to a museum where others now may enjoy its beauty, and I suppose it is fitting that her name is to be found among the others inscribed on the marble slabs that line the grand staircase. But I am saying that the accumulation did not seem in the end to make her a happier or more fulfilled person.

There is also a difference between collecting and hoarding. For some people collecting is emotionally neutral; hoarding carries a sense of secrecy and greed. Hoarders squirrel their stuff away, they stockpile it so that no one will deprive them of it. When I hear the word "hoard," I think of a dragon stretched on top of its hoard. Dragons aren't depicted as happy. (A hoard of metal and stones must be an uncomfortable bed!) And everybody in the story is scared to death of them and is either trying to avoid them or kill them. Who is going to love a cold, dangerous and scaly monster? Is it because dragons are deprived of love and friendship that they accumulate or hoard under their soft, vulnerable bellies, great piles of gold and jewels? I think deprivation breeds a scarcity mentality, and fear of scarcity, in turn, breeds an inordinate need to accumulate and then to defend our hoard. No matter how much precious stuff we pile up, the fear of scarcity persists, and it persists in depriving us of contentment, and even more, of happiness.

Doug: How do we go about emptying ourselves of the belief that wealth will buy happiness?

ES: Emptying ourselves of any of our belief systems takes a lot of doing. The first step is a commitment to awareness. By that I mean a resolve to face the facts, to look at things as they really are. At one time I believed Marilyn Monroe had everything that made for happiness. She was, even more than the daughter of my stepfather's friend, beautiful, young, famous, truly talented and wealthy. Her death was a shock. When she died it seemed that none of those things had been sufficient to make her happy. I began to look at the wealthy people I knew or read about, to see if in fact they *did* seem happier than other people. Most of them didn't. The next step was to look at myself. What was the real reason I wanted to possess more things? To win respect? Love? Power? Independence? Self-worth? Identity? Even immortality? Could wealth really buy those things?

> The land of a rich man produced abundantly. And he thought to himself, "What should I do, for I have no place to store my crops?" Then he said, "I will do this: I will pull down my barns and build larger ones, and there I will store all my grain and my goods. And I will say to my soul, 'Soul, you have ample goods laid up for many years; relax, eat, drink, be merry.'" But God said to him, "You fool! This very night your life is being demanded of you. And the things you have prepared, whose will they be?" (Luke 12: 16-20)

That's a classic example of the false promise that wealth will bring enduring happiness, or immortality. Another classic and haunting reminder is Shakespeare's "Golden lads and girls all must,/ As chimney sweepers, come to dust."

Once we have become aware of the need for emptying ourselves of the myth that accumulating things will make us happy, it's time to take a closer look at how "emptiness" will bring peace rather than more stress. There are at least two kinds of emptiness. The emptiness that comes from force or misfortune isn't good news. The emptiness that will make us free must be *chosen*. It cannot be deprivation, even self-deprivation; it must be a voluntary giving away of a lesser good in order to make room for a greater good.

Mary Ann Schmidt wrote about this in the Winter 1994 issue of *Communique*, the newsletter of The Foundation for Community Encouragement, after her house burned down: "Emptiness is not the barrenness of despair...nor is it the wresting from your grasp or mine of possessions. Emptiness is a CHOICE—not something out of our control."

The key word in any stripping away of possessions is choice. Saint Francis chose, in the public square in Assisi, to strip off all his expensive clothes and return them to his angry father, and stand there naked before God. He chose to strip himself. If you choose to give something away it is not violation, it is freedom. And what it is freedom *from* is not things—things are neutral—but the attachment to things. It is not money itself but the *love* of money that is the root of all evil. The point of emptying ourselves is freedom to discern which good things will contribute to our deepest happiness in the long run.

Doug: In the conversations you have with people, is accumulation an issue that comes up? If so, how?

ES: A few people talk to me about not having enough, especially to keep up with the needs and demands of their children. But most of what I hear is uneasiness about having accumulated too much. This often becomes a conscious issue when a person is about to make a move, or to make the Big Move—death. The striking characteristic of this issue is guilt.

Often when people are faced with a move, especially when they are faced with moving out of this life "sooner rather than later," it becomes clear that the things they have squirreled away are going to be brought to light and picked over. People dread comments like "You should have seen his basement!" or "Guess how many jars of face cream she had stockpiled?" Even in a minor move, it's not too pleasant to face such things oneself.

Another thing I often hear, explicitly or implicitly, is akin to what has been called in the military "survivor's guilt." People say to me things like: "When millions in the world are starving, why should I have so much to eat that I have a problem with obesity?" The seed of this kind of guilt was sown in my own experience as a child; when I didn't finish the food on my plate I was reminded of the starving Armenians. (Undoubtedly that dates me! For different generations there are different starving peoples.) Or, "When so many people die in the streets of Calcutta, or in unimaginable living conditions, why do I have this big house on three acres, with a hot tub?" Or, "When others do not know how to read, why do I have a wall full of diplomas and certificates?" These are painful and complex questions, and it is understandable that they are often

repressed until a crisis (such as a major move) is imminent. It seems
that one reason why over-accumulation doesn't make us happy is
because of the guilt that develops in connection with it. It is just
possible that in our current culture we feel more guilt about our
stockpiling than about our sexuality, and so it is less taboo to inquire
about someone's sex life than about their bank account.

It will be appropriate to tackle the social and environmental
aspects of these issues of accumulation further on in our dialogue.
Right now I'd like to mention another concern that people
sometimes bring to our conversations—a sense of guilt about their
hidden or semi-hidden motives for accumulation. This issue is
related to one we talked about previously: the danger of investing
one's worth or identity in something external to oneself. Some
people become aware that they are in danger of identifying their
worth, or even their understanding of themselves, with what they
possess. The gold Cadillac, the golden throne, the gold medal, and
the pre-Columbian gold collection can become more than status
symbols; such acquisitions, or what they signify, can take over a part
of who their owners *are* to the world, and most dangerously, who
they are to themselves. What would they do if they lost these things?
Who would they be? Who would remember them after they are gone?
Often, when these questions become conscious, persons may feel
guilt at using external things to define themselves. At the same time
they may begin to grieve the loss of these ego props. Such grief is
realistic.

However, as my conversations with people have proceeded, the
"good news" eventually surfaces. The first part of the good news is
that the *awareness* of the problem is the most effective step toward
its resolution. Secondly, awareness will lead to freedom—in this
case, freedom from misplaced attachment to things. Misplaced and
inordinate attachment leads at worst to addiction and exploitation;
even at best it may result in doing oneself out of guilt-free
enjoyment.

Guilt about accumulation is insidious. I used to carry it
unconsciously. Then once, many years ago, I was sent on a team
mission to a Native American reservation in southern Canada. I had
a break-through there. The comparison between what I and the other
team members had, and what the native people had was shocking
enough to make me painfully aware both of my good fortune and of
my guilt about it. Then I asked myself, "What would I wish for the

children of this household I am billeted in?" I realized that I would
wish for them basic food, clothing and education. And I would also
wish for them some "extras." And then I thought, if I truly would
want extras for them, is it wrong to want them for myself? And I
answered myself—"No! I am to love my neighbor *as* myself—not
better than myself."

It is true that many people, and I was one of them, need to go
through a certain period of rigorous discipline and self-denial in
order to be able to get to the desired goal of "sitting loose" to things.
However, assuming moderation and sharing, good things are created
to be delighted in, and our appropriate response to them is not guilt,
but gratitude and generosity.

**Doug: Can a person have a lot of money and continue to
accumulate and still grow spiritually? Or as Jesus said, is it
really easier for a camel to go through the eye of a needle than
for a rich person to go to heaven?**

ES: If you remember, just after Jesus said that bit about the camel, he
concluded with: "...for God all things are possible." So I would say,
yes, it is *possible* for a person to continue to accumulate and still
grow spiritually. But it isn't easy. Scholars through the ages have
fretted over the saying you quoted (Matthew 19:24; Mark 10:25;
Luke 18:25). It has been suggested, for example, that "The Eye of a
Needle" was the name of a very narrow gate in the city wall through
which it was impossible for a heavily laden camel to pass—
something like one of our overpasses which can only accommodate
vehicles under a certain height. The Anchor Bible mentions such
explanations, but concludes: "...it seems certain that this is simply a
proverb cast in hyperbolic form." In any case, taken in context, the
point of the story is to show that having many possessions, or as you
put it, "continuing to accumulate," may pose a strong, if not an
irresistible, distraction to finding the true treasure of one's life.

I expect each human being must discern for herself or himself
where their heart is: which of the world's goods are nurturing to
their spiritual growth and which diminish spirit, even while
fattening their bodies or their egos or their wallets. There is a fine
description of the distractions of possessions in the Old Testament
book of Ecclesiasticus, or The Wisdom of Sirach. It also includes the
statement there that it is *possible* to be rich and also to be blessed:

"Wakefulness over wealth wastes away one's flesh, and anxiety about it drives away sleep...One who loves gold will not be justified; one who pursues money will be led astray by it...[But] Blessed is the rich person who is found blameless, and who does not go after gold. Who is he, that we may praise him? For he has done wonders among his people" (Sirach 31: 1-24) .

Doug: What is the balance we should strike in accumulating or not accumulating, based on Spitzer's levels of happiness? Do you buy this model at all?

ES: The Ecclesiasticus passage quoted above is a good lead-in to responding to this question. (One who *loves* gold will not be justified," etc.) It is perhaps not so much a question of balance but of attitude. That is, it may be less important whether we have much or little, plain things or costly, than whether we can sit lightly to them or, on the contrary, hoard them for purposes of self-worth, the approval of others, or greed born of the scarcity myth. I once learned a hard lesson about this.

Years ago, I was stationed in our Convent in Georgia. One Christmas a neighborhood child brought the Sisters some ball-point pens as a present. She spilled them out of a bag onto the table where we were having tea. The one that fell in front of Sister Josephine was black and silver; the one in front of me was exactly the same pen, but a garish orange. I envied Sister Josephine's black and silver pen. For three days I fretted about whether I should ask Sister Josephine to trade with me or not. I hated myself for being so petty and greedy. I tried to forget about it but I couldn't. When I stopped worrying about the black pen, I started worrying about my attachment. Here was someone who had given away a small fortune and who got hung up on a black plastic pen! No, I finally realized, it is not the amount or value of the stuff we have or don't have; it is how it entraps our attention and our spirit. After three days, what I learned was that I did not want my heart to be enslaved by the "treasure" of a ball-point pen. Or any other *thing*.

Spitzer's four levels of human desire and happiness are splendid, and I think they march along very well with the levels of love and the process of "ripening" we talked about in Chapter One— the journey from narcissism to self-gift.

I think one needs to be careful, though, how one interprets "Good Beyond Self." It is all too easy, especially in some later forms of the Christian ethic, to interpret that as meaning we should be less good to ourselves, or even beat up on ourselves. I once ran across the rather cute but misleading saying: "**JOY** means: Jesus first, **O**thers second, and **Y**ourself last." That sort of thing can lead to a very false kind of humility and a very false kind of imposed austerity. It is no good seeing myself "last" as a way of condoning a poor self-image. As one wise person put it: "If you have a shabby self-image, how are you going to love your neighbor, if you love your neighbor as yourself?"

Ultimate reality is indeed beyond self—but it is good to remember that it means joy and good things for all, including oneself. Like any true community, ultimate reality is completely inclusive. In fact, in the early Christian tradition, heaven is described not only as a grand party, but as the feast at a wedding reception, the nuptial supper of the Lamb. If we want to have eternal joy, we need to start practicing enjoyment now. Perhaps some capacity for delight and enjoyment is the appropriate "wedding garment" for that banquet.

Doug: The simplicity movement says that we should all just sell everything we have that is a luxury and live a minimalist or ascetic life. But in my experience, that does not guarantee fulfillment either, does it? I mean monks and nuns and ascetics aren't always happy are they?

ES: Actually, I think there may be a number of questions here. First a word about the "simplicity movement." As the Shaker hymn states, it is a gift to be simple. As our culture and the human race as a whole "ripens," it is to be hoped that we will collectively as well as individually receive and cherish that gift, and learn to delay gratification. If we do not simplify our consumer demands and distribute the world's wealth more equitably, we will mortally deprive huge segments of populations. If the human race doesn't move up Spitzer's scale to considerations of "Good Beyond Self," our heedless accumulation and consumption of the world's resources may be felt in our own time, and not just our great-grandchildren's. Of course we try to repress such considerations. It is hard enough to come to the point of death and realize, "I can't take it with me." To realize that the human race may die, and that we would not even be remembered as we remember the dinosaurs, is even harder. The unconscious or semi-conscious guilt that we may be abettors in humanity's and in our planet's death is almost greater than we can bear.

Ecological concerns are very closely related to the simplicity movement, and they are of both practical and spiritual significance. There are many excellent books on treating our earth, Gaia, and her natural resources with love and respect, by writers from Thomas Berry to Al Gore. There is one book I will mention for its clarity about the importance of the spiritual attitude toward worldly goods: *The Gift* by Lewis Hyde. One of Hyde's points that struck me most forcibly is his contrast of our prevailing consumer society with the gift society of the early Native American people. When, for instance, they needed to consume the bison, they first gave the beast their worshipful respect and gratitude, and the bison in mutual gift offered its life to them for food.

But we are part of *our* society, and there is a limit to how simple we may be and still remain a part of it. It is crucial to remember that guilt, and its consequent beating up on ourselves, will not in itself help anything. What will help is awareness, acceptance of the realities involved, and doing what we can.

In my community there are certain things we agree to do communally, like recycling and eating less high on the food chain, and then each of us individually does what she can. For instance, Sister Ruth is able to use a minimal amount of face tissue; she washes and irons her handkerchiefs. Over the decades, I don't know how many trees she may have saved. I haven't gotten that simple yet, but I am quite good at "recycling" clothes and wearing "hand-me-downs" without, I am told, looking unkempt or dowdy. One thing we all can do is approach the things we own or use with gratitude and delight, and not as things to be consumed and exploited for self-aggrandizement.

There is another point about simplicity. Simplicity comes in two stages. The "second simplicity" lies beyond and not this side of complexity. Scott Peck develops this point splendidly in *The Road Less Traveled and Beyond*, basing his insight on a quotation from Oliver Wendell Holmes, Jr.: "I don't give a fig for the simplicity on this side of complexity, but I would die for the simplicity on the other side."

I first became aware of the two simplicities decades ago when I was in a museum in front of a late Picasso drawing of a woman's face. Two people came up, and one remarked to the other, "My three-year-old could do that!" I thought to myself, "No. Your three year old couldn't." A child's drawing of a circle with minimal lines for eyes, nose, and mouth would be completely different. The Picasso drawing has behind it a lifetime of observation and draftsmanship; the placement of these simple lines reveal the anatomy and expression of the face they represent. Shakespeare came to the second simplicity of *Lear* and *The Tempest* on the other side of *Titus Andronicus* and *Measure for Measure*.

Sometimes I think the "simplicity movement" is rather simplistic, more like the first of the two simplicities, in that it seems to negate the complexity of living in our present day world. (Sister Ruth may save trees, but eliminate jobs.) True simplicity sometimes takes a lifetime of conscious concern and action to achieve. In my experience, only the second kind of ripened simplicity, informed by experience and chosen in grace, can lead to fulfillment.

A word about "ascetics." The word comes from the Greek meaning "discipline" and was used to refer to training for the Olympic games: stripping down and getting in shape. Asceticism, like any practice, is of no merit in itself—it is for the purpose of attaining. In the Olympic games it was, as St. Paul put it, to attain a perishable wreath; in the spiritual realm we train for imperishable prizes like ripeness, spiritual freedom and peace.

You might say that monks and nuns are professionals in this spiritual "race": we are supported and sponsored to run it. But as in all athletic events, the professionals do not always compete for virtuous reasons; they can be as caught up in greed and self-aggrandizement and pride as anyone else. So, also, monks and nuns. The stripping down of the monastic lifestyle must be chosen, and chosen for good, healthy reasons if it is to lead to fulfillment and freedom. Monastic poverty is not meant to be masochism, degradation or indigence. It is not rightly an imposed deprivation. It has to do with gift and humility—the respectful and appropriate approach to and use of things.

The holy men and women who lived in the wildernesses of Egypt and Palestine in the fourth and fifth centuries C.E. knew a lot about living simply. They knew that rigorous external practices, though sometimes useful as a way to begin to change one's life-style, meant very little *in themselves*. Theodora was one of the great "Desert Mothers." Amma Theodora said, "There was an anchorite who was able to banish the demons, and he asked them, 'What makes you go away? Is it fasting?' They replied, 'We do not eat or drink.' 'Is it vigils?' They replied, 'We do not sleep.' 'Is it separation from the world?' 'We live in the deserts.' 'What power sends you away then?' They said, 'Nothing can overcome us, but only humility.' Do you see how humility is victorious over the demons?" (*The Desert Christian*, translated by Benedicta Ward, S.L.G.)

To the degree that it is joyfully chosen, simplicity can be a way of emptying the vessel in order for there to be space for the joy and peace that "dancing with the spirit" invites. Happiness is a by-product neither of acquisition nor of deprivation; happiness is a by-product of the mutual self-gift of mature love.

Doug: To me, the reason for accumulating things like praise from others is that it is providing me with love that I need. And I know we have discussed the fact that God already unconditionally loves me, but my God is very often a silent God and if she loves me, I don't hear it enough. So to give up the need for approval from others in order to listen for approval from a silent God is scary and often unfulfilling. Is my preoccupation with praise from others drowning out the voice of God?

ES: It is true that our God is most often a God of silence and invisibility. The wonderful new translation of the "still small voice" passage in the book of Kings (I Kings 19:12) is: "...but the Lord was not in the fire; and after the fire a sound of sheer silence." "Truly, you are a God who hides himself [or herself], O God of Israel, the Savior" (Isaiah 45:15). It is a built-in part of our humanity to yearn to see the face of Divine Compassion and to hear the voice of Love.

There is a story which I connect with the writer Madeleine L'Engle, though I've heard it attributed to other sources. It's the story of a small boy who was afraid of the dark. One night he kept thinking of excuses to keep his mother with him. "I want a glass of milk," and then when the milk was gone, "I have to go potty," and after that was done, "Read me another story." Finally the patient mother said, "That's enough, now try to go to sleep." "It's dark," came the quavering little voice, "don't leave me alone." "You don't have to be afraid, love," said the mother gently, "you're not alone, God is with you." After a moment the child answered, "But I want someone *with skin on!*"

It is human to want "someone with skin on." (As we have noted, perhaps that is the reason for the Incarnation.) Sometimes, though, in the mystery of Love, the Absolute does seem to leave us in the lonely, scary dark. Even Jesus, being fully human, felt this to the point of agony and dereliction in the garden of Gethsemane and on the cross.

It is not a bad thing to desire people's love, and their good opinions of us, any more than it is a bad thing to desire the material goods we have talked about. The trouble comes when we accumulate human praise and good opinions *as a substitute* for God's love, for true friendship or for our own self-acceptance. We are then, once again, stockpiling treasures which may fill us but not nourish us in the long run. And the anxiety that attends our driven, or even addictive, need for these good opinions will keep us from freedom.

Here is an example. When I was young and living in New York City I had a friend, who had first been a friend of my mother's, and of whom I was in some awe. She was a member of the European aristocracy who, as a girl, had been sent to England and then to this country to escape the war. She now lived alone in an exquisite apartment on the Upper East Side, cultivated white azaleas on her balcony, devoutly attended the nearby Roman Catholic church, and prepared meals that were fit for royalty. This was definitely a person whose good opinion I craved. The story begins with the sad fact that I had arrived late to one of those elegant repasts, and the meat had been the slightest bit overdone. Nothing, of course, was said, but I had felt terrible.

And now, about a month later, I had been asked to dinner again, and I was on the 79th Street bus crossing to the East Side. Before we got through Central Park I realized the traffic was very heavy, and, in fact, we were soon in a traffic jam. I had not allowed sufficient time for unforeseen delays. My anxiety level, always fairly high in those days, began to rise. By now the bus had stopped and I began to perspire and feel the blood drain away from my head. I *couldn't* be late again! What would she think of me? What would I think of myself? Five minutes later the bus still wasn't moving and I had all the classic symptoms of a panic attack. I started fantasizing: if I got off the bus and tried to run, could I get there in time? No. If I got a taxi? No, the taxi would be caught in the same traffic. If I went home I could call her and say...I had sprained my ankle? I was looking forward so much to coming *next* week? Anything but admit I had not left enough time *again*. My need for approval at that moment was certainly "drowning out the voice of God" and even of sanity. At the height of this panic state, I came to some sort of brink of choice. And I did something entirely new for me—I gave up. I emptied myself of the demand for approval and praise. I chose to surrender to the reality of the situation and face the worst: I was going to be late and it was my own fault. Period. And then, standing in that bus in the middle of Manhattan rush hour, the most tremendous feeling of relief fell upon me. All the panic symptoms left me, and I was simply there on the bus between Madison and Park, fallible but free!

As it turned out I was about fifteen minutes late. I walked into my friend's apartment, said, "I'm sorry," and she accepted my apology graciously as my rational mind had known she would. The roast chicken was perhaps the tiniest bit less moist and tender than it might have been, but we proceeded to have a lovely evening. Whenever, now, I am tempted to scramble after the approval of others as a substitute for God's love or my own self-esteem, I remember the 79th Street cross-town bus. I am fallible. For those who feel unkindly towards me, my fallibility will add fuel to their fire; for my friends, it will be matter for forgiveness.

Doug: If I give up much of my preoccupation with accumulating material things, what is there to replace it? Am I to become empty for the sake of emptiness? What is the quid pro quo for following the "road less material"?

ES: We said asceticism has no virtue in itself, but only in what it is the training *for*, and similarly there is no virtue in emptying for the sake of emptying. First, let's look at what we're emptying ourselves *of*. In our Community Building work we have identified five aspects of emptiness. We may empty ourselves of:

1. The biases, prejudices, cultural lies and images that keep us from seeing the truth about ourselves and others.

2. Our own pre-determined and unyielding agenda.

3. The need to control, fix, organize, or convert oneself, another or a group.

4. The fear that keeps us from the kind of surrender "to a higher power" of which the Twelve-Step groups speak.

5. The demand for certainty, security and perfection.

James Wilkes, in discussing Paul Tillich's theology, has written: "The truth is that [human beings] cannot have absolute security, certitude, or perfection. To want them is understandable, to demand them is diabolical, and to believe that one has already attained them is madness" (*The Gift of Courage*). In other words, it's human, and O.K. to want things, but unless we empty ourselves of the *demanding*, we will never achieve the freedom and peace such as that which came to me on the 79th Street bus.

The point of emptying a vessel is to provide space for that with which you want to fill it. Empty space is basically neutral, and it can even be dangerous. The natural order abhors a vacuum, and so does the supernatural. Remember what Jesus said about the unclean spirit that went out of a person? When it came back, it found its house "...empty, swept, and put in order. Then it goes and brings along seven other spirits more evil than itself, and they enter and live there" (Matthew 12:43). If a vessel is emptied, if a space is cleared, then it should in due season be filled with the desired good. If a person makes a clearing in a field to plant a garden, then they should get on with cultivation, or the land will revert to its former state. We will talk more about "filling" the vessel in Chapter Nine.

But there is one very important point to be made here. Both in gardening and in human spirituality there is a crucial time between the clearing out of the old growth and the planting of new growth. It is a harrowing time. In the dictionary the first definition of "harrow" is "an implement of agriculture...to stir the soil," that is, to break up the hard crust and clods. A later definition states that metaphorically to be "under the harrow" means "to suffer affliction or distress."

In classical spirituality this time is called "the dark night of the senses." It may well begin when a person has realized that the myth of "more is better" is a cultural lie, that more stuff or acclaim is not, in fact, providing happiness. That person may start to divest himself or herself of accumulated "stuff," both of material possessions and of over-reliance on public honors and the good opinion of others. But the knack of inviting spiritual good into that empty space takes time, just as the land, after it has been cleared, must be harrowed and otherwise prepared before it can receive the good seed.

If I may switch images, it's like being in the state where a tadpole is turning into a frog. I would imagine that is a very uncomfortable or at least an awkward experience. The little amphibian is losing its gills and having to breathe a rarefied atmosphere with brand new tiny lungs; it is losing the long tail that was so handy for swimming, and it is not yet proficient on these clumsy new legs for land use.

The only choice is to wait it out. But it is very helpful to many people to realize that this decision to move from "stuff" to spirit is a transition, and the transformational stage of "neither still here nor yet there" is a recognized experience in the spiritual life. Just because it doesn't feel good doesn't mean it's not working. If the intention, the yearning, is for ripeness, wisdom, and freedom in the spirit, they will come in God's time—in due season. And that is the harvest, the quid pro quo. An acorn falls into the ground and dies— empties itself—becomes a husk. A caterpillar withers itself into a chrysalis and the chrysalis in turn is emptied in order to free the butterfly. We empty ourselves, die to certain things, *in order to* make room for a more mature stage, a new freedom to live.

4

The Myth of Limitlessness

Myth: "In this book, I'll show you how to be a no-limit person, a winner 100 percent of the time! I can prove to you in very practical day-to-day terms that the only things holding you back from happiness, super health and fulfillment are the limits you impose on yourself!" From the Wayne Dyer book, *The Sky's the Limit.*

Truth: Each of us has a particular set of skills and talents that by definition limit what we do and where we go. Such limits are among the most important assets we have because they allow us to focus on that particular path which requires our unique skills and to let go of those paths which require skills we do not possess.

> **In the world to come, they will not ask,**
> **"Why were you not Moses."**
> **They will ask "Why were you not Zusya?"**
> **-Zusya of Hanipoli**

Our use of Wayne Dyer's quotation here is not meant as an attack on him. In fact, I am a big Wayne Dyer fan. We quote him in this context because the title of his book and his own description of it so clearly reflect the thinking on which so many of us have been raised. Dyer wrote this book in 1980, at a time when the human potential movement had been in full swing for a couple of decades. Those of us raised during this era are acutely familiar with the belief system that suggests anything is possible and the only thing holding us back is—well—ourselves.

In this chapter, we will explore the myth of limitlessness and the huge stress it creates in our lives. We will also explore, as in previous chapters, the spiritual dimensions of this belief and suggest ways to reframe how we view our own limitations.

Family Systems and The Myth of Limitlessness

One of the generations most indoctrinated by the myth of limitlessness is the baby-boomer generation. Blessed with unprecedented prosperity during their childhoods in the '50s and '60s and further gifted with unprecedented prosperity in the '90s, this generation of Americans has been infused with the belief of limitlessness and has on some level experienced the reality of it.

The baby-boomers' parents after all had made it through the great depression; they had fought and won several wars; they had, in the aftermath of those wars, built the United States into a world economic power second to none. All of these were legitimate and impressive accomplishments which reinforced the idea that anything is possible if you just put your mind to it.

As I was growing up, I certainly believed that I was capable of anything if I just put my mind to it. And most things I put my mind to did work for me. But very early in life, I noticed that not all human beings are created equal. I had friends who were not gifted in everything or even in many things. Some didn't seem to have any gifts at all and we would make fun of them and call them "losers." Because if you couldn't make it in the land of limitless opportunity (as America clearly was seen to be), you couldn't make it anywhere.

The definition of what "success" meant back then was quite narrow. The successful kid in my neighborhood was one who excelled at athletics, was a straight "A" or at least a straight "B+" student, was attractive and had loving parents who catered to their every need and want. Going to college was, for us, not only expected, it was required. And not just going to college but graduating and probably going on to graduate school. The theme was that we were people who had been given tremendous gifts and we were taught to challenge ourselves to maximize those gifts.

As my socialization continued in this way, I always wondered what would happen to the kids who didn't have the same kinds of gifts required by this very narrow and specific path where the standards were set so high. Last fall, I was doing a series of workshops for my employer, AARP, on computers and seniors. The workshops were co-sponsored by Microsoft and the goal was to expose older folks to the computer by holding introductory or "beginner" courses. The first such classes were held in Bellevue, Washington, where I grew up. At one of the breaks, a woman came up to me and introduced herself as the mother of one of my grade school classmates whom I had not seen since I was in sixth grade, some 25 years before. We exchanged pleasantries and then, when I asked how her daughter Alice was doing, she said, "Oh, we lost Alice two years ago. She had struggled for years with bulimia and anorexia and finally she was found dead of a heroin overdose in her apartment." I tried to mask the shock and utter horror I felt upon hearing this. Searching for something to say, I clumsily blurted out, "I don't know if you knew this or not, but I had a really big crush on Alice when we were in 5th grade."

As the seminar was about to resume and the woman started to walk away, I began to think about why people like Alice fall victim to such maladies as bulimia and drug addiction and what role coming from a community where there are high expectations of everyone contributes to it.

In Bellevue, Washington, in the 1960s, the sky was the limit. It was like Garrison Keillor's Lake Wobegon: "...where all the men are strong, all the women are beautiful and all the children are above average." But all the children weren't above average. And those who were merely "normal" in academic or social achievement were at great risk either of becoming workaholics to try to meet the exaggerated expectations of others or spending the rest of their lives simply feeling like failures.

For people like Alice and other kids I knew during that time, expectations were astronomical and many of them never came anywhere close to meeting those expectations. It caused many to blame themselves for their inability to take advantage of the land of limitless opportunity. And for some, that self-blame was more than they could carry and they self-destructed.

Self-blame is one of the most insidious and destructive phenomena humans can experience. The fundamental self-talk is: "I am not good enough" or "I should have done..." or "I must ..." Such self-talk is a manifestation of limitless thinking. For if, as the belief holds, *anything* and *everything* is possible for *any* individual, then there is really no one to blame besides oneself.

Peer Groups and The Myth of Limitlessness

I have come to believe that one of the primary forces driving me in my quest for success and fulfillment is how I compare to others in my own age group. Juliet Schor has written an insightful book entitled *The Overspent American: Upscaling, Downshifting, and the New Consumer,* in which she describes how Americans are spending money and acquiring things in order to compete for status within "reference groups." She says that these reference groups change over time but that throughout our lives, we are taught to compete with others in the group by acquiring things. As we pointed out in Chapter Three, and Schor also reminds us, Americans are engaged in a kind of mass overspending, where "large numbers of Americans spend more than they say they would like to…more than they realize they are spending and more than is fiscally prudent."

Part of the explanation for this kind of behavior is the belief held deeply by millions that there is no limit to the amount of stuff one should have. If, as Wayne Dyer says, "The sky is the limit" in everything we do, then why not consume unprecedented amounts of stuff? Add to this belief the combination of Schor's point that a lot of the consumption is a competitive response to winning out over one's reference group and the idea that we are finite creatures who yearn for the infinite, and the human engine is bound to be barreling along on overdrive most of the time.

Peer influences exacerbate this phenomenon because the more I seek limitless success and accumulated wealth, the more individuals in my peer or reference group seek to compete by amassing their own wealth. And each step up the ladder is a point of no return because, at least in American culture, there is no path downward, no route down the mountain which is viewed as successful. We are forced through competition and peer influence to keep going, even if the pressure created by such efforts is killing us.

Culture and The Myth of Limitlessness

Lest we think that only the baby-boom generation is engaged in no-limit kind of thinking, consider a recent graduation speech given at Seattle University in 1998. A high percentage of the 1,400 graduates this warm June day were young adults in their early twenties, as was the student speaker selected by faculty and her fellow students to address those gathered.

The speaker began by talking about how excited she was to be coming up to the podium later in the day to receive her $60,000 piece of paper. She talked about how her education had been fantastic but she did feel anxious about the student loans she had built up and the need to find a good, high-paying job and soon!

Later in her talk, she described something that happened to her on an exchange trip to Mexico the previous summer. She described how she only had a short time to see things while she was there and she remembers wanting to "see it all." This, she said, was reflective of her generation which wanted to do it all, see it all, and have it all in a hurry. She recalled taking a bus out into the countryside to do some sightseeing. When she boarded the bus, the only seat available was the one right behind the driver and it had a dark-stained glass partition between the seat and the driver, making it impossible for her to see the road ahead. This was frustrating to her because she described herself as a person who always liked to see into the future and know what was coming down the road. This seat forced her to look only to the sides as the bus passed the rural countryside.

On the trip back, she boarded the bus again, and this time she was lucky enough to get a seat on the other side of the bus where she could see the road ahead. But as they were arriving at the town where she was staying, she realized that she had been so engaged in looking down the road that she missed all the beautiful countryside she had seen when her view of the front was blocked. Her point was that in this fast-paced world of seemingly "no-limits," where people want to experience the maximum amount they can, they risk missing the richness of the everyday things. It is the dilemma between the western view of spirituality (life is a journey) and the eastern view (life is here, right now, in the present moment).

Our culture glorifies those who have gone the furthest the fastest. Even though we are finite creatures, we get the message that those of us who seemingly defy our finiteness and accomplish feats of limitless proportions will be heroes. Perhaps we feel so confined by our finiteness and so thoroughly yearn for infinite reality that we will worship those who seem unfettered by such human limitations. But such beliefs ignore the natural cyclical nature of our being, where some days we have high energy, and other days not so high energy. Poet David Whyte, in *The Heart Aroused,* addressed the struggles we have with working at full throttle all the time:

> We might think of the moon as being the natural cyclical reminder of our own internal ebb and flow. The wish to keep the moon full all month, imposing

> our will on the body of the heavens, is the wish to stay
> in the addicting and forever-youthful light of
> masculine "peak performance"…There is tremendous
> pressure in the modern business world to ignore the
> changing cycles of our native energies.

The myth of limitlessness suggests that even if our bodies are only a quarter-moon full, we are nevertheless expected to perform as though we were "full" every workday. This insight has been helpful to me on days when I beat myself up for feeling less than "on." It allows me to think that perhaps it is the natural cycle of things to feel "on" some days and half-on or three-quarters-on the next day. It gives me permission to be—human.

We also are impacted by the myth of limitlessness in thinking about our careers. We are led to believe that in the land of limitless opportunity we can be and do anything we want, an idea which is not only untrue, but enormously stress-producing. Parker Palmer, in writing for the journal "Weavings," once said that as a youth, he saw all paths in life as open. None of the various options or "ways" to go were yet closed. Then as he grew older and realized he probably was not going to become a professional baseball player, for example, he would mourn the loss of a "way closing."

But over time, Palmer says he realized that as more and more "ways closing" occurred, his level of stress and anxiety about what to do with his life declined. As it became more and more apparent to him what he clearly could not do, he found he had more time to pursue those few things he knew he was here to pursue. And he didn't spend all his time on one road wondering if the other roads would have been better. He also discovered he did those few things with much greater force and impact.

As I was thinking about this, the image came to me of water running through a hose. When you run water through a hose without a pressure nozzle, it comes out at a slow, even pace. But when you put a spray nozzle on it, thereby covering up most of the opening and forcing the water to travel through a narrow passage, the water comes out with much greater force and impact. So too it happens that when we focus our gifts on those activities for which we seem truly called, we tend to increase in intensity and impact.

Dialogue on the Myth of Limitlessness

Doug: Why do you think we are so filled with the belief that anything is possible?

ES: We are hard-wired for it. Every culture with a written history reports that human beings have an innate yearning for the infinite—which is another way of saying limitlessness. In Chapter One, I quoted my favorite definition of the human soul: "The capacity for infinite reality to be held finitely." It's not surprising, then, that we feel ourselves longing to embrace infinity, or to attain limitlessness.

Paradoxically, we get in trouble not because we set our limits too high, but because we set them too low. The cultural myth does not promote *true* limitlessness, which is in the dimension of spirit, but rather unrealistic goals (like the sky) which are still finite. The sky's the limit? The sky is not even much of a metaphor anymore for a frontier; after all, we have walked on the moon and explored space. To be captain of the Enterprise and travel to worlds unknown seems to affirm our built-in belief that anything is possible, but not even a time-warp leap will satisfy the soul's hunger for the limitlessness which is the spirit's freedom. Neither will imperial power satisfy, nor universal acclaim, nor any lofty attainment in this world or other worlds. But we persist in attaching our desire for the infinite to finite though unrealistic ends. Yearning for what we cannot have is stressful. Even when we get what we think we want, we are often not content: "Neurosis is wanting what we can't have, and not being able to bear what we've got."

Maybe a reason that our particular culture is so filled with the belief that anything is possible, is that we have inherited a large dose of pioneer spirit. Many of our forebears traveled west to break out of extremely limiting structures, some from literal imprisonment, some from prisons of ideology or caste. The "Westward Ho!" mentality assumed that there was vast, unlimited territory to be conquered, and nearly unlimited drive and stamina to conquer it.

America's pioneer spirit is simply our brand of a universal drive. If there is any Everest to be climbed, any record to be broken, any frontier to be exceeded, then human beings have always striven to do so. Witness the Empire State Building, the Pyramids, the Colossus of Rhodes, and the realm of Alexander the Great. Not to mention the Tower of Babel, which may be the supreme example of the myth of "the sky's the limit." It's evident that human beings are filled with the belief that anything is possible. The catch is that we expect that exceeding physical, spatial, or even intellectual limits will satisfy the soul's capacity for the infinite. It never has.

Doug: What is the role of choice in discussing this business of limitlessness?

ES: The ability to choose is essential to being human. It is a divine attribute, like the power of love. To be able to choose and to love proclaim that we are created in the image of the Creator. As far as we know, other creatures have instincts which direct their behavior, but only humans seem to have *both* instinct and conscious choice. The faculty of choice is on the one hand our glory, and on the other our tragic flaw. With choice comes the freedom to cooperate in our own "ripening," to share in crafting a particular life out of theoretical limitlessness. As you have pointed out, we can see "ways closing" and choose fruitfully from among our realistic alternatives.

Alas, this great gift of choice bears with it the inalienable option of choosing poorly. And that can have dire consequences. We can recognize our limits in a helpful way, but we can also limit ourselves to our diminishment by, for example, choosing to drop out of school rather than graduate. C. S. Lewis wrote: "...human beings, all over the earth, have this curious idea that they ought to behave in a certain way, and cannot really get rid of it...they do not in fact behave that way" (*Mere Christianity*). We can choose the good, or choose the lesser good, or even choose what we know is evil. Many times bad choices are prompted by our old friends: addiction to control, and narcissism.

Examples of the dire consequences of human willfulness go back to the creation myths of many cultures. In the Greek creation story, Prometheus, the Titan, chooses to steal fire from the gods (predominantly a choice for humanity's good); his sister-in-law, Pandora, the first woman, chooses to open the box which contains all the world's ills. In the Judeo-Christian creation story, Adam and Eve choose to disobey the divine limitation on edible fruit. Milton's Satan in *Paradise Lost* says, "Better to reign in Hell than serve in Heaven." Reigning anywhere may *seem* more unlimiting than serving, but actually, by choosing control over community, Satan is locking himself away from the God "in whose service is perfect freedom."

The infant narcissism in each of us tempts us to choose what is immediately gratifying. It is not easy to resist those temptations and choose values in the dimensions of Spitzer's third and fourth levels. It usually takes many decades of experiential learning to foresee even partially the consequences of one's choices. If you want to read a superb fictional account of a creation story in which an intelligent race chooses willingness over willfulness—and does not "fall"—read C. S. Lewis's science fiction trilogy: *Out of the Silent Planet, Perelandra,* and *That Hideous Strength.*

Fortunately, along with the divine and dangerous gift of choice, human beings have been given a faculty designed to help us choose the good. It is called *conscience.* According to Webster, conscience is: "...a faculty, power, or principle, conceived to decide as to the moral quality of one's own thoughts or acts, enjoining what is good."

I like to think of conscience in a more homey way—as the kibitzer at a game of poker. The kibitzer, for instance, can whisper to me over my shoulder that I know it's foolish to draw to an inside straight—the odds in my favor are minuscule. I can then *choose* either to listen and sensibly fold, or to disregard the advice and say to the dealer, "One card, please." Conscience does not make the actual decision—our own will does that; perhaps conscience might be described as the capacity for accumulated experience and insight, informed by grace.

Conscience can grow just as libraries can grow and, like good libraries, the increase should be qualitative as well as quantitative—there needs to be judicious weeding out. Such cultivation of our conscience is of great importance; in a real sense we become what we choose, and in making our life choices we need all the help we can get.

Doug: One of my favorite quotations is, "You can have *anything* you want; you just can't have *everything* you want." The idea is that we need to make choices but within the context of those choices, we can have whatever we choose. Is this true in your view?

ES: Up to a point. I, too, have experienced the grace in accepting "ways closing." I remember when I was twelve years old I wanted to be a poet. My mother had always wanted to be a painter, and she sent me to an excellent local artist for lessons in watercolor painting. It turned out that I had some talent. So now, did I want to be a painter or a poet? Even at the age of twelve, I knew in my heart that to be the best artist I could be, I must make a serious commitment to one or the other discipline, not equally to both. At that early age, I chose words over paint, and I have never regretted it. I enjoy painting, doing calligraphy, copper enameling, and other forms of art whenever I get a chance, but my first artistic choice and primary commitment has remained with the written word.

So part of the answer to your question is "Yes." Having what we choose involves the great life-skills of *discernment* and its sister *prioritizing*.

One of the prevalent sub-myths in this area is that choosing is, or ought to be, easy. Sometimes it is. I don't remember agonizing about choosing words over paint. But sometimes it isn't. It is tempting to put the blame on God for the gift/burden of choice, and chafe about how to figure out "the will of God" for our lives. The fact is, we have been given the gift of choice, and it cannot be returned without loss of our humanity.

There was an Episcopalian priest named Homer Rogers who is reported to have told the following story on himself. One time he received a call to another parish. The new place offered opportunities for challenging ministry, but on the other hand, he was involved in significant work where he was. He prayed about this choice, trying to see the will of God for his life, but no answer was forthcoming. He consulted with persons he trusted, he weighed the assets of both alternatives, he prayed again, but to no avail: he still had no clear direction. He began to get a little frantic to know the will of God for this next stage of his life. He went into the church and knelt before the altar. He prayed, "God, I want to do your will, but I can't until I know what it is. I'm not getting up from my knees until I have some clarification." And then it came. Quite clearly he was aware of God's answer: "Homer, *I don't care* which parish you choose!"

God's grace and the vicissitudes of life notwithstanding, we arc left with the lion's share of responsibility for our own decisions. And sometimes making a choice *can* be agonizing. It may or may not be consoling that every mature human being, including Jesus, has had to go through such times. That was what Gethsemane was about. Jesus knew the authorities were out to get him. At supper that

Thursday evening, Judas had in some way made it quite clear that he was going to act as informer. Jesus went out to the garden of Gethsemane, where his closest friends proceeded to fall asleep, leaving him alone in the dark. The choice he faced involved staying to teach in Jerusalem, within fatal reach of his strongest enemies, or fleeing once again to be able to continue his ministry.

I fantasize that his prayer might have run something like this: "Father, I can't figure out what you have in mind! I've been so sure that your will was for me to bring in the Kingdom. But I'm young— not thirty-five yet—it's only been three years since I started my ministry. You know that these friends of mine here, sleeping this hour away, haven't really caught on yet. If I don't escape again *right now*, the authorities will nab me and have me killed. I can't believe that Peter and the others are ready to carry on without me—I'd bet anything that if I'm murdered, they'll be confused and despairing, and if they don't just run away, they'll huddle together in upper rooms behind closed doors for fear of the authorities. Do you really think they can do the work of bringing in the Kingdom if I'm gone?" What to do? Stay and be killed, or go underground once more and continue to lead the mission? Well, finally the choice he had to make became clear to Jesus, but not before he had sweated blood over it.

If Jesus had to sweat blood over a decision, chances are we may have our moment as well. Freedom of choice is perhaps the greatest gift of human nature, but nobody ever promised it would be a rose garden—or at least a rose garden without thorns.

Sometimes it's too hard to choose well, and despite our best intentions we can't see our way clearly. It is a very difficult and adult process correctly to identify our real alternatives, prioritize them, and take responsibility for our choices. One thing is very important in making choices: not to be so hard on ourselves that we demand certainty before we act. Augustine Baker, a 17th century monk, gives us some excellent advice on this in his great book, *Holy Wisdom*: "In doubtful cases the soul must not expect to obtain absolute certainty…an inclination, however slight, towards one side, affords sufficient indication of God's will to be adopted. If there is no perceptible leaning either way, the soul should seek advice or supply the deficiency with her unbiased natural judgment."

It is good to hang in there with the agony of the decision, with the reality of the paradox, the dilemma, until things become clear. We can try to think it out, pray, talk to wise people and pray some more, but eventually the time comes simply to do one thing or the other. Father Stephen Langton once said to me, "If God can forgive our sins, God can surely forgive our mistakes."

So far I've gone into the bad news about the human faculty of choice. There is great good news. Once when I asked my Novitiate Director Mary Michael Simpson about this, she replied, "The will of God is identical with your own deepest desire." This shocked me at first, until I realized that the catch word was "deepest." (That harks back to our point about intrinsic and extrinsic values.)

Another wise woman named Sister Catherine Josephine once gave me a superb analogy. She had been used to thinking, she said, that trying to find the will of God in making choices for her life was like using a "paint by numbers" kit. Filling in little numbered areas on a printed board with correspondingly numbered colors. She tried to figure out what God wanted, and then tried to match her choices and actions to it. One day, however, in a flash of divine insight, she realized that wasn't the way it was at all. It was much more like God giving her a blank canvas and a palette full of colors and saying, "Dear one, paint me a picture!"

One of the most helpful quotations to me in this area is that of St. Irenaeus: "The glory of God is a human being fully alive." God's glory—God's will for my life—is nothing less than the fullness, the richness, of my particular humanity. I don't have to *get* anywhere; I just have to be who I most fully am.

Doug: Have you talked to people who are frustrated by the number of choices they have, who in effect have trouble deciding which apple to pick off the tree?

ES: Yes, many people are frustrated by the number of choices they have, and for some it goes beyond frustration. Choice becomes not only frustrating, but intolerable. A story comes to my mind which may not be the best example in response to your question, because in it the "trouble deciding" comes from a place much more serious than frustration. However, the story does illustrate an *extreme* of paralysis in the face of choice.

I once knew a young man who had been diagnosed at an early age with schizophrenia. When I knew him he was well on the way to recovery and off almost all his medication. He was writing about his experience of the disease, and shared with me some of what he had written. Several analogies he used struck me forcefully. He told me that when he was in a schizophrenic break it was as if he were in dark outer space where he could see planets and stars, but did not know where *he was* among them; it was like being able to perceive things around him quite clearly but not understand his relationship to them. To further illustrate this, he said it was like being in a restaurant with a menu of delicious foods in front of him, and not being able to choose what to eat. For him, schizophrenia was the ultimate manifestation of the inability to choose.

For many of us the "trouble deciding" is not so extreme, but stressful enough. Part of that stress, I believe, comes from the pressure of our culture on the individual. There are too many choices—from cereals on the shelf, to job ads in the paper.

I graduated from college in the fifties, and I felt there was a great deal of pressure on the women graduating with me to pursue a career and/or go on to graduate studies. The world was not only our oyster, but a whole bed full of oysters. There was, at my college, what seemed to me at the time a silly custom. The graduating seniors ritually processed through an arch covered with daisies, and each announced what she would be doing after graduation. Only one of us said she was going to get married and have babies. I thought at the time how brave she was to say it—there was tremendous peer pressure against being "just" a home-maker. This, mind you, was back in the fifties. I also remember thinking that in order to grant freedom to those of us who wanted careers, the option of family and children, as a respected and fulfilling life-choice, was being snatched away from many. As I began graduate studies and teaching, I saw numerous undergraduates—men and women in their late teens and early twenties—stressed to their limits by having to choose what to do, and almost whom to be. I wondered if the old system of having the option—indeed the expectation—of following in one's parents' footsteps was such a bad idea. Maybe not everybody is constituted to, or really wants to, forge a world-view, a role, a career for him- or herself. In most cultures, if you were, say, a Thomas Wolsey, you could have the option of being a butcher in Ipswich like your father, *or* you could rise through the ranks of the Church and become a Cardinal.

As I talk to people who are frustrated by "deciding which apple to pick off the tree," I notice another source of frustration, which is a consequence not of having too many choices but too few. It is an either/or dilemma where neither alternative is acceptable. It often takes the form of "Do I give in, or do I fight?" I told the story in Chapter Two about my friend who felt that the acceptance of death was a "cop-out." She only saw two alternatives: capitulation or fighting a war she was doomed to lose. Neither alternative was acceptable; both caused stress and denied peace.

I have talked to a number of people who felt trapped in the same dilemma of two intolerable choices, not at the time of death, but in life situations. In Chapter Two I indicated that chosen surrender might be a third option to being either a victim or an oppressor. But surrender is hard to understand, much less to choose, particularly in the stress of a relationship that is breaking down. "Do I just lie down and take it, or do I fight back?" In an attempt to widen the choices, I have sometimes used the following analogy, which is not unlike the concepts behind "Assertiveness Training."

Suppose someone throws a dart at you. (This might be an image for a put-down or a sharp criticism.) One choice is to throw it back and make war. Another choice is just to leave it embedded in your flesh, where it will soon begin to fester. A third, more effective, choice might be to take it out, put it in a safe place where it cannot hurt you or anyone else, and tend to your wound. What is such a safe place? For believers in God, the heart of God is such a safe place; for anyone, a human friend who is capable of confidentiality and trust is another. The relationship with God which we call prayer is perhaps the best medicine and healing power for such wounds, and it goes hand in hand with self-acceptance.

This does not mean that one never chooses to prevent the aggressor. Often the dart-thrower must be stopped. But there are ways to do this without becoming hostile oneself. First, don't give the aggressors power; don't vote for them. If they must be confronted, confront with firmness and compassion—"tough love." The spiritual principle here is one which The Foundation for Community Encouragement teaches. If hard things need to be said, they can be said as an *ally* rather than as an *adversary*, and when they are said from the ally stance they are more, rather than less, powerful and effective. Remember, hatred is like swallowing poison and hoping the other person will get sick.

Facing either too many choices or too few choices can cause major stress. The good news is that discernment is a life-skill that can be learned and acquired. It is possible to practice widening or limiting our perception of alternatives in accordance with the reality of the situation. What needs to be emptied here is the sub-myth that choice should either be limitless or so limited that we virtually have no choice. Learning to choose well not only leads to peace, but to true adulthood and holy wisdom. Meister Eckhardt, a 13th century Dominican Friar, wrote: "Wisdom consists in doing the next thing you have to do, doing it with all your heart, and finding delight in doing it." That kind of wisdom doesn't come cheaply, but it is worth the cost.

Doug: With the belief system that says "the sky is the limit," doesn't that attitude add anxiety and stress to people who feel that since anything and everything is available, they ought to be taking advantage and going for it all the time?

ES: As we have noted, stress often comes from being trapped between contrary messages. Such messages may seem contradictory and also equally imperative. The general and cultural message is, as you noted: "Anything and everything is available—you must take advantage of it all the time." The personal and specific message is too often: "The sky *may* be the limit, but *you*, personally, haven't a chance—you are a) not acceptable, b) stupid, c) ugly, d) underprivileged, e) a born loser," etc. That is, "You can do anything you want to, but you can't really do *anything* right." The effect of these conflicting messages can make a person react like a squirrel in a cage or a rat racing around a maze. There is a need to strive endlessly, while feeling doomed to get nowhere.

To make matters worse, we have conflicting messages not only about pushing limits but also about the faculty of choice. The cultural myth implies that you have limitless choices and that taking advantage of them is effortless—doors will open ahead of you as for royalty on an official visit. Things will fall into your lap or spring out of your laptop. If you do have to make a few choices, like which job to take, which person to marry, or where to go on vacation, such choices should be easy. The opposite, internal message can be that you don't have any choice at all—you are trapped. Even more stressfully, one can be faced with only two alternatives, both of which are unacceptable. (This is like being caught on the classic "horns of a dilemma.") We have already talked about one example of this dilemma: capitulation or war.

The reality is that choosing isn't easy. It is, rather, a great virtue (from Latin *virtus,* strength). To be a winner in discernment takes as much pain and practice as any Olympic training or martial art. The good news is that, like any great art, it is part gift and part discipline; some people have a natural talent for it, but choosing rightly is a skill that can be acquired and practiced by all. It is possible to learn that, as we have said, there may be a third alternative to an apparent dilemma, and it is possible to learn how to prioritize. It is even possible that, though choice may still be difficult, there will come a shift from neurotic anxiety about it, to a more existential concern which is not inconsistent with internal peace.

There is something we can do to promote this shift from stress to serenity. It is a kind of emptying. We can try not to force decisions, not to "push the river." We can try to empty ourselves of the driven need for immediate answers and control, in order to make space for the wisdom of the spirit—our own spirit and Holy Spirit.

It is in that sort of space where we can pay attention to our dreams. The time between sleep and waking is called the hypnagogic state. Our consciousness is more receptive then, because what Zen calls "busy mind" is not yet, or not still, in full gear. Have you ever been stressed out over a problem or situation and "slept on it," and on waking known clearly what choice must be made or action taken? The point of practicing the art of discernment is to be able to experience that openness and clarity even during our more active hours.

Discernment is a sister of prophecy. Both describe seeing ever more clearly *what is*, recognizing probable consequences, and identifying appropriate action. Perhaps today we use the word "vision" more than "prophecy." Leaders with vision have mastered the art of discernment—of seeing *what is*, and therefore having a better chance at making right choices about how to act from that viewpoint. Well-tuned discernment is not only a gift for leaders, but also for those for whom they are authorities and prophets.

There is another sub-myth under limitlessness which I hinted about in the dialogue following the first question. This sub-myth is that if we feel limited in daily life, we just haven't gotten spiritual enough. The myth is that there is no limit—but we feel oppressed by limits, and this is a contradiction. If limitlessness is a myth (that is, in reality our resources and choices *are limited*), what about infinity?

The way I hear the question from a lot of folks is something like "If God is infinite/limitless, and my spirit (made in God's image) has the capacity for infinity/limitlessness, how does this relate to my feeling so limited in my everyday life?"

This sub-myth fosters polarities that seem at best paradoxical, and at worst irreconcilable. Some examples of such polarities are: time and eternity, three-dimensional space and infinity, matter and spirit, body and soul, reason and faith, secular and sacred, everyday and Sunday. For some people, at some points in their journeys, trying to reconcile these apparently separate modes of being is very stress-producing. Am I the same person at work or in a bar as I am at church? If I have to get this report done by five o'clock, and the sitter has just called to say my child has a temperature of 102°, and I have to shop before I go home, how do I relate these real limits of time/space to the notion of limitlessness? How does my stressful dailiness relate to eternity?

I once had an insight into this. I was on a train, idly watching the telephone poles going past the window at fairly regular intervals. I decided to clock them, and in fact they did go by in approximately the same number of seconds. I noticed that the mountains in the distance went past "much more slowly." Then I realized that was only one kind of truth; another was that neither telephone poles *nor* mountains were going past at all—I, that is, the train, was "going past." Then I thought that another truth was that I, train, telephone poles and mountains were all on the surface of a planet that was "going" around its own axis and also around the sun. Who knows if the sun was going around something—whether space is or is not curved? At what point is space taken into infinity and time into eternity? The important insight was that *there is no existential break between the truth of timing the distance of telephone poles, and the truth of the "space/time" of the absolute or God.*

A paradox is a seeming contradiction of two truths. Mystery goes beyond paradox, in that it holds together infinite seemingly inconsistent truths.

If we can hold in creative tension the mystery of the limits of our five senses and our limitless spirit instead of subscribing to the sub-myths of duality, then the stress of trying to hold together seemingly contradictory realities can be alleviated. Mystery does not oppose "everyday" reality; it is the medium by which our dailiness can be embraced by cosmic or divine reality. It offers us an expanded stage, a way beyond the squirrel cage.

Doug: Do you believe that each of us is born into this world for a particular purpose or purposes and that we should try to determine that purpose as soon as we can and focus on it to the exclusion of other things?

ES: In a sense, yes, we each are born to a purpose or purposes. Perhaps we are born with them as the particular acorn is born with the purpose of becoming a particular oak. But how a particular acorn/oak actually turns out is determined by a multitude of internal and external factors: soil nutrients, weather, position among other trees, squirrels and the logging industry. With human beings another whole dimension is added: the capacity to choose and to participate in the discernment and crafting of our life-purpose. As we have implied above, this responsibility is one that many would like to forego. Some people feel they are not up to it, and perhaps some do better given a clear model to follow, like the one woman at my college who was going to be a wife and mother like her own mother and grandmothers before her. Some, as we also have indicated, put all the onus for their purpose in life on the will of God or the whim of the Fates or their guru or horoscope. Some go to the opposite extreme of claiming all the responsibility for purpose or lack of purpose, as Shakespeare wrote in *Julius Caesar*: "The fault, dear Brutus, is not in our stars, but in ourselves that we are underlings."

Some people seem to have a stronger call and a greater ability to cooperate in the discernment of their purpose. Their attitude is not "I don't have to do anything, it's just my fate, or God's inscrutable will"; neither is it "I have to forge my destiny all by myself," or as William Ernest Henley wrote: "I am the master of my fate; I am the captain of my soul."

If there is a God, and if God is love, then there needs to be a loving *mutuality* in the project. At the risk of seeming irreverent, I think of the human spirit and the Holy Spirit asking one another: "Honey, what do you feel like doing? What picture shall we paint?"

For myself, my purpose has on the one hand revealed itself very early, and on the other hand deepened and broadened with every opportunity for choice and every challenge, so that in my sixties the focus is still sharpening. I spoke earlier in this dialogue of my choice when I was twelve years old to be a writer. Very early I had another conscious purpose as well: to be a seeker of the truth. These were not so much laudable ideals as survival techniques. Many aspects of my life seemed so crazy that to find out what was true meant sanity; many times when I did not feel heard when I spoke, I would write things down for myself. However, these "purposes" have gone down many seeming detours which looked at the time like distractions. In fact, they were enrichments. For instance, seeing myself as a truth-seeker and a writer, I never imagined myself as an administrator. I rather looked down on administration. But recently I have served on the Board of Directors of two non-profit organizations, and of one I am currently the President of Corporation. These experiences have not deterred my "purpose," but enhanced it. So I don't know about "focusing" on a purpose "to the exclusion of other things." If the purpose is a good fit for you, it will be able to be broadened and deepened by the *inclusion* of almost any experience.

The most important thing to remember about all this is that *our ultimate life-purpose is who we are and how we love, not what we do*. Who we are is often enriched by experiences and activities that may seem at the time to be totally extraneous to anything we might have thought would further our life's purpose. As some wit said, "We are created to be human beings, not human doings."

Doug: To what extent is this idea of self-blame a factor in an individual's sense of stress and dis-ease? In a land with so many "successful" people and so many opportunities, how does not "making it" or blaming oneself for not competing impact one's mental health?

ES: Self-blame causes major stress. I'd like to talk about it in a general way before responding to the particular question of "blaming oneself for *not competing*."

One reason why self-blame is stressful is that it is hard to know whether the blame is justified or not. In other words, it's hard to tell the difference between true guilt and false guilt. False guilt and true guilt *feel* almost identical. True guilt is perhaps easier to recognize and deal with: it is when you really hacked down the cherry tree, or you deliberately stole away your friend's partner and you admit it, at least to yourself. False guilt is harder to name and describe. Here's an example. From my earliest years I felt guilty about how I *looked*.

I got the message that I should have been pretty like my mother and not have the heavier features and darker hair of my father. Also, somehow I got the idea that I should have been a boy. I felt as if I had done something terribly wrong to make my mother so disappointed in me. Or worse, I felt I *was* somehow terribly wrong.

Another example of false guilt is the classic one around the early death of a parent. My own father became fatally ill with cancer when I was eleven, and as far as possible his illness was hidden from my younger brother and me. While he was actually dying, the overt message was: "Your Daddy is resting a lot because he is getting well from an operation." So it seemed sudden when he died two years later. It *felt* as if what was unacceptable about me was connected somehow to his death. If only I had been better, he might not have had to abandon me this way, or at least I might not need to feel guilty as well as forsaken by his dying.

False guilt is an insidious and deadly thing. We can attach it to anything—not the least of which might be "not making it" when we have gotten the imperative message that we ought to "make it," in fact, *must make it.* I don't know about people with psychoses and social disorders, but for the majority of us typical neurotics, the weight of false guilt can make us just as anxious and stress-ridden as if we were really to blame.

Now, what can we *do* about true guilt and false guilt? Though they may feel the same, they are quite different and they need to be healed differently. True guilt is an ethical and spiritual problem; false guilt is primarily a psychological problem.

The best way to resolve true guilt is recognition, admission, forgiveness and reconciliation. This can be done within oneself, with another person, and/or with God. Some people fear this exercise because they see it as a breast-beating or masochistic sort of affair; after all, strong men don't cry, strong women don't admit weakness, rugged individuals don't need to confess. However, for me and for many, confession has had just the opposite effect. It has proved to be a way to love ourselves better, a way to growth and freedom. It is one of the most profound kinds of emptying.

I was very lucky (or graced) in my introduction to dealing with *true* guilt. I was baptized as an adult in the Anglican Church in London, England. The Saturday before my baptism, I had an appointment to make a "sacramental confession." I was given instructions on how to prepare. Everything I had heard about this sort of event was distasteful if not horrifying. To make a long and doleful story short, I appeared in church at the appointed time and went into an old-fashioned box-like "confessional" and knelt down in front of the grill, feeling like a caged animal. I proceeded, however, dutifully to pour out the significant sins that I could remember from 28 years of pagan, and if not riotous at least unruly, living. It took me about fifteen minutes. When I finished, there was a moment of terrifying silence. Tears were running down my face. Then my mentor, Father Langton, said one word: "Splendid!"

I was stunned. The stuff I had emptied out to him, that I was truly guilty of, was so horrendous! But then his enthusiasm when he had said "Splendid!" let me know that I had done a fine job of recognizing and admitting it. An image came into my mind: a medical team called in to tend someone who has swallowed poison. The poison is pumped out. The medics, of course, pay no attention to what has been emitted, but only to the patient, who is well-purged and on the way back to health. Ever since that day so many decades ago, the sacrament of reconciliation has been for me a growth tool— a spiritual emptying—making space for the freedom of getting on with life.

Of course, sacramental confession is only one way of dealing with true guilt. There are other ways to recognize, admit, and ask and receive forgiveness, so that we can, to use a computer analogy, empty our Trash or Recycle Bin, and make space for new wisdom.

The healing of *false* guilt has in common with that of true guilt a recognition of the cause of the guilt-feeling. But here the trick is to identify that for which we should *not* claim responsibility. My experience is that false guilt is best dealt with in a therapeutic situation.

I have talked to a number of people who were oldest children in a family where the parents were severely dysfunctional, and who grew up with the conviction that they were globally responsible, that if anything went wrong it was *their fault*. And that they would be punished dreadfully for it. Of course, things did sometimes go wrong, no matter how hard they tried. The tendency to self-blame and the fear of the worst-case scenario can persist long after childhood. The consequent anxiety has roots, of course, in specific past events. One of the most poignant instances I've heard was a man's memory of being a little boy with a father and mother who for different reasons were not good at coping. One day he was told the family had to get to somewhere extremely important, like a train station, and that there was a flat tire on the car. The little boy didn't really know how to change a tire, but he stood in the middle of the driveway *feeling* that if he didn't somehow accomplish it, his world would fall apart and *it would be his fault.* Later in life he knew how to change a tire, but he still at times got the same dreadful feeling.

Good psychotherapy can, by creating an atmosphere of safety and trust, enable a person to remember such key incidents and identify their feelings at the time. Then, when similar feelings are evoked in current living, one can better see where they came from. A helpful and important thing to realize is that what seemed to be life-threatening when one was a child, isn't necessarily so now. Now we know how to get the tire changed.

The particular self-blame around the issue of "not making it" or "not competing" has a couple of interesting aspects. One is a sub-myth of our culture: "Busier is better." There are roots of this sub-myth in some very early cultures. In the Christian West it has been called "the Martha/Mary syndrome." When Jesus went to these sisters' house for dinner, Martha was busy and, as the New English Bible translates it, "fretting and fussing" about many things. Mary chose to empty herself of distraction, and listen. Jesus named Mary's contemplative presence "the better part." Through the ages, this little incident has been used to support those people who choose the road less traveled and carry the banner: "Busier is *not* necessarily better!"

It must be noted that there is a great gulf of difference between contemplation and "navel gazing." The first is the hard work of listening for and seeking the truth, the second is close to laziness and narcissism. Undoubtedly Mary had her turn at cooking or fetching the water to wash up. As it is written in the original rule of our Order, "Love must act, as light must shine and fire must burn." (James O. S. Huntington, Founder, Order of the Holy Cross). The wisdom that is the fruit of contemplation must be offered in ministry. As a sense of authentic community makes doing a task smoother for a group, so, in an individual life, contemplation makes one more efficient, not less.

Contemplation and action are not opposites, they are complementary necessities—like systole and diastole, breathing in and breathing out. Without either, one would be dead. Even the Desert Fathers and Mothers preached the necessity of balancing contemplation and solitude with manual work and hospitality.

A lot of stress and self-blame, a lot of false guilt, can attach itself to not being busy and competing, pushing the limits, all the time. How often do you ask someone how they're doing and *don't* get an answer like "busy," "over my head," "swamped," "way behind," or "exhausted"? Often we manage to be proud of being over-busy. The implication is that, despite all, we're "making it!"

Of course all this stress impacts one's mental health. I am not an expert on mental health, but I have noticed one thing that can happen. If early on the compulsion "to make it, to push the limits" is too strong, and the self-blame for "not making it" is too painful to bear, a kind of split can take place in one's personality. The lousy and deflated self-image who can't "make it" is banished to the caves of repression, and the inflated "I can do anything better than you" image is given the place in the sun. That wouldn't be so bad if the klutz image never made itself heard or felt—only of course, it does. Like any trapped or mistreated creature it can become vicious and aggressive, and, in a desperate attempt to alleviate its suffering, often transfers the blame onto other people and/or external events. This causes mutual hostility and fear. Or the deflated self-image can be expressed in bottomless-pit neediness and all sorts of manipulative behaviors in attempts to get its needs met.

The split, opposite images of klutz and kingpin, are of course both lies, and lying to oneself is detrimental to one's psychological and spiritual health. I wonder if the experts would say that this split in images is related to the sickness called bi-polar. It does seem that when the "I've made it" or "I'm going to make it" image is in the sun, a person can have all the souped-up energy of the manic state, and conversely when the "I'm never going to make it" image howls out of its darkness, depression can strike.

The reality is that we are limited, and that it is O.K. It's not only O.K., it's glorious. It's glorious because it is the truth, and the truth will make us free.

Doug: The idea of the "myth of limitlessness" and "maximizing human potential" are not the same, right? I mean we are called to make the most of our potential, but within the confines of our abilities and talents. So we are not saying "Don't try to maximize your potential," are we?

ES: Right. The Myth of Limitlessness is very different from maximizing our human potential. One thing about all cultural lies—what we are calling myths—is that they are hazy and generalized. Truth is particular and unique. The Myth of Limitlessness implies vaguely that everybody could "make it," any child can grow up to be President of the United States, anyone can be Cinderella, everyone can go from rags to riches. We ended the dialogue on the last question with the quote that the truth will make us free. But for me to maximize my potential, for you to maximize your potential, it is not truth *in general* but my own personal truth, your own personal truth, that we are talking about.

One of the big troubles about myths is that they are so generalized as to be dangerous. In Community Building work, the first stage is what we call "pseudo-community." In this initial stage of group process, one myth or assumption is that we are all nice people, everyone is "making it," and we are all pretty much the same. In true community we have recognized our differences and hold them in respect. And most often our differences lie in our limitations. To be known for who I really am, to be accepted for where I really am in the hard process of maximizing my potential, is to be free. Individuation, which is another way of talking about maximizing human potential, is hard work. I have never heard of its being done without pain. It is perhaps the narrow way that leads to life. It does seem to be the road less traveled.

It takes costly attention and perseverance to realize my own truth, my extremely particular limitations and my entirely unique endowments. Only the truth for my life—*not for yours*—will make me free. And *vice versa*. For example, celibate chastity may be a vehicle for me to maximize my potential, but it might be an obstacle for you to maximize yours. The myth or cultural lie of limitlessness would like to brainwash us into a vague compulsion that we should do it all—or at least get to the top of some unnamed Everest; that we must keep pushing the rock up the mountain like Sisyphus, who was damned, and admit no limitations.

Let's stop a minute. Are we swallowing the propaganda that being limited is bad? Could it be that having limits is good, even wonderful? What, after all, is a limit? My own skin is a limit and I'd be dead without it. My psychological boundaries are limits and I'd be insane without them. The frame around a great painting is a limit, the dimensions of the Globe Theater were a certain kind of limit for Shakespeare, the shores of a great ocean or a small stream are limits. My birth and my death are the frames, boundaries, and shores— the limits—of my life. It is the stage, as Shakespeare said, upon which my absolutely distinctive and gloriously-delimited life is played out, with all its tragic flaws, to fill its unique human potential. If there is life in eternity, it will perhaps not be limited. But for now let us glory in our limits, because they are what make us splendidly and uniquely ourselves. The Sufi poet Rumi writes:

> *a journey to the sea*
> *is horses and fodder and contrivance*
> *but at land's end*
> *the footsteps vanish...*
>
> *a million galaxies*
> *are a little scum*
> *on that shoreless sea.*

──5──
The Myth of Individualism

Myth: I am solely responsible for my own destiny, captain of my own ship and master of my own fate. Any reliance on others is a sign of weakness.

Truth: All human beings are interconnected and part of a larger system known as the human species. This species has the paradoxical characteristic of having the capacity to become separate individuals, and yet to be dependent on others. It is "a predicament."

> **The problem with...rugged individualism is that it runs with only one side of this paradox, incorporates only one half of our humanity. It recognizes that we are called to individuation, power and wholeness. But it denies entirely the other part of the human story: that we can never fully get there and that we are, of necessity in our uniqueness, weak and imperfect creatures who need each other.**
> **—M. Scott Peck**

There is no society on earth that places more emphasis on the importance of individualism than the United States. It is a concept that is so ingrained in us that we almost take it for granted, discounting the need for relationships as a source of essential health and wholeness. Yet we are indeed creatures who need both togetherness and separateness. The question is how to do both in a dualistic, either/or world, and particularly in a culture that places such total emphasis on "making it on one's own." This chapter explores the myth and paradox of individualism and attempts to unpack the complicated ways in which we come to embody the belief in doing it all ourselves.

Family Systems and The Myth of Individualism

I had a classmate who once described to me what it had been like for her when she and her husband and young daughter lived in

Japan. They had very tiny quarters since housing was expensive and space was at a premium. In Japan, the shortage of space was only part of the difference with American culture. The Japanese place high value on family and the importance of establishing close relationships. These relationships last for a lifetime and individual family members' primary obligation is to the family unit more than to themselves.

My friend described how for the first several years their daughter slept in their bed with them and they thought nothing of it. But when they moved back to the United States and their daughter was still sleeping in their bed, their parents and neighbors expressed shock and concern that it would damage the self-esteem of the child.

We inculcate our young with the myth of individualism almost from the moment of birth. In fact, a common ritual, which many refer to as the nesting instinct, is to prepare the baby's room during pregnancy so that the moment the child is born, he or she can have a separate room, separate bed, separate closet and so forth.

We buy the young toddler his or her own clothes, his or her own bicycle, a lunch box with his or her name on it. Whereas in Japan it was quite common for children to sleep in the parents' bed and feel in the first instant that being a part of the family was more important than establishing one's individual identity, in the United States. individual identity is all important.

We learn that the goal of our existence is to build up an individuated self, a self that has credentials, unique skills, talents, sexual attractiveness, athletic abilities and so on. Once the self has been nurtured and shaped and established, then we spend huge amounts of time making sure that our separate and unique identity is preserved. All of this takes enormous energy and has the effect of isolating us from others.

Peer Groups and The Myth of Individualism

One of the consequences of our cultural focus on individualism is competition. The call to individuate and become separate entities who must make it on our own is often dependent on beating out the other. If I alone am master of my own fate and others are masters of their own fate, then I am destined to see the other as an "it" at best and as "the enemy" at worst. The myth of individualism precludes our ever moving from "I-it" to "I-thou" to "I-Thou" as Martin Buber has described it: seeing the other as a divine act of creation.

Competitiveness is a key component of American culture and we have learned it from our families and also from each other. As a young teenager trying out for the basketball team, I learned very quickly that there were only 12 players who would make the team and the rest of us would be out of luck. When I applied to colleges, I learned that certain prestigious colleges would accept only about 5% of all the applicants and the remaining 95% were out of luck. This had the effect of making me see others as competitors, not as collaborators or even brothers and sisters. The idea that we are all interconnected and interdependent was about as far from my thinking as the planet Pluto.

My socialization with classmates was that we must pull ourselves up by our bootstraps, work hard and *individually* achieve success. Asking for help was for wimps and collaboration was okay in team sports, but otherwise one must do it on one's own. And collaboration even in team sports was muted by the fact that at the end of the season, the team would have a leading scorer, all-star teams, all-state teams, and other measurements which put individual players on a hierarchy.

The fact that we are taught to compete against each other dramatically alters the way we interact. Since I was taught to see the game as one in which there were only a handful of winners and most everyone else loses, I learned to react to others as a threat. It is almost never okay to let down my guard or trust those against whom I am competing, since my getting what I want is dependent on your not getting what you want. Competition makes me less likely to help my fellow human beings because they become the enemy. No wonder so many more of us no longer trust each other. No wonder so many more of us are living alone and feel a sense of isolation in the 1990s.

Recently I attended a high school track and field championship event with a friend of mine which illustrates the obsession we have with winning. My friend's grandson, Timmy, was a leading contender to win the meet and, as a sophomore, he not only won but also set a state record with his score in the difficult ten-event decathlon competition. Throughout the day, other state championship events were taking place, each time ending with a medal ceremony for the top ten finishers. I couldn't help noticing how when they gave out the medals, the athletes who finished in places 2 through 10 were merely announced and received their medal. But then when it came time to announce the winner, instead of just reading his or her name, the announcer would build it up, saying in a loud and dramatic voice "and now, your new, 1998 state decathlon champion, with a score of xxxx points, is..." and they would read the name. In other words, the winner is a "champion" and everyone else is not. This is one of the many ways we ratchet up the intensity of competition among individuals, making it that much harder for kids to place the importance of individual awards and winning in its proper perspective.

Culture and The Myth of Individualism

More than any other myth, the idea that we have to make it individually is the single biggest source of stress in our culture. We are continually told that the successful person is the one who individually achieves the greatest feats. And while service or good beyond self, Spitzer's Level Three activities, are certainly respected by society, the accumulation of *individual* achievement or ego gratification (Level Two) is far more respected and glamorized by the media and the culture.

The reason such reliance on individual achievement causes so much anxiety is because to achieve something literally on one's own is a fallacy. Human beings, as Scott Peck says in the quotation which opened this chapter, are creatures who are inherently dependent on one another. Even the most brilliant playwright needs help at some things, so does the strongest boxer, the most decorated soldier, the cutest girl in the school, the strongest boy, the wisest scholar. But we have internalized the idea that each of us has to be good at everything.

As a male, I am given the impression that I have to be smart, earn a lot of money, be aggressive, yet sensitive to the needs of others, and, most annoying of all to me personally, able to fix any kind of mechanical thing that breaks. One of the underlying reasons for the immense popularity of television shows like "Home Improvement" is that here you have a guy who is supposed to be the ultimate handyman, but when he is off the air and trying to make simple repairs around the house, he is a disaster. Many men and women can relate to the disparity between the expectations we project onto all men as handy and mechanically gifted compared to the reality.

The myth of individualism places enormous pressure on the individual to be good at everything and to be in control in every situation. Because both of these are impossible, we become very good at faking it. We employ a sophisticated series of social masks to give the impression that we are on top of every situation, while secretly we are paralyzed with fear that others will find out the truth. A recent poll of chief executives of major U.S. companies revealed over 50% of those surveyed said their biggest fear was that one day people would find out they were incompetent and unqualified to do their job. Apparently, many CEOs have mastered the art of faking it but in so doing have isolated themselves from others and precluded ever being able to be who they really are.

One of the reasons community building workshops and other kinds of group work are so powerful is that they create environments where people can remove their social masks and be themselves, often for the first time. Imagine what it would be like to spend a day being able to be exactly who you are without having to worry about being judged for not living up to the image you have created for yourself. This is what happens in community building.

The workshops are three days long. During the first two days, typically twenty-five to forty individuals sit in chairs in a circle. The wisdom of sitting in a circle is that everyone can see everyone else's face. Two facilitators convene the circle and provide instructions to participants. These instructions are brief and outline some of the rules of engagement such as:

> **No fixing
> **No judging
> **Speak in "I" statements
> **Speak only when moved to speak

The facilitators then read a story and say that each session will begin with three minutes of silence. The facilitators instruct the group that, after the three minutes are up, anyone who is moved to speak may do so. They are told to begin by saying their name and to speak in the first person, using primarily "I", "my" statements. For a complete description of this process, see *The Different Drum*.

The first time I attended one of these workshops, I was absolutely blown away. I had just come from a meeting of a task force on elder abuse where people from different government agencies had been sitting around all posturing about how they were going to end abuse of our elderly population. I remember thinking afterward while I was driving to the community building workshop how inauthentic and pretentious everyone had been, including myself.

After the first couple of hours in the community building workshop, I remember telling the group how I wished the people on the task force could have been there to experience what it was like to communicate authentically.

The community building workshop encourages individuals to empty themselves of the barriers they have developed over years and years of being judged which stand in the way of meaningful communication and spiritual growth. In my case, I realized after my first workshop that I was spending huge amounts of energy projecting a particular persona so that people would think I was successfully achieving what my parents and others expected of me.

I remember on the third day of that first workshop, we did an exercise where we were supposed to draw the social mask or masks we employ to hide from people. I drew a picture of Superman, complete with a giant "S" on the chest and a cape. When it came time to describe my mask, I said that I spend most of my time trying to convince people that I am Superman, the ultimate successful, all-powerful, super-action hero of comic-book fame.

As we went around the room, everyone had drawn a social mask which they used to hide behind. The point to this exercise was not to say it is bad to employ social masks from time to time. In fact, in a harshly judgmental world, the social mask can be and often is a necessary protective shield. But by becoming aware of the masks one wears, one can better cope with the extent to which they block authentic interaction with others.

Prior to that first workshop for example, I had never even heard of the concept of a social mask. Once I had become aware of my own masks and had seen others share theirs, it was a huge leap forward in understanding myself and how I relate to others.

Another thing the community building workshop does is to allow people to experience unconditional acceptance, albeit in an artificial environment and for a limited time. This makes an incredible impact because once you get a taste of unconditional acceptance or love, you want to experience it all the time and many people are *permanently* changed by it. I have become a much more accepting person since experiencing the workshop; I am more accepting not only of others but also of myself. Why? Because once I realized that everyone, no matter who they are or where they come from, has experienced pain and struggle as well as success and happiness, then maybe—just maybe—it is okay for me to have experienced it. ES has a saying: there are only two kinds of people—those with pain who know it and those with pain who don't know it. One cannot sit through a community building workshop and fail to understand what she means by this statement.

The myth of individualism, with its consequences of competition, social masks, and mutual judgment, has the effect of making individuals withdraw further and further into themselves, becoming less and less open and authentic. We do this because since everyone is wearing the social mask of success and "having it all together," we begin to feel we are the only ones who are not "all together" and therefore we can't let anyone else know the truth. The community building workshops and other forms of group work allow individuals to see each other as they really are and the first thing one realizes is that everyone struggles from time to time.

Irving Yalom, in his classic study of group psychotherapy, has identified "curative" factors: elements of the group process that improve an individual's sense of health and wholeness (see *The Theory and Practice of Group Psychotherapy*). One of the primary curative factors which group therapy participants report is "universality," the idea that others have the same kinds of problems I do. What is so comforting about seeing others who have the same kind of problems is precisely what is so limiting about the myth of individualism. If we are never allowed to show ourselves to each other as we really are and we get all of our cues about how to be from television images of happy people, then we will come to believe that we are the only souls on earth who are in pain. In short, misery does love company.

Universality can also come back to bite us however. A ten-year study recently released by the John T. and Catherine C. MacArthur Foundation created headlines such as "Mid-life Crisis a Myth" and "Researchers to Baby-Boomers: No Mid-life Crisis." This study surveyed some 3,000 people between the ages of 30 and 70 to see if they experienced a mid-life crisis. The study concluded that close to 77% of respondents said they never experienced anything like a mid-life crisis. In fact, many said the middle years were very good.

Putting aside questions about how authentic people are in responding to such surveys, what do the headlines from such a study do to the person who is in fact in the middle of a mid-life crisis? They will likely feel marginalized and ashamed that they uniquely couldn't cope with the modern world in which they find themselves. And what about the person who is in crisis but has denied it and convinced himself he has it all together? Doesn't such a survey just re-enforce such denial, leaving the individual to conclude falsely, "See, I'm fine just like everybody else."

I remember reading about this study and thinking that this is merely another example of how thoroughly enmeshed we are in the culture of rugged individualism, where if you need help, you don't ask for it and if someone asks you if you need help, you tell them "I'm fine, thank you very much." I asked ES for her take on this business of individualism and how we can live the paradox of needing both an individual identity and connection to others.

Dialogue on The Myth of Individualism

Doug: First of all, ES, I would like to ask you how you would define "individual?"

ES: My short definition may sound a little obscure: I once defined an individual as "a discreet locus of potential consciousness."

However, the word and concept of "individual" deserves a longer look. It comes from a Latin word meaning indivisible, not able to be divided. This is strange, because in almost every culture human beings *have* seen themselves as divided—not only from other individuals, but within themselves. Most often this division has been described as body and spirit, or body, mind, soul and spirit—at any rate, into that which is material and goes back to the earth, and that which is spiritual and may live on in some fashion apart from the body. I am told that the ancient Israelites were exceptional in *not* making such a marked distinction.

On the whole, however, human nature seems to have known itself as divided, sometimes to the point of internal warfare—what the ancients called "psycomachia": the battle between body and soul.

Often this battle is focused on the contrary impulses in human nature to good and to evil. Saint Paul names the struggle that of "flesh" (*sarx*) and "spirit" (*pneuma*). The Greek words refer to those aspects of human nature which are opposed to, and in alignment with, the true God-created self (cf. Romans 7: 14-25).

The Faustus legend is a classic example of this apparent human duality. I remember the scene in Marlowe's play (*Doctor Faustus*, scene V) where the Evil Spirit is whispering to Faustus in one ear and the Good Spirit is whispering opposite advice in the other ear. Hildegard of Bingen wrote a whole liturgical drama on the battle for the human soul between Satan and the Virtues. The human creature, far from feeling "indivisible," most often feels fragmented. Extreme cases of this are multiple personality disorder and demonic possession. It is very stressful to feel that I *ought* to be unique and integrated, and at the same time feel at odds within myself.

Another way in which humans see themselves divided is into genders—male and female. Not only are there men and women, but there is seen to be the feminine element in every man and a masculine aspect of every woman. Many writers, classic and modern, have written of androgyny—the merging of, or desire to merge, both genders in one individual. Coleridge wrote: "The truth is, a great mind must be androgynous." Some writers have suggested that the yearning for the opposite sex is part of a yearning for a disunited human nature to become whole. An example of this from Greek mythology is the story of the blind prophet, Tiresias, who as a result of killing coupling snakes was turned into a woman and lived as one, until seven years later he met the same two snakes and was turned back into a man. The inference is that his experience of androgyny contributed significantly to his wisdom of the human condition.

The human individual is not a simple integer, but a complexity of many dimensions and aspects. As you point out in the introduction, the feeling of *internal* conflict is intensified by an individual's sense of him/herself in relation to *external* demands. Working out how to relate to others, or worse, *not* working it out, is very stressful. Does an individual have a completely separate existence? The word "existence" comes from the Greek, meaning "to stand out from" (*ex histemi*). And yet we can't stop the world and get off. We are part of the world and the world is part of us. We can't be completely separate, and, except for moments of great enlightenment, we can't be completely one.

It has been said that the human individual is caught between two primal fears: the fear of being abandoned, and the fear of being overwhelmed. In our earliest, most vulnerable state, these are realistic fears of life-threatening proportion: an infant can be deserted, or it can be rolled over on and smothered. Later, although we grow physically less vulnerable, the primal fears may remain or return, especially in moments of stress. The fear of abandonment may show up as needy loneliness or a feeling of being marginalized; the fear of being overwhelmed can manifest itself as a fear of being taken over or crowded out. The remnants of these contradictory fears cause more than a paradox; they hold the individual in a very stressful dilemma: how to be a separate individual with one's own boundaries, and how to become connected with another individual and with a community. Those others! We can't live with them and we can't live without them!

Part of the answer to separateness and connection has to do with the stages of maturity that we discussed in Chapter One. At first the infant cannot distinguish itself from its environment; it is not yet consciously an individual (though it has all the potential to become one, as an acorn has to be an oak). Later it learns that it is an individual and others are individuals in their own right. What Plato implied was "the examined life" is the long process of integrating the divisions that we feel within ourselves and coming to the "ripened" state of integrity where we can risk and offer this individuated self to others in relationship.

Another way of saying it is that an individual is not born; she/he is developed. That's why I defined an individual as a discreet locus of *potential* consciousness. The good news is that when a person is fully ripe (grown up, enlightened, mature, holy), we could say that she or he does live up to the root meaning of the word and can no longer be divided. Such individuals have integrated and transcended (though not denied) their inner and outer divisions, and have become one in themselves and at one with the world.

Doug: What is the primary effect the myth of individualism has on people today?

ES: I see three primary effects. The first two refer back to the fears I just mentioned in the response to question one: the fear of being abandoned and the fear of being overwhelmed. The third is a loss of the gift of discipleship. I'll say a little about each of these.

First, the fear of being abandoned can manifest itself in feelings of isolation or loneliness. My brother once said wryly, "It may be true that 'no man is an island,' but sometimes I feel like a very long peninsula."

My brother and I spent our early childhood in an apartment building in the middle of Manhattan. We didn't know the people who lived behind the door across the small elevator lobby. When I was growing up I never knew what most people meant by "a community." The school bus picked us up and brought us home, and we knew other children at school, but there was not what most people know as *neighborhood*. There was no girl or boy next door. Later it has seemed to me that my "neighborhood" was more like a coral reef made of concrete. All those tall buildings were like giant exoskeletons housing little bits of human protoplasm. And I wonder whether suburbia, with its show of neighborliness, is, in fact, very much better at counteracting loneliness. The myth of individualism fosters isolation.

But secondly, the same myth can cause an individual to feel overwhelmed and stressed-out. A person can feel like Atlas holding the world on his shoulder all by himself, and further, as you pointed out, in competition with a host of other Atlases trying to grab the world as if it were a beach ball so they can do the same thing. "Host" in the last sentence is the right word; "host" originally meant an enemy, hence an army, and we get "hostility" from the same root. For being a Rugged Individual, there is not even the camaraderie of soldiers fighting a common enemy. The stress of competition can make a person feel driven, trampled on, and marginalized. The dilemma here is that the individual is both segregated and racing to keep up or get in front of the pack.

The Rugged Individual who claims "I can do it all by myself" has to be pretty much on the go all the time. There is little or no time and space to get out of the race, just *to be*—no "down-time." Maybe commuting once partly performed that function, but now with cell phones and laptops even that time has been usurped. I wonder if this is why golf has become so popular. The golf course is one place, along with the trout stream, where one cannot be "got at," where one doesn't have to be so rugged and can have some space just to be oneself. Unfortunately there can be competitive and cell-phone-bearing golfers and even fisher-folk, but the links and the stream invite the kind of space that allows one to be just a human being and discover the true difference between isolation and solitude. Isolation implies anxiety or stress about what one is not a part of; solitude implies contentment in one's own chosen time-out.

The third major effect that I see the myth of the Rugged Individual having on people today is the loss of the gift of discipleship. In your introductory definition you stated: "Any reliance on others is a sign of weakness," and later you noted, "Asking for help was for wimps." With that attitude one cannot be seen sitting at anyone else's feet. Sometimes I think we should change the motto on the U.S. dollar bill from "In God We Trust," to "No Problem."

Some people do find teachers and gurus, but this is generally seen as counter-cultural, and the myth-mentality is broadened to something like "Asking for help is for wimps and weirdoes."

In almost all other cultures people have not only been willing but eager to sit at the feet of someone more experienced and usually older. In the Renaissance, an aspiring young artist would become an apprentice in a master's studio and learn by painting cherubs in the corners of the master's works, until his skill was sufficient and he had developed his own style and could set up a studio himself. It was more or less the same in every branch of the arts and crafts. From another culture we have the popularized example of Kung Fu—when the disciple is ready, he takes the pebble from the master's hand. And, of course, in the Star Wars cosmology, there is the rigorous discipleship of training to be a Jedi Knight.

In almost every culture except our prevailing one, there are elaborate rituals of discipleship for the young of both sexes which culminate in being received into womanhood and manhood. In our times the myth of Rugged Individualism has no doubt affected even Jewish Bar and Bas Mitzvah and Christian Confirmation, so that the element of learning from the elders is minimized and only the celebration is maximized.

One of the best positive examples of modern discipleship I have heard of is the Frank Lloyd Wright community at Talliesin West, where young aspiring architects came to sit at the great man's feet. They carried in his firewood and did his other chores so that they could hear his wisdom. Rugged Individualism shrinks at that sort of thing. If it must learn something it will *pay* for it. If you pay for it, the sub-myth runs, you are not indebted and are *not asking for help*. This allows Rugged Individuals to go to high-tech training programs, or to psychiatrists. They are not asking for help or submitting themselves to somebody else's greater wisdom, they are simply hiring professionals. Which means they are in charge, still ruggedly in control.

Another way to get around asking for help is what we call co-dependency. One or both parties may be offering help or care-giving, but it is a kind of Rugged Individualism *à deux*. The two merge into a sort of dyadic entity that isolates itself, does not seek outside help, and often is hostile and corrosive to community. The co-dependent dyad is typically born out of fear and weakness and only wears a mask of self-sufficiency. There is a great deal of difference between a symbiotic neediness of this sort and a mature exchange of gifts.

Where Rugged Individualism prevails, it is not okay to ask for the invaluable insights of wisdom and experience. For to do so is to be called a wimp, a weirdo or a loser. And in the context of this myth, to be a loser is to have "dropped out," "bottomed out," or "burned out." Rugged Individualism robs us of the knowledge of our elders and much of the richness of our "roots" and traditions. In place of our deep truth, Rugged Individualism offers us a veneer of self-sufficiency. The myth robs us of our human nature as "social animals," of our capacity to give and receive gratefully and gracefully; it robs us of community.

Doug: What does community building do to help people overcome the myth of individualism?

ES: Human beings who live or work together as a group have a tendency to move through phases or stages of interaction. As you note at the beginning of this chapter, The Foundation for Community Encouragement uses a model to work with this premise based on the writings of Scott Peck, as described most fully in his book, *The Different Drum*. What I'll do here, in answer to your question, is first to see briefly how the first two stages which Peck describes relate to the myth of Rugged Individualism, and then explore what has to happen in the third stage in order to reach the

fourth stage where Rugged Individualism is traded in for a sense of
true community.

The opening stage in our Community Building work is referred
to as "pseudo-community." At first a group of individuals are either
too fearful, or too competitive (or both), to risk expressing their real
thoughts and feelings. Admission of inadequacy or pain is
unacceptable to the Rugged Individual and so must be either
repressed or inhibited. The group's motto at this stage is "No
Problem." This, of course, is a lie. Even if a person's life is
currently as good as it can get, there is some problem, some
limitation, somewhere. There are people at this moment dying on
the streets of Calcutta; sooner or later we will all die. Because denial
of all problems *is* pseudo, it is not healthy to settle for pseudo-
community as a life style, although such superficial pleasantry can be
appropriate at a cocktail party or with waiters in a restaurant.
Revealing our true selves indiscriminately is not the goal; the goal is
to become in ourselves more and more aware of our true nature.

At some point in a group the "No Problem" aspect of Rugged
Individualism usually wears thin and breaks down, because, as we
noted, the myth doesn't offer much in the way of relating to others
except for competition or exclusive twosomes. When the veneer
wears thin enough, what we call "chaos" breaks out. Here, people
tend to express their feelings of isolation by excluding themselves or
others from the group. Or as competition surfaces, they may try to
put down or fix others. In either case the group is fragmented into
individuals trying to control their environment or exclude themselves
from it—either to be captain of the ship, or give up and abandon
ship with the rats.

If enough individuals in the group trust the process and stop
trying to fix or organize it, the group may move into a third stage
which we call "emptiness." Naming and creating ways to bring about
this stage of a group's development is one of the major contributions
Peck has made to building community. Emptying is also perhaps the
most significant factor in helping people to overcome the myth of
individualism.

There are many levels of emptiness—some of which we have
discussed in Chapter Three. Here are a few more notes on emptiness
as it specifically applies to community as opposed to individualism.

Emptiness is a risky business. It involves giving up the need to
control. It consists, among other things, of emptying myself of my

"rugged" self-image, what my unyielding agenda is, what I want to push through. This kind of letting go isn't easy, and it takes a considerable degree of trust. It's risky to trade individualistic control for openness and vulnerability. At the beginning, emptiness often feels like frustration or dejection. But it offers the most effective way to "help people overcome the myth of individualism." It means the shedding or emptying of what some people call "the false self" and others call the "ego."

This kind of self-surrender feels like death and in fact it is a kind of death. *But what dies?* Does an acorn die to become an oak? Does a caterpillar die to become a butterfly? "Unless a grain of wheat falls into the earth and dies, it remains just a single grain; but if it dies, it bears much fruit" (John:12: 24). Again, what dies? The husk, the chrysalis, the outer coating; we might add, the social mask. These protective shells are no longer needed when the new creature is strong enough to outgrow and naturally shed them.

Consider the lobster. I have heard that a young lobster develops a hard carapace or shell, which, as the lobster grows, becomes too small and must be shed. On the one hand, shedding the shell is the only chance the lobster will have to live and grow; on the other hand, the shell-less lobster is very vulnerable until it grows its new shell, and may get eaten by predators. However, if it hangs in there, shell after shell, it will one day become a mature and formidable creature. The point to be made is that the cycle of dying and renewal is both necessary and risky if we are to move towards wholeness.

When the immature husk, the mask, the defense, the shell is cracked open and emptied, new growth, new choices and new life can emerge. Then a person can have a taste of the fourth stage of "true community," where, paradoxically, one is not less individual, but more so. I am no longer either isolated or absorbed. Being more myself, I can relate more consciously and authentically with others.

Doug: What strategies can we give people for walking through the world living as authentically as possible? Is living life wearing a social mask a barrier to spiritual growth and wholeness?

ES: Well, I can think of a couple of *tips* to mention—though I don't know if they qualify as "strategies." First, there is a discipline which virtually all spiritual paths teach. It has to do with paying attention.

One way of putting it is "Wake up! and be there!" This is related to seeing *what is* (not what society and culture says ought to be) and to living fully in the moment. However, being aware is far from easy. In fact it is a discipline that takes a lifetime of practice. When one has matured or ripened in this art of being conscious, one has emptied oneself of the old spiritual cataracts of isolation and competition and has come into a sense of presence and interconnectedness. St. Paul uses the word "empty" of Jesus in his letter to the church in Philippi: "He...did not regard equality with God as something to be exploited, but emptied himself, being born in human likeness..." (Phil. 2 :6).

In fact the discipline of dying to the Rugged Individual self is generally such a long, hard process that we all have to make fun of it sometimes. There is the story of the Zen monk who went up to the street vendor selling hot-dogs and said, "Make me one with everything." The vendor did so and the monk gave him a twenty dollar bill which the vendor put in his cash box and shut it. "Where's my change?" asked the monk. The vendor replied, "Change must come from within."

But though the discipline of awareness, of living "the examined life," is difficult and often costly, it is the way both to freedom and to relationship. As we have noted before, "The truth shall make you free." (*First* it may make you miserable, but *then* it will make you free.) So one "strategy," for those who are called to it, is to practice paying attention to your life. Who are you, actually and particularly, and what is really going on for you? Far from being "navel-gazing" or narcissistic, awareness will put us in touch with the reality of others and with our environment. Without self-knowledge there can be no true compassion.

This leads us to the second tip or "strategy." Because self-awareness is, God only knows why, the less traveled road, it can sometimes get very lonely indeed, and in fact there may be a danger of taking a wrong turn, of getting lost. So the second strategy is to find a guide.

St. John of the Cross pushes the road analogy just about as far as it can go: "Wherefore, upon this road, to enter upon the road is to leave the road; or, to express it better, it is to pass on to the goal and to leave one's own way and to enter upon that which has no way, which is God." Or as Eastern wisdom puts it: "If you see the path in front of you, it is not your path." In these spaces of spiritual non-seeing, rugged individualism fails and one needs a trusty guide. The traditional name in Western spirituality for such a guide is a spiritual director. I used to dislike this term, not only because it sounded pompous but because it sounded a bit bossy. I didn't want to be directed—told what to do—I mostly wanted to be listened to and given confirmation that I was on the right track. And indeed, that is the right and proper mode for such a relationship. I had an experience one day, though, which made me think the term "director" was not so bad after all. I was driving, and had gotten off the interstate for a meal and, when I was ready to continue my trip, found that I had gotten totally lost in some small town's industrial district. I pulled into a gas station and asked for directions. They told me, "Turn right out of here, go three stoplights, when you get to the main street with the bus station on the corner turn left, and in about three blocks you'll see the on ramp. If you come to a school on your right, you've gone too far." The directions were fine and I got back on the interstate.

What I realized was that the gas station attendants didn't tell me where I wanted to go—I knew where I wanted to go; they helped me figure out how I might get there. They weren't necessarily wiser than I, or superior, much less holier—it was that *they were familiar with the territory.* So also with spiritual directors. If they're worth their salt they will not tell you where you want to go, much less where you ought to go, but being familiar with the territory of spirituality they can help you keep going there. Pick somebody for a spiritual guide who has been saying their prayers for a couple of decades, and whose opinion you trust in other areas.

Living with a social mask on all the time is surely a barrier to growth and spiritual health—if not spiritual life. Continuing to be confined in our social mask when we are ready to outgrow it would be like a lobster who wouldn't/couldn't shed its shell. If we feel the call for our spirit to expand beyond the tight carapace of its rugged individualism, then we must risk being open in a new way. That's why it's a good strategy to stay alert, and also to listen to someone who has been there and knows the territory. We might even find it's refreshing to be a disciple after all, and that learning from others is the quickest way to get further on our own unique journey.

Doug: What does God want us to do with regard to this question of individuality versus togetherness? Is it okay to be who we are even if society and everyone around us rejects it? How do we know when to be authentic and when to employ a social mask?

ES: The way I respond to any question beginning "What does God want us to do…" is to remember our quote from St. Irenaeus: "The glory of God is a human being fully alive." This is especially relevant in the area of "individuality versus togetherness," because individuality and togetherness are both about love.

Scott Peck's wisdom about individuality and togetherness was quoted in Chapter One: "…a major characteristic of genuine love is that the distinction between oneself and the other is always maintained and preserved. The genuine lover always perceives the beloved as someone who has a totally separate identity…" The respect for the separateness of oneself and of the other is the *sine qua non* of the love of two mature persons. It is, however, the exact opposite of rugged individualism. The rugged individualist lives in a state of isolation, competition, and the need to control; the mature lover lives in a state of communion, mutual exchange, and self-gift.

Another way of putting it is that rugged individualism (including co-dependency) insists that one and one equals one. And that one is ME. The next step, involving justice and cooperation, recognizes that one and one equals two. The mystery of love can bring us to a place where one and one equal three! There can be two separate individuals and the separate reality of their relationship: of what they are to and with one another. One of the best analogies I know for the Christian doctrine of the Trinity makes exactly this point about the "individuality versus togetherness" at the heart of divine love. Archbishop Anthony Bloom wrote the following about what I have just called self-gift:

> The word which I would use is self-annihilation; the ability to accept not to be, no longer to exist in a situation because something else matters more. By this I mean the following: John the Baptist said about himself, 'I am the friend of the Bridegroom.' The Bride is not his bride, neither is the Bridegroom his bridegroom, but such is his love for both of them that he brings them together—he is their witness and their companion in the marriage feast; he brings them to the

chamber where they will meet face to face alone in a fulfilled relationship of soul and body, and he remains outside lying across the door so that no one should disturb the mystery of this love...in God we find...the exulting joy of three persons who love in giving perfectly and receiving perfectly, but who being a Trinitarian relationship, if I may put it in this form of speech, are not in the way of each other, in which each of them accepts every single moment not to exist for the two others to be face to face—the miracle of total communion, fusion and oneness.

Speaking of God we must consider things in the simultaneity of events and not in temporal succession. The three simultaneously give, the three simultaneously receive, the three simultaneously place themselves in such a situation that the others are alone with each other (*God and Man*).

This is pretty heady stuff. The thing that makes this kind of self-giving good news is that it can be chosen for the sake of love. The reason why God would want this for us is that we are made in God's image, which is the individuality *and* togetherness of divine love.

The response to the next part of your question follows naturally. Self-gift implies that you have a self—a ripe self—to give. A lot of us don't yet have such a self to give away (some call it sufficient ego strength) and are working on building up and cultivating such a self. If folks are in—especially if they are *stuck* in—the state of rugged individualism, then they will not understand that the point of becoming an individual is to give oneself away and receive the other in love. So of course they will reject giving the self away, or shedding the mask, as very bad news indeed. But even if "society and everyone around us rejects it," it is okay, and for those who are called, it is imperative, to proceed to grow into who we really are.

If we have come to the point of giving ourselves to others in relationship and community, it's good to remember that we can't fix other people or society. If they are not there yet, they aren't. We can plant seeds and water, but, as St. Paul reminds us: "God gives the growth" (1 Cor. 3:6). They either will or will not come to the point of acceptance.

The last part of your question concerns knowing when we are to be authentic and when to employ a social mask. This, too, is a matter of life-long growth in discernment. As we ripen in love, we will ripen in discernment. St. Paul has a wise word here. "To the weak I became weak, so that I might win the weak. I have become all things to all people..." (I Cor. 9:22). At first this might sound like hypocrisy, but it isn't. I can only be weak with the weakness that I actually find in myself. If I meet people on their own level, even if that level is a social mask, I can only use the aspect of social mask that I have known in myself. When Elisha revived the child of the Shunammite woman, he "got up on the bed and lay upon the child, putting his mouth upon his mouth...and his hands upon his hands; and...lay bent over him..." (2 Kings 4:34). The prophet made himself small to fit the child. This was not hypocrisy; it was healing love.

God meets us where we are, in order to go with us to where we long to be. I think we are called to do the same in the acceptance of ourselves and of others.

— 6 —

The Myth of Happiness

Myth: The reason we are here on earth is to find eternal, blissful happiness and, once discovered, keep it for our entire life. A corollary principle is that if one is not happy, one must become very good at faking it in order to avoid the judgment of others.

Truth: The reality is that happiness is only one aspect of what it means to lead a fulfilling and meaningful life. Ignoring life's difficulties and pain in order experience happiness can paradoxically become a barrier to its achievement.

All beings are seeking happiness. It is the purpose of life.
—The Dalai Lama

When we are in community building workshops with people who have never experienced the process, a comment often heard at breaks or afterwards is: "Why do people spend so much time talking about pain? Where does the joy come in? I thought being in community meant to be joyful with each other?" These questions are understandable since most of us grow up with the culturally-installed belief that the goal of life is to be happy all the time. The short answer to this question is that often the pain people express in community building workshops is something they need to get rid of to clear the way to joy. Our culture does not encourage people to express pain, so when presented with a safe place to do so, people can pour it out like an overheated boiler.

In this chapter, we discuss the myth of happiness and how it can be a barrier to true joy. We are not saying one should never be happy. What you will find us closer to saying is that to lead a full life, one must be willing to experience both pain and joy. At best, to experience only the latter and not the former is to limit the experience of both. At worst, attempts to totally avoid pain can result in depression, rage and even neurosis.

Family Systems and The Myth of Happiness

A professor of mine was asked by one of his students if he thought it was a good idea to have children. The professor, who had four kids, thought about it and then said, "I know a lot of people who have chosen not to have children because they are afraid of the responsibility and the emotional pain it might cause them. I believe children do cause more pain because one exposes oneself so totally by loving so deeply. But kids also bring more joy. On the pain/joy continuum, people with kids get more of both; people who decide not to have kids get *less* of both. It just depends on what one wants."

I mention the decision to have children because it reflects one manifestation of the myth of happiness: avoid pain at all costs. The aging baby-boomer couple, seeing the problems some of their friends have had with their children, decide to cut off that entire experience in order to avoid pain.

The pain-avoidance approach is applied to all kinds of situations in our culture. I may decide not to take a new job assignment which involves more risk but also more potential rewards because I make a comfortable living doing what I do now, even though it no longer challenges me. Or I might decide not to commit to a relationship of marriage because it might fail or because I might have to limit my freedom in some other way.

The reality is that the more open one is to experience, the more one experiences both pain and joy. Great thinkers have pointed out that once we know that parts of life are difficult and involve pain, then we can deal with it. It is when the cultural myth claims you can live without pain that we begin to run around looking for ways out of it. The Outward Bound motto comes to mind: "If you can't get out of it, get into it." There is no getting out of pain or joy, so we might as well get into both.

If one of the beliefs or sub-myths of happiness is pain-avoidance, then another one is conflict-avoidance. After all, if I am in conflict, I am not happy, right? The belief in conflict-avoidance, like pain-avoidance, can block one's growth and, more significantly, one's relationships.

As I was growing up, my parents avoided both conflict and pain. For example, I almost never saw my parents fight. It was not because they did not fight, but they wanted to protect us from the reality that their relationship occasionally ran into conflict. While they thought they were doing this for our own good, it made me incapable of dealing with conflict in my own life. The belief was to always smooth over conflict, to make things okay, to change the subject when something bad or emotionally painful came up.

My parents weren't the only ones in my world running away from pain of all kinds, including emotional pain. One example is still as clear as though it happened yesterday. When I was about 24, I was visiting a friend and his family at their cabin for the weekend. My friend Roger had always been the pillar of strength in his family and his brother at the time was struggling with his life. Having just gotten out of the military and taken a job first at a fast food restaurant and then as an overworked and underpaid retail clerk in a department store, Roger's brother was a bit lost. He had not yet found a mate and had responded to his struggle by isolating himself from most everyone including his family. Roger's dad, who is a very compassionate man, felt worried and also a bit offended when his younger son did not show up until late in the afternoon that day.

I remember just prior to the brother's arrival, his dad, feeling a considerable wave of emotion, ran off into the bedroom and we could hear him sobbing. Roger got up to go into the room to see how he was doing and his mother immediately ran into his path and said, "Don't go in there, your father is not feeling very well." Roger said, "I know, that's why I am going to go in to see if I can comfort him." She said, "No, don't. He'll be all right if you just leave him alone for awhile."

The message was clear: let people experience their pain behind closed doors, away from the light of scrutiny, alone. Roger's mother was not unconcerned about his father in this situation. In fact, in her own way, she was trying to protect him from having others see him in a weak position.

Roger's parents and my parents had a lot in common, but so did many others of this particular generation. Everyone was exceedingly concerned with the way they looked to others, especially when it came to hiding pain. For being in pain meant weakness, failure, vulnerability. It meant one was failing at rugged individualism. My parents may have been unusually sensitive to what people thought of them because they were "famous" in their day: my dad a network anchorman and my mother a model, both professions which required that one look "perfect" and "together" all the time. I often think about how much energy that must have taken to look perfect all the time under all conditions. But to one extent or another, my entire generation has bought into the belief that you hide weakness and appear happy all the time. It's almost as if the appearance of happiness will attract happiness. Indeed, the AA folks, who have helped an enormous number of people out of chemical dependency, have a saying "fake it to make it." We'll ask ES about this later in this chapter.

So when my family and friends taught me through modeling that conflict and pain were to be avoided (and again they did so with the best of intentions), whenever I felt conflict or pain, I repressed it. In my first marriage, I could have gone to the Olympic Games in the 100 meter dash away from conflict. I was so good at not arguing and not working out obvious differences my wife and I were having, that someone should have given me a medal. To the outside world, of course, everyone who saw us thought we were the perfect couple. I say "of course" because that was the goal: to look perfect, and happy—to look perfectly happy.

The dynamic which drove me was: "I have to be a successful husband and a successful father," and the only modeling I had seen of successful husbands and fathers was of people who *never* argued. This is not to say that I had no role in the problems I faced during my marriage; I did. I made enormous mistakes, fatal ones. But the paradox was that in my search for the perfect, happy marriage, I thought I could get there by pretending it had already happened. Instead, I got just the opposite. I got a divorce.

Peer Groups and The Myth of Happiness

One powerful part of the belief system operating here is that, even if one is not happy, one is expected to fake it. Pretend to be happy even when you are not. This may be one reason why so many people skim along the surface of life, going from one superficial activity to another. Blaise Pascal called life an "endless series of distractions." I think it is why we spend billions of dollars watching professional sports. I know I use sports as a distraction. Since finishing graduate school, I have started watching baseball. I realize that one reason I do this is to detach from the stress of my busy life. ES and I have talked about this before, how some people have trouble unhooking the brain. Some unhook by watching baseball, others do crossword puzzles. Still others use chemicals like drugs and alcohol to unhook. It is not necessarily bad to look for ways to calm the mind so long as it does not cause physical damage to one's vessel or become a method of completely ignoring what is going on inside. For too many, the latter is the pattern and what is being avoided is the reality that life is not happy all the time.

The general pattern of faking it or "pain-avoidance" is the reason so much depression is surfacing in our culture. For if our culture almost institutionally prohibits the authentic expression of negative or painful emotions, they have to go somewhere, namely underground. Eventually such repressed emotions will erupt, often at a time and with a ferocity that the individual cannot control.

The fact that we all wear the social mask of "having it all together" and of being happy increases the risk that repressed negative emotions will one day erupt with dangerous force. This is especially true for teenagers who are so dependent upon the opinions of peers for self-esteem. What does a teenager do who is feeling depressed because his father won't talk to him or because his girlfriend just broke up with him? In our culture, he can't tell his friends he is depressed, because they will call him a "loser" or otherwise make fun of him.

What does the upwardly-mobile business executive do who is feeling an existential crisis of meaning even though, by all outward appearances, he is highly successful? Does he tell his boss and risk being taken off the fast track because he can't handle the pressure? Does he tell his wife he is thinking of quitting his six-figure-income job and becoming a school teacher and risk being seen as a poor provider?

Too often, what happens to these people is they simply swallow the pain and grin and bear it. But just as I was able to keep up the outward facade of success, the social mask of "having it all together," only to see my life implode, so too will others run the risk of implosion. Or, as has been the case with a number of troubled teenagers, explosion. Consider the collateral damage caused by two repressed teenagers in Arkansas who went to school one day armed with guns loaded with ammunition, pulled the fire alarm and then lay in wait for hundreds of innocent school children to come running outside so they could mow them down. When they were later described in the newspaper, one reporter said they seemed on the surface like quiet but otherwise "normal" kids.

Culture and The Myth of Happiness

It is not just families and peers who reinforce the myth of happiness. Stephanie Coontz has written a book entitled *The Way We Never Were*, which documents the ethic of the 1950's of sweeping pain and conflict under the carpet. That decade, which was seen as an idyllic postwar boom time, according to Coontz actually had higher levels of teen pregnancy than any decade since and alcoholism and domestic violence were rampant. We were just very good at hiding these social ills. Books by Norman Vincent Peale and others reinforced this idea by suggesting we should just "think positively" all the time and our troubles would go away.

But as Jung and many others have pointed out, when we repress negative emotions they do not go away, they just go underground. They become part of the dark or shadow side: "Neurosis is always a substitute for legitimate suffering." By this, Jung meant there is a legitimate role for suffering, especially when it has the effect of emptying one of pain. More on this later.

I saw an interview conducted by Katie Couric on NBC's Today show with Bill Cosby, whose son Ennis was murdered in 1997. The killer had just been sentenced to life in prison without the possibility of parole. Katie spent a lot of the interview asking Cosby about justice issues, but also how he was forced to grieve publicly. At the end of the interview, Cosby turned the interviewer into the interviewed by saying, "I am glad to see your smile back—cause the cancer is not fun." Cosby was referring to Couric's husband who had died of cancer around the same time Ennis Cosby had been murdered, leaving her with two small children. Couric, looking a bit startled by this, said, "Well, I am giving it the old college try."

I had noticed earlier that day that she looked quite worn-down, with her normally beautiful face heavily covered with makeup to cover obvious black circles under her eyes. I remember thinking at the time that we reward people who, despite horrible pain and loss, are able to cover it up and put on a stiff upper lip and "give it the old college try." But what are we modeling for our children when we perpetuate this kind of covering up of emotions? There is clearly a value in being able to tough it out in difficult situations. In fact, such toughness is an inbred survival instinct without which we would most certainly perish. But all of us need an outlet to express such grief, release such pain, just as the doctor seeks to cure food poisoning by removing toxins from the patient, to borrow from ES's image of her experience with confession.

How can we be happy? Is it just as simple as avoiding repressing one's emotions? How can we get off the treadmill of having to look as though we are happy which, in the end, will guarantee that we are not? I posed some of these questions to ES.

Dialogue on The Myth of Happiness

Doug: Why do people run away from pain and conflict? How is running away from it related to finding joy?

ES: The quick answer to the first part of your question is that people run away from pain and conflict instinctively. Everyone snatches their hand away from a hot stove; all creatures will try to run away from a forest fire. All creatures, including humans, when faced with conflict will experience instinctual feelings of "fight or flight." If we feel we might get the worst of it, we flee.

The longer and more complex answer must include the fact that under certain conditions a creature may *not* run from pain or conflict, in order to obtain an extrinsic or greater good. Some animals will risk pain, conflict, and even death to obtain food or to propagate the species. In animals this "crazy" behavior is as instinctual as the avoidance of pain. It may at times seem bizarre to humans; for example, the salmon killing itself swimming upstream or the male praying mantis being eaten by its mate in the very act of copulation. But unless there is an overriding instinct not to, sensate creatures instinctively avoid suffering and any conflict they are not confident of winning.

However, human beings, made in the image of God, have an innate capacity that can override instinct in any circumstance. We call it free will or choice. And one thing we can choose to do is to face pain or conflict, not only for the purpose of self-preservation or species preservation, but because it most clearly manifests our present truth, and because it will nurture our spiritual growth or that of others. We can choose to face and bear pain for love.

In Chapter Two, on the Myth of Control, we talked about surrender. What we said there is very important to remember when we are dealing with whether to run from conflict and pain or to stay and risk it for the cause of a greater good. We can't give away what we do not have. We can't take on what we cannot bear. We need to think very carefully, and if we are people of prayer, pray very hard before we choose *not* to run from pain or conflict. It was Jesus who said: "For which of you, intending to build a tower, does not sit down and estimate the cost? Or what king, going out to wage war against another king, will not sit down first and consider whether he is able with ten thousand to oppose the one who comes against him with twenty thousand?" (Luke 14:28-31). If I make myself vulnerable, I need not only to count the cost, but also to be sure of the value of my choice.

One of my favorite examples of the razor's-edge nature of choosing to face pain and death itself is in T. S. Eliot's *Murder in the Cathedral*. Archbishop Thomas Becket is informed that his assassins are waiting in the church to kill him when he comes in. Should he escape by a back door and run away? Or should he do what he always does at this time of day, and go into the church to say Evening Prayer? The question is not whether he will be killed or not—he knows he will be killed if he doesn't run away. The question is, will walking in there be martyrdom or suicide? "The last temptation is the greatest treason: To do the right thing for the wrong reason."

I think this is much the same question which caused Jesus to sweat blood in Gethsemane. To run away or to face the pain? It is also the choice each human being has to make at some time or another. Would this action be heroism or wasteful recklessness? Is this particular avoidance of pain healthy or neurotic? Is this evasion of conflict the peace-making of the Dalai Lama or is it conciliation covering passive aggression? Is this death "laying down my life for my friend" or is it Jonestown?

One can see why one of the most prevalent sub-myths of the happiness myth is "Ignorance is bliss." That is, if you don't know it, you don't have to sweat it. But it is the experience of the wisest human beings throughout history, that true joy lies not on this side of knowledge but on the other side. Ignorance sometimes may result in avoidance of pain, but *choosing* ignorance over knowledge will never bring us to the wisdom that bears fruit in true peace and joy.

You ask how running away from pain relates to finding joy. The answer lies in much we have written before about extrinsic value and self-gift. It may not *always* seem more blessed to give than to receive, but there is no doubt that human beings do find joy in giving. Giving often involves some sort of giving *away*, some loss, some emptying. We speak about making a sacrifice. The thing to emphasize about sacrifice is that it is never pain for pain's sake; that is close to masochism. Sacrifice is also never waste; it is never throwing away something that is worthless. It must be the very best, the lamb "without blemish or spot," and it must be cherished before it is given. It must be given voluntarily and with the intention of praise and love. This is supremely true about the ultimate gift, which is the gift of oneself. If we have too poor or too damaged a self-image, or if we are giving under any coercion, we probably should not attempt self-sacrifice. But when we do give ourselves freely, for the right reason, the fruits of this offering are liberation and joy.

Joy is a by-product of choosing the good. Sometimes the good comes easily and gracefully; often it comes as a result of sweating blood, of enduring, and not running from the pain. The joy of an Olympic winner crowns all the pain and rigors of the training. Olympic contestants go through all the agony for a "perishable wreath," as St. Paul reminds us, or, as we would put it today, for the gold medal. It is also possible to choose to endure pain to obtain a spiritual reward which brings holy joy.

It is written of Jesus: "...who for the sake of the joy that was set before him endured the cross, disregarding its shame, and has taken his seat at the right hand of the throne of God" (Heb. 12:2).

Doug: Is the goal of life really to be happy, as the Dalai Lama has said? And if pretending to be happy doesn't work, then what does?

ES: The Dalai Lama speaks very directly and simply. I imagine what he means by happiness is what we are calling joy, or blessedness, which is often translated as happiness, as in Jesus' sermon on the mount. In fact you could almost say that Jesus preached the sermon on the mount against what we are calling the myth of happiness. Blessed (or happy) are those who mourn? Blessed are those who are persecuted? Notice that to "persecuted" Jesus adds "for righteousness sake." He is not suggesting that persecution in itself is a good thing to choose. He is suggesting that true blessedness does not deny persecution or conflict, but can embrace and transcend them.

On a first level the Dalai Lama's words may sound comforting; on a deeper level they can be disturbing. Both in Jesus' time and now, the happiness myth would have us believe in a simplistic reward and punishment principle: be good and you will be happy; be bad and you will be miserable. Unfortunately when this is turned around we have the myth that if you are happy you must be good, and if you are miserable you must be bad. This is very stressful. The temptation is to fake being happy so you can tell yourself you are good, you are okay.

A person looks around and sees that other people—the ones who don't look like losers, who are "making it"—seem to be okay, to be happy. Or at least they don't seem to have the secret, unacceptable kind of rotten pain that he or she does. Happiness is presented as deceptively easy to attain. In fact, if we have a sneaking suspicion that we don't have happiness, we feel we *should* have it, and so we tend to convince ourselves and others that we *are* happy—in other words we fake it.

Each person may have a slightly different reason for faking it. When I was a kid, if I wasn't happy, if I was sad or angry, my mother would say something like: "Pull yourself together. I'm not going to talk to you when you're like this—come back when you've stopped crying." So in my case not being happy, or at least not acting happy, essentially meant to be abandoned. I learned early to fake being happy. I got so good at it that I learned how to get the attention I needed by being a clown. I got my acceptance needs met by being "Good old ES whom you could tease and dump on and she never showed pain or hit back, she just kept on smiling." I was 45 years old and in therapy before I knew I could be angry—or indeed what real conflict felt like. For a long time I had told myself and others that mine had been a perfectly happy childhood. I knew people who had had a traumatic childhood were unhappy and thus not okay. I was okay, wasn't I? So I must have had a happy childhood. In therapy I grew strong enough to surface past unhappiness and finally grow beyond it.

This issue of "faking it" is not a simple one. There are at least two ways we can look at it. The first is denial of pain and conflict, which means succumbing to the cultural lie. The second, as you have noted in the introduction, is the sense in which AA uses it: "Fake it to make it." This is also the way Hamlet uses the concept when he says to his mother, "Assume a virtue if you have it not." The first dictionary definitions of "assume" mean to receive, adopt, take or put on, which is how Hamlet meant it. Only when you get down to the third definition do you find the implication of pretense.

It is possible to "pretend" to be happy in the sense of *practicing* or *preparing* to be happy. Roberto Assagioli has a great insight about this in his book *The Act of Will:*

> If for example, we are sad or depressed, it is difficult if not impossible, to become cheerful or serene through a direct act of will. On the other hand, it is within our power to smooth our forehead, lift our head, smile and speak words of optimism, confidence and joy. That is to say, we are able to behave "as if" we were cheerful and confident...More important, the use of this technique will actually change our emotional state. Little by little, and sometimes rapidly, the emotional state will follow.

This kind of "assumption" of happiness can only be done when we don't lie to ourselves. *First* there is a need to recognize the sadness or pain. I am hurt. I am angry. I am depressed. *Then*, without denying that knowledge, one can try to practice happiness. Sound impossible? People have told me of various ways they have found to practice happiness in the midst of depression.

Here's an example from my own life. When I was in my twenties I went through a very painful period which felt as though the bottom had dropped out of my world and I was in "the pits." It was as if no one could reach me. Then I found J. S. Bach's Concerto for Two Violins in E Major. I found that when I listened to it—the second movement in particular—I felt understood. It seemed to me the saddest piece of music in the world, and at that time Bach was the only human consciousness who was able to reach down to the place of *my* sadness and be there with me. Having felt my pain met and acknowledged in this way, I was then ready for the third movement, which is brighter and lighter. It helped me practice happiness, in the best sense of "fake it to make it," and pick myself up and get on with my life.

So I would say pretending in the sense of lying to oneself won't work, but exploring what happiness might be for you, even when you know you have cause for unhappiness, can be good practice for learning how to open up to joy. And that *is* the purpose of life.

Doug: What does God think about the whole idea of being happy? I keep thinking of the Book of Job where the devil convinces God to test Job's faith by first removing good things from him and then bestowing horrible tragedy. Job seemed to be empty of the notion of happiness: he was faithful regardless of what events occurred in his life. Are we saying this is something to strive for?

ES: Responding to the first part of your question, as I've said, I don't pretend to know what God thinks about anything. But, as the theologian Ray Hart has written, "We are invited into knowledge and received into mystery." Only *after* he had written his entire *Summa Theologica* did St. Thomas Aquinas say something like "It all seems to me like a bunch of straw." ("Straw" is a euphemism for the Latin.) We can talk and write about what we think God thinks, as long as we realize that all our theology is finally taken into mystery, and that it would be easier for Hamlet to understand the mind of Shakespeare than for us to understand the mind of God!

All disclaimers notwithstanding, we trust the spirit of wisdom and truth to speak to us through Scripture. We can glean some hints about what God thinks about "the whole idea of being happy."

You mention the Book of Job. But before we get to the Book of Job, which is a real poser, let's look at a couple of other things. The first thing that comes to *my* mind is the 53rd chapter of the book of Isaiah, where we find the description of "The suffering servant." The whole Chapter is a poetic antithesis of the happiness myth. The cruelly disfigured "servant" who will be exalted by God is taken by scholars as meant to be Israel, and has been adopted by Christian writers as a prefiguring of Christ. "He was despised and rejected by others; a man of suffering and acquainted with infirmity." This is the man (or people) whom God will exalt and lift up. It is clear that God does not expect us or particularly want us to be serenely happy all the time in this life. God's chosen servant, God's chosen people, God's most beloved son, are characterized as miserable. God is truth; God calls us to *be real*. It is our faithfulness to our reality, no matter how harsh, grief-stricken, or even unjust it may be, that God will reward with compassion and exalt. Richard M. Benson went so far as to write: "If we could have loved God in some better way than by suffering, Jesus would have chosen that better way" (*Look to the Glory*).

Now about Job. This great work certainly deals with the doctrine that righteousness *should* bring happiness and prosperity, and that wickedness *should* bring unhappiness and misfortune, and that obviously this is not always the case. This is not the place to analyze the subtleties of the purpose and teachings of the Book of Job (for which the curious may be referred to the scholars, e.g. to the Anchor Bible introduction to the work). The point is that humanity has always been plagued by the idea that if you are good you should be rewarded by being happy, and if you are bad you should be punished.

Perhaps consequences of reward or punishment for being good or bad are passed down from parent to child, as the infant is toilet trained and generally civilized.

Inevitably there comes a time when one is punished when one *hasn't* been bad, or has gotten away with a bad act that has not been punished. Where is parental justice? It is natural that we first see God as Parent. Where is Divine Justice? Why are good people not always rewarded by happiness, and why do some bad people get away with murder? On the first and rational level there is no answer. Unfairness happens. But there is one important thing to remember. The "happiness" that can come to the "wicked" (as when we see such a person wielding great power and "flourishing like the green bay tree") is not true joy. Good fortune is not necessarily identical with good cheer. Remember Marilyn Monroe—she had it all, looks, riches, talent, popularity. Remember Midas. Were they *joyful*? Just as things will not necessarily make us happy, so also with behaviors. There is nothing we can *do* to assure happiness.

Some human beings have focused on trying to overcome, or "tough out" or discount pain. In classical times they called themselves Stoics, after a philosopher named Zeno in about 300 BC who taught in the *stoa* or covered porch. There are still Stoics today. The trouble with being stoic is that if you manage to become indifferent to pain, you also become indifferent to delight. I sometimes think that only to the degree that one has experienced suffering can one experience joy.

I think that there may be two dead-end roads in this matter of striving for happiness. One way that will not get us very far is refusing to move beyond the stage of bitter rage at pain and injustice. It may be appropriate to be angry *at first*, even angry with God, but eventually we do well to stop shooting ourselves up with adrenaline, and take the turn toward reconciliation and peace. The other dead end road is to give up and become a compliant victim of our pain. The alternative to strive for is to look to the larger picture, and find the glory at the heart of reality. That sounds pretty highfalutin; here's a homey example of the good news of "the larger picture."

My brother Paul is a very good poker player. I am a lousy poker player. When I go on my vacation to my brother and sister-in-law's house, we often play family poker. When I am dealt good cards I am happy; when I am dealt bad cards I am unhappy. Now Paul enjoys every hand. When he gets good cards he is happy in the usual sense of the word, but when he gets a bum hand he is not unhappy in the usual sense, because it presents him with a challenge. He can show that he's a really good player because he can play a bad hand just as well as a good one. Sometimes he chooses to fold. Over the course of the evening he usually wins, because he knows how to deal with every poker situation most effectively. And over all he really enjoys the game. I haven't learned how to do that in poker to any great extent, but that is what I am striving for in life. In the larger picture, over the long haul, or as the theologians say, "*sub specie aeternitatis*" (under the aspect of eternity), life is a splendid adventure and challenge, and I am learning to play even the "bum hands" with greater skill and enjoyment.

Doug: When is it okay to wear the social mask and when not?

ES: I would say it's okay to wear the social mask when you need to; when you need to either out of love for yourself or out of love for others. Let me say a little more about these two reasons for wearing the social mask.

First, as I have said before, there is a kind of foolhardy vulnerability which crosses over the line from salutary risk to reckless waste. As we have said, taking one's mask off can be dangerous. It was created in the first place to protect us from what may then have been life-threatening situations; we need to know that they are not life-threatening now. Remember the little lobster. You don't want to strip yourself of protection until you are fairly sure you will not be destroyed or irreparably damaged. This takes a lot of hard discernment. It means knowing the difference, as Scott Peck has said, between being hurt and being damaged, and ultimately (as we have noted) discerning the difference between martyrdom and suicide. It also means knowing whether this is the *time and place* for you to show yourself as you really are and speak your truth as you see it. Will it do any good? A wise person once said, "You can only be crucified once." What he meant at that time was that if you burn your draft card and go to prison, you have lost credibility with the larger section of the public. Henceforth you will be preaching to the choir. Has my hour come? Is this the time to speak my truth, to get fired from my job, to burn my bridges or my draft card? Will the greater good be accomplished? It may be true that we can "only be crucified once," but we can certainly have more than one Gethsemane!

Some people might say that wearing the social mask is "a crutch." Some people say religion is a crutch. The thing to remember about crutches is that when you have a broken ankle they are very good things indeed, and wise people learn to use them well. The other thing to remember about crutches is that they *are* crutches, and that hobbling along on them is not the preferred way to walk freely through life. The same thing is true about masks. Remember when you said that before the Community Building Workshop you didn't realize you *had* a mask? The important thing is to know it is a mask; that it is your mask. Then you can start deciding when you can choose not to wear it.

Secondly, a person can wear a social mask out of consideration and love for others. One of the things pseudo-community is good for is to put people at their ease. One of my mentors, Father Langton, was a wonderful example to me in this. A few weeks before he died he was bedridden in a London flat, having had a stroke that impaired his ability to speak and even to think very clearly. Many people, some of them bishops and theologians, came from all around just to be near him, as if he blessed each visitor just with his presence. A good friend of mine brought her little son to see him. Father Langton managed to smile radiantly, put his hand on the child's head, and say, "You're a good little brat."

By the time one is as integrated and "ripened" as Father Langton was, it is somewhat misleading to call his behavior a social mask. Yes, he was smiling on the outside while he suffered inside, and yes he was talking "small talk" when he was most probably preoccupied with eternity. But such action had by that time become his chosen way of being—to offer himself, regardless of cost, for the well-being of others. A person doesn't have to be as "ripe" or holy as Father Langton was to know when wearing one's social mask is not only the most expedient, but also the most loving thing to do. Sometimes it can be practice, or foreplay, for a more profound interaction to follow.

Doug: Is it possible to think positively and "fake it to make it" and not be in denial?"

ES: One question here is "What are we thinking positively *about*?" The danger is in trying to think positively about something that is, in fact, negative. That is the road to self-deception and lying. Take the example of Father Langton above. He did not think positively about his pain, his helplessness or his dying. He thoroughly disliked them. But he thought positively about the larger picture. I do not mean by "larger picture" the sentimental idea of "pie in the sky when you die," where this life is seen as "a vale of tears" and *then* you get to be happy in Heaven. (That is the way a "level two" sort of love looks at it: happiness/unhappiness as a punishment/reward situation.) No, he saw his own real suffering *in the present moment* in the larger context of love and glory. This glory is manifested in the particular moment; for instance, in the curious eyes of a six-year-old redheaded brat, coming to be blessed by Father Langton. At one point in his early years as a parish priest Father Langton might have had to "fake" such selflessness; now he had "made" it. He had, by a long process of becoming empty of self, become free of self-protection. And in that freedom he had found joy.

Doug: Are you a happy person? Has that always been the case? If not, what has changed that makes you happier now?

ES: Yes, I would say that I am a happy person, and no, that has not always been the case. Hardly! In my early decades I spent the greater part of my time trapped in anxiety and residual fears of being abandoned. I tried to make every man who was attracted to me into a parent who would pick me up in his big strong arms and tell me that I was special, that I was his own little sweetie-pie. Naturally the men tended to flee in panic, leaving me feeling even more abandoned. And another thing: I was distressed by the idea that life *should* have some meaning, and that I might kid myself into thinking it did, when actually the truth was that life was meaningless. Also, of course, I was beset by the oppression of the cultural myths we have been discussing. Not only wasn't I perfect, popular, accomplished, in control, and so on, but I was in anguish about whether these *were* myths, or if it was just me who was crazy.

One of the most freeing insights in my life came when I was in therapy. I had entered into analytic psychotherapy not because I had broken down, so I thought, but as a kind of "growth tool." About two years into this hard discipline of truth-seeking, I realized that I was in fact crazy. (It took me two years to become strong enough to admit that weakness!) The freeing thing was that I realized I was crazy, and *also* that the cultural myths were lies. In other words, even being crazy, I had been able in some degree to recognize truth and falsehood when I saw it. However, I had to get somewhat stronger and further healed before I understood how the cultural myths had trapped me personally and particularly, and what emptying I had to do to get disentangled from them.

You asked "What has changed that makes you happier now?" Almost everything has changed. I've heard that we change every cell of our bodies every seven years, so I suppose something like that can happen with the mind and spirit without losing our personal continuity.

One part of that shift towards happiness lies in the change in my self-perception, and that was largely brought about in therapy. Therapy was, for me, above all, a safe place where I felt secure enough to risk and empty. It was a place and a discipline where I identified and faced all the ways I saw myself. I described these images in detail in Chapter Two.

What my therapy became was not unlike what FCE means by "true community." It became a place, physically and emotionally, where I felt met and known the way I had felt years before by the music and spirit of Bach. It was a space that was safe enough and respectful enough of where I truly was, that I might risk moving out into the unknown, the un-guaranteed territory of freedom to be myself.

The other thing that changed to bring me further into happiness was my relationship to God. For me, the journey, the seeking, the exploration into God, was the search for truth. I needed to know what really *was*. This was not for me an academic exercise, it was survival and sanity. I say it was not an academic exercise, yet I had become an academic, and my mind, crazy and off-track as it was, was the best tool I had. So I suffered a long and very intellectual kind of conversion. But God is not only Truth, God is Love. I would never have come into an experiential relationship with Divine Reality if God had not broken through my controls, defenses and intellectualizations with grace. God did that. Jesus broke in upon my unlit chaos as the living light of divine compassion. This brought a kind of happiness in relationship beyond description, and it is taking me a lifetime to venture into its fullness. I am only beginning to understand that at the heart of God, the Lamb slain from the foundation of the world is at one with the power of love and glory.

It has sometimes seemed to me that the Holy Trinity contains within itself the mystery of suffering and joy. God the Father-Mother is the glory; God the Son, Jesus, is the suffering and the passion, God the Holy Spirit is the dailiness. Being an intense sort of person, the dailiness has been hardest for me to grasp. But I am coming slowly to see in the delight of each moment the true answer to the human yearning for happiness.

There is some truth in the myth of happiness, as there is in all myths. The purpose of life *is* to find happiness, or as Joseph Campbell put it, to follow (and find) our bliss. The trouble is, we don't have a very clear idea of what or where happiness will be when we find it—as is shown in the old tale of "The Blue Bird of Happiness"—and we haven't a clue what to do with the unhappiness we encounter on the way. Tragedy, pain, injustice—they just don't fit in.

All through my seeking I have been plagued by this question that has haunted humanity down the centuries, and which brings us back to why we have constructed the myth of happiness. Why pain? What is the purpose of suffering? One day a sort of response to this question came to me. You might call it "How to get from suffering to glory in five not-so-easy lessons."

> The purpose of suffering is wisdom,
> The purpose of wisdom is freedom,
> The purpose of freedom is compassion,
> The purpose of compassion is love,
> The purpose of love is glory."

—— 7 ——

The Myth of Being Good

Myth: The most important thing we can do is to be good and do good things as prescribed by a specific set of moral codes.

Truth: The most important thing we can do is to become increasingly aware and accepting of our nature: our nature in relation to God, in relation to ourselves and in relation to each other.

> **You do not have to be good. You do not have to go through the desert on your knees for a thousand miles repenting. You only have to let the soft animal of your body love what it loves.**
> **—Mary Oliver**

ES and I discussed at length whether the myth of being good is different enough from the myth of perfection to merit its own chapter. We decided it was, for this reason: whereas the myth of perfection is about images in the culture which suggest we need to perform perfectly and has more to do with "doing," the myth of being good is more about who we are and has more to do with "being." It is the message that says we have to *be* morally good all the time and if we are not, we need to walk on our hands and knees for a thousand miles repenting.

In this chapter, we will discuss good and evil, the role society plays in our definitions of them and the link between "doing" and "being" good. We will also discuss two important conditions which are related to the myth of being good: guilt and shame.

Family Systems and The Myth of Being Good

When I look back on my own childhood, I see that a lot of activity I engaged in was to cover up a feeling of not being good enough for those around me. There were many expectations that I be good at activities like school and athletics, but also that I be morally good, that I never have an evil or immoral thought. Since I had evil and immoral thoughts all the time, this created some real angst within me. But as I looked around at the people in my environment, I never heard anyone say they too had evil thoughts and "thank God I never acted on them," as I had thought. Everyone just seemed to be "on board" or to use another phrase that was common to my WASP culture, they had agreed to "get with the program."

The "program" was to look like one had it all together all of the time. The pressure both to *do* good and *be* good was enormous and I was not even a regular church-going person nor was anyone in my nuclear family. For many people who had a regular diet of Catholicism or other mainstream religious experience, the issue of being good was associated with nothing less than salvation: you will not get to heaven unless you "straighten up and fly right" and when you don't, you must be sure to confess with contrition.

I saw a lot of the fallout of the sins of institutional religion when I was taking classes at Seattle University where often half of the class would be comprised of cradle-Catholics. Many of these folks had issues with the way their parish and the larger institution made them feel about their own self-worth growing up. In our class discussions, the issue of a judgmental God was a common topic.

Beyond Seattle University, there is a huge segment of the population that apparently views God as a judge as opposed to a lover. Longitudinal studies conducted by the Roper Center for Public Opinion ask a cross-section of the population each year to describe their image of God on a scale of one to seven, with one being God as "judge" and seven being God as "lover." Each year, an average of 37 percent of respondents say they view God as "judge" and only eight percent say they view God as "lover." This is significant because if four of ten people see God as a judge and if we are made in the image of God, then it should not be surprising that many of us judge ourselves and others harshly.

In my own experience, my sense of self-blame or shame came from the fact that everyone around me looked so together. A primary reason why we pretend to have it together is to avoid judgment. For example, I never told *anyone* the kinds of thoughts I was having as an adolescent boy because I thought people would think I was a weirdo. Since I was the only one who knew that I was having bizarre fantasies about girls (and other things, but mainly girls), and because no one else ever said they were having such thoughts, I concluded that I must indeed be weird.

Once I grew up a little and studied the science of developmental psychology and realized all boys have such fantasies, driven by a new chemical in the body called testosterone, I realized that perhaps I wasn't quite as bad as I had originally thought. This again leads us back to Yalom's curative factor of universality. If others have similar things happening to them, then I am more likely to accept what is going on in me. If the way everyone looks and acts is different from the way I look and act, I feel shame.

I have used the concept of universality almost every day in raising my son. Each step along his developmental path, I try to mirror back to him that the things he feels and thinks and is experiencing are completely normal, despite what others in his peer group might say. A common phrase in my household when I am frustrated with something Nick has done is, "Nick, would you just stop acting your age for a moment!" It is important for us in our family systems to affirm that it is okay to *be* the way we are, even if we have impulses that seem abnormal or socially unacceptable.

There is a classic scene in the movie *Parenthood* which illustrates this point. One of the characters is a 13-year-old boy named Gary. Gary's mother is divorced and he is at the age where he is starting to experience his sexuality. He begins acting very strange and secretive and his mother is worried he might be on drugs. One day she looks in his room and finds a number of adult sex videos. She is worried about this and since his father is not around, she asks her daughter's 18-year-old boyfriend to talk to Gary.

In a powerful scene, the boyfriend comes out after talking with Gary and explains to Gary's mother [excuse the indiscreet language], "Several months ago, Gary got his first boner. Do you know what that is? Anyway, since then, he has been, well, slapping the salami. Apparently he was going for a world record. He thought there was something wrong with him. Like he was a pervert or something. I told him 'that's what little dudes do.' And that made him happy."

In the quest to avoid being bad, we often retreat into our own worlds out of fear that someone will discover how bad we are. Labels of "good" and "bad" are placed on what is most often simply human nature. Yet if we ignore our human impulses totally and pretend they are not there, they can become what Joseph Campbell calls a devil:

My definition of a devil is a God that has not been
recognized: a power in you to which you have not given
expression and then like all repressed energy, it builds up
and becomes completely dangerous to the position you
are trying to hold and so it is a threat.

We are not saying that "anything goes" in terms of one's
behavior. Many post-modernist thinkers argue that since everything
is relative and based on perception, it is okay for humans to do
anything they want. The fact is there are moral codes and systems of
conduct which, if followed, can lead to a more fulfilling and
complete life. Conversely, there are systems of conduct which can
lead to a disastrous life. C. S. Lewis addressed this point in *Mere
Christianity*:

> People often think of Christian morality as a kind of
> bargain in which God says: "If you keep a lot of rules,
> I'll reward you, and if you don't, I'll do the other
> thing." I do not think that is the best way of looking at
> it. I would much rather say that every time you make a
> choice, you are turning the central part of you, the part
> of you that chooses, into something a little different
> from what it was before. And taking your life as a
> whole, with all your innumerable choices, all your life
> long you are slowly turning this central thing into a
> Heavenly creature or into a hellish creature: either into a
> creature that is in harmony with God, with other
> creatures, and with itself, or else into one that is in a
> state of war and hatred with God, and with its fellow
> creatures, and with itself. To be the one kind of creature
> is Heaven: that is, it is joy, and peace, and knowledge,
> and power. To be the other means madness, horror,
> idiocy, rage, impotence, and eternal loneliness. Each of
> us at each moment is progressing to the one state or the
> other.

We are, each of us, "progressing" towards one state or the other.
But progression is not the same as arrival. The movement is often
slow and the journey long and we need to be patient and accept our
progress, even if it is molecule by molecule.

Peer Groups and The Myth of Being Good

Scott Peck tells an interesting story about how everyone has a murderer inside them. He has one which he keeps in a fairly well-appointed jail cell, with a big padlock on it. He describes how he goes down to feed his murderer every so often and takes good care of it because he wants to be able to consult with it from time to time. He says there are things he can learn from that dark part of himself.

The idea is that the human organism is capable of doing every kind of behavior that has ever been done, good and bad. The best way to ensure that the murderer and other characters which represent undesirable behavior stay locked away is to acknowledge their existence, to accept the reality of the whole of our self. To use Joseph Campbell's idea, turn the spotlight of awareness on the devil (repressed human forces), and he loses his hold over you. Another way of putting it is: evil is only evil if it has not been brought into awareness. If it remains in the dark shadowy byways of the unconscious, it gets thicker and darker, more unpredictable and also more uncontrollable.

The problem is that our culture does not allow human beings to acknowledge these dark byways. This lack of acceptance for the unacceptable is nowhere more prevalent than among teenagers who are all looking for validation. More and more, their validation seems to come not from compliments from each other but by winning the contest to shame and ridicule each other.

My own teenager is a very sweet kid with a big heart, but he has become masterful at making fun of other people including his dad. And when I see him around other kids his age, I can see why he does this. It is a defense against the onslaught of shaming criticism: your best defense is a good offense.

The effect this has is to make it absolutely impossible for kids to talk to each other in any kind of nurturing, accepting way. When I was on a fishing trip with Nick and one of his friends, at one point I said to Nick, "You know, I am getting tired of you two guys making fun of me." Nick said, "Oh come on Dad, we're only teasing."

And you know what? They were only teasing. And I will acknowledge that I might be more sensitive to teasing than some others, but then I got to thinking about the whole concept of teasing. There is no reason why I or anyone else has to accept teasing as a mode of interaction that is acceptable. All it does, in my view, is make it less and less likely that human beings will ever get to the point where they will be able to accept each other and possibly even reveal some of the things about themselves that are not very good. Teasing ensures that the social masks will stay on, the defenses will remain up and the parts of all of us that are "bad" will remain hidden from view where they can do the most damage.

What would happen if the public school system had a day set aside each year called "no teasing/no kidding" day? How would the average junior high school student's day be different if on just one day, no one in the entire school was allowed to tease them? How would the overweight 13-year-old feel about going to school? How would the pimple-faced 14-year-old feel? How would the shortest kid in the school feel? How would the tallest kid feel? Acceptance of imperfection fosters change. As Carl Rogers put it: "The curious paradox is that when I accept myself just the way I am, then I can change." The converse might also be true: if I do not accept myself the way I am, I will never change. Perhaps this was the inspiration for the Jesuit prayer/meditation: "I do not have to change for God to love me."

Human beings lose self-esteem by verbal abuse and it starts when we are young and gets worse and worse. I recall being at a friend's 20-year high school reunion. My friend and a number of others were sitting around commenting on how fat some of their classmates had gotten. This went on for several hours until finally I said, "Why don't you just have an electronic reader board at the registration table and a scale and you can announce each new arrival by stating their name and new weight?"

We are responsible for our behavior, yes, but verbal abuse of ourselves and one another for falling short of our own standards does not move us in the direction of wholeness. Thich Nhat Hanh, in a poem of tremendous self-compassion, describes the notion of accepting all parts of the self:

Please Call Me By My True Names

I am a frog swimming happily
in the clear water of a pond.
And I am the grass-snake
that silently feeds itself on the frog.

I am the child in Uganda, all skin and bones,
my legs as thin as bamboo sticks.
And I am the arms merchant,
selling deadly weapons to Uganda.
I am the twelve-year-old girl,
refugee on a small boat,
who throws herself into the ocean
after being raped by a sea pirate.
And I am the pirate,
my heart not yet capable
of seeing and loving.
Please call me by my true names,
so I can hear all my cries and laughter at once,
so I can see that my joy and pain are one.
Please call me by my true names,
so I can wake up
and the door of my heart could be left open,
the door of compassion.

Culture and The Myth of Being Good

At the writing of this book, the investigation of the U.S. President and his alleged affair with a young intern was just coming to a peak. After being investigated for seven months by the Office of Independent Counsel, the President finally admitted that he had had an inappropriate relationship with the young intern. At issue was not the fact that he had the affair but that he had lied to the Grand Jury about the affair. As I was watching this drama unfold, I kept thinking, of course he lied about the affair hc had with a 21-year-old intern inside the Oval Office. What choice did he have? Tell them the sordid details and then be banished from the kingdom?

The moral issue of a president's sexual improprieties is not the point here. Rather, it points to the larger issue of a society in which we judge each other all the time for things which, let's face it, are human things. They are not good things; they are human things and being human is about being both good and bad. Great leaders throughout the ages have had idiosyncrasies which ranged from having extramarital affairs to chemical addiction to out-and-out corruption. They also did great things for the country. In this sense, many of our leaders have, to use C. S. Lewis' image, moved back and forth between becoming hellish creatures and heavenly creatures. We will discuss in the dialogue section the relationship between good and bad and going to heaven.

The political arena is merely an exaggerated example of the judgmental nature of humans. In my own experience, I felt the scrutiny of judgment as a political appointee. The whole time I worked for the Attorney General of Washington State, I felt anything I did could end up in the news. In fact, my boss once told me, "While you're on my watch, just be sure you never do anything you wouldn't want to see on the front page of *The Seattle Times.*"

Once I left the political arena and was able to have a normal kind of life where I didn't feel my own behavior was going to be scrutinized and judged at every turn, I was much more open to people, much less inclined to hide my flaws and, ironically, much less likely to criticize others.

Another set of dynamics that play out in this business of being good are the concepts of shame and guilt. Guilt is about feeling bad for things one does. Shame is about feeling bad for who one is. Rabbi Harold Kushner in his book *How Good Do We Have to Be?* tells the story of his going to a county spelling bee and losing in the first round because he misspelled the word "judgment" (of all words to misspell!) by putting an 'e' in the middle. He said the mistake itself was not that remarkable but what was remarkable was the fact that forty years later he still beats himself up over the mistake. Kushner wrote that he often completely ignores all of the positive things he has done with his life, which far outnumber the mistakes or "bad" things. This relentless self-blame has the potential to turn "doing" mistakes into "being" mistakes, guilt to shame, if they are internalized enough. Beat yourself up enough over mistakes you've made and the mistake you *made* becomes the mistake you *are.*

I used to get teased relentlessly by my brother and father for not being particularly handy with tools and manual labor. So, at about the age of 31, on a very unconscious level, I refinanced my house and bought a completely dilapidated "fixer" rental home. I spent over six months completely remodeling the house myself.

I later reflected on why I had done this and the answer was clear: I had to remove the belief that I could not fix things or be handy with a hammer. Up until that time, I had been enormously self-conscious about fixing things, so much so that I approached such tasks with a sense of dread and, of course, usually reinforced the belief by botching the job. This belief of not being able to do manual labor soon became something more: maybe I was somehow intrinsically flawed, maybe my inability to use a hammer was reflective of a deep defect in my character. Since men were supposed to be good at construction and I clearly wasn't, what was wrong with me? This is a kind of "slippery-slope" logic where once you get going in the direction of thinking you're no good, you start to gain speed and before you know it, you find yourself in a heap at the bottom of the hill.

Once I had remodeled a whole house and done a reasonably good job at it, the weight of that stigma was lifted and I now routinely work on projects with ease. Once I emptied myself of the belief that I was a home improvement klutz, I was free to use my authentic skills to do good work in that area. And believe it or not, my sense of well-being improved once I had removed this negative belief. And once my self-esteem improved, I found myself starting to do other things that were good, like running and returning to school.

So if we should accept ourselves as we are and try to empty ourselves of negative beliefs, does this mean we should not try to be good? And if we should try, to which set of moral values do we subscribe? Should we follow the creed of the Boy Scouts to be trustworthy, loyal, helpful, friendly, courteous, kind, obedient, cheerful, thrifty, brave, clean and reverent? How should we respond to prescriptive exhortations about the kinds of moral values we should live by?

Some of these beliefs make a lot of sense and would probably constitute good news. But what if I can't always be cheerful or kind? What if there are days when I am clearly not brave or friendly? We need a set of moral guidelines for how to move towards positive beliefs. But, if I look at them as absolute states or dualities, where I either am or am not kind or courteous all the time, then I will be asking for self-blame and shame.

One alternative is to choose to see beliefs and values as different manifestations of the same reality or as being on a continuum along which we are moving. Viewed this way, I can simply check my progress based upon the direction I am going rather than whether I have "arrived." This alternative view would not only allow me to exercise more self-compassion but would also mean living closer to truth, which means freedom. I asked ES about these issues.

Dialogue on The Myth of Being Good

Doug: What about this business of people's images of God. We have said throughout the book that God is love, but many people say their image of God is as "judge." Are these people wrong?

ES: I would say that imaging God as judge is not so much a question of right or wrong as it is a developmental issue. As you no doubt know better than I, a child is not necessarily *wrong* in seeing a parent as dispenser of rules, rewards and punishments, and an adult is not necessarily *right* in moving beyond rules and laws. Also, it is a necessary and a very good thing to have judges in this world, and there can be very holy judges. To the people of the First Covenant, the Law and justice and righteous judges were very important. And they still are to all of us today. There is nothing wrong with seeing God as a righteous judge.

But humanity is called beyond *only* living by law to being mature lovers. We are called beyond Level Two Love which is justice, to Level Three Love which is mutual gift. We are made in the image of God, and as we become more capable of mature love, we are able to image God as the ultimate mature lover—as perfect, complete love itself. When this happens, it may naturally take precedence over less mature or less "ripened" imaging. Since no individual or group or nation functions on any of the three levels *all the time*, it is good to have judges and nurturers as well as friends and lovers. Jesus said, "Do not think that I have come to abolish the law or the prophets; I have come not to abolish but to fulfill" (Matthew 5:17). Jesus does call us to be friends. It can be very bad news to image God only and permanently as a severe (not to say unjust) judge. We may not need to abolish that image, but we need to develop others.

It is very important to remember that *any* image we have of God is by definition untrue. The best chance we have is to use as a model the noblest and best of human love we have ever known.

Doug: Does God accept me regardless of what I do? A related question: Did God accept Adolf Hitler the way he was or the Oklahoma City Bomber Timothy McVey who slaughtered hundreds of innocent men, women and children?

ES: The answer to this question can be both very simple and very complex. The simple way of looking at it is to think of the many parents and lovers who have "accepted" significant others even when they have perpetrated criminal and even appalling acts. If it is conceivable that, say, Eva Braun accepted Hitler the way he was, is it not conceivable that God could? If I know even one other person in my own life who accepts me as I am, regardless of what I do, why not God?

The question that follows logically is "Then why should I or anyone take the hard road of trying to choose the good?" Some people do seem to take advantage of the principle of unconditional love, and defend their unacceptable behavior by saying "You need to accept me just the way I am." It is all very well to say, "Love the sinner and hate the sin," but it is not always so easy to do. Especially if a person who acts violently or abusively claims,"How I act is part of who I am." Such persons need to be told in love, "I accept *you*, but what you are doing to yourself and others is not acceptable." To love them does not necessarily mean to vote for them, to put them in power, or to put weapons—material or verbal—at their disposal. To love them may mean, in extreme cases, to lock them up.

The next question might be: "Even if I can accept this person as they are—should I?" This leads us into the more complex aspect of the issue. Even if God *can* accept me or others no matter what we do (after all, God is all-mighty) *ought* God to accept badness? (God is all-goodness.)

The ancient theologians came up with a formulation that states that God has two wills: God's will of good pleasure, and God's will of permission. This echoes in a sense the distinction we made earlier in talking about surrender: to accept a bad thing is not necessarily to condone it. God does not condone or take pleasure in evil; God accepts the reality which God permits. Of course the next question we can ask is "If it is not God's *good pleasure*, why does God *permit* evil?" The final answer to that is that we don't know; the ancient theologians called this whole problem "the mystery of iniquity."

But this mystery may have something to do with the nature of love. (God is love.) To be worth anything at all, love must be freely given. If "love" is demanded or imposed, it comes close to manipulation or rape. We've talked a good deal about mature love, and how it is the free and chosen mutual gift of two independent persons. In order to be free to choose to love God and to love the good, there must be a real alternative. We must *really* be free to choose the lesser good, to choose away from love, to choose evil. Only the freedom of that decision gives our option for love its value.

There is another dimension to this complexity. We might ask: "How much free choice did Timothy McVey or Adolph Hitler really have?" To what extent were the cards stacked against them by nature or nurture or both? What about children—even infants—who are so damaged and traumatized, so inhumanely treated by parents and/or peers, that they have little motivational recourse beyond the animal instincts for survival and domination? We read, for instance, that Hitler was raped and brutalized by his father. This in no way exonerates his actions, but it opens the discussion of how much choice there is in every evil act and how much force of circumstance.

Another way to put it is to speak of positive and negative programming. What is the ratio in any given human being between negative programming and the freedom to choose? When you come down to it, how much is my own behavior shaped by nature and nurture; what models for good choice have I had? How much grace have I been given? God only knows how well I have done with what I have been given. Jesus said, "From everyone to whom much has been given, much will be required" (Luke 12:48). This reminds me of my family's poker game: how well has each one done with the hands he or she has been dealt?

Here's a story about something that happened to me once which I often recall when issues like these arise. Once I was involved as a material witness in a rape and murder trial. A piece of jewelry I had made—a copper enamel medallion with a fish on it—was found at the scene of the crime. The suspect was a young man who had been convicted of rape and murder several years before. He had been an exemplary inmate and had been let out on parole. They had arrested him for breaking parole and were trying him for a second incident of rape and murder. At the first crime scene they had found a religious medal, though it was of the mass-produced type that anyone could have obtained. Where I came in was that mine, found at this second scene of the crime, was obviously hand-made and therefore traceable. The police hoped that by tracing its provenance they could establish an evidential link with the defendant. In fact, that wasn't hard. The prison chaplain had purchased the medal from the shop where I had placed it on consignment, and was present at the trial to testify that he had given it to the defendant. All I had to do was to witness that I had made the medallion, and that it was one of a kind, which I could do with confidence, since I noticed I had made a mistake on that particular piece, in how I placed the fish's gills.

The point of the story is that when I got into the witness box I had my first glimpse of the defendant. It was a shock. He was a pleasant-looking young man in a blue sport shirt, looking very ordinary and vulnerable. I wondered what it was like for him. Had he possibly fought with his demons all his short life, and perhaps gone wild and given in to them these two times? Who knew how many times he might have fought against his demons and won? To what extent were the cards stacked against him? And what about his leaving religious medals at the scenes of his horrible acts? What sort of guilt, conscious or semi-conscious, would that indicate? What kind of terror and even repentance might he feel? And then I wondered if perhaps this young man might have done more with the circumstances he had been given than I had with all that had been given to me. That perhaps in the eyes of God, this murderer and rapist might be a holier person than I.

I thought, then, of an analogy with Pharaoh and the ancient Jewish people in Egypt. Pharaoh, he of the hard heart, ordered that the Israelites should make bricks without straw. But God would never do that. We are each called to make as many bricks as we have been given straw to make them with. And we don't know how much straw anyone else has been given. I didn't know how much straw that young man in the dock had been given. I don't know how much anybody I live or work with has been given, and I am even unclear how much I have myself. That's why it's useless to compare oneself to anyone else. Much less to judge oneself or anyone else.

When it comes to self-judgment, perhaps all I can do is commit myself to a continual discernment of the gifts I have been given so that I may extend myself in understanding, choosing, and acting for the good. If, for all my discerning, I cannot finally know how much straw (grace, and/or lack of negative programming) I have at any given time, then I cannot, without being as hard-hearted to myself as Pharaoh, demand of myself such and such a level of goodness.

But part of the mystery is that we can, in cooperation with grace, learn how to be conscious, grow in discernment, learn better how to choose the good. Perhaps the only reason for accepting a person as they are, regardless of what they do, is to create an atmosphere where they can take the risk of trying to be different and choose better. Not only can God's grace help us with this transforming process, but we can help one another. Acceptance, withholding judgment, makes possible the movement from compulsion to choice: the way to mature humanity.

Doug: One of the things I have seen in working with older people is they tend to believe strongly in the idea that good works will get them to heaven. Is there truth to the idea that the more one does for others, the greater their chance of going to heaven or of being with God?

ES: Before we go into the question of "good works," let's talk a little about what "heaven" could mean. The usual concept of heaven has a lot to do with what we talked about in the last chapter—freedom from all suffering, happiness, joy, bliss. This holds true in many spiritual traditions. Celebration, feasting and banqueting are frequent components or symbols of paradise.

In the Christian tradition a splendid image of heaven is found in the Book of the Revelation to John (19:9) where we read: "Blessed are those who are invited to the marriage supper of the Lamb." Celebration, music, feasting, joy—in honor of what? Of the consummation of love in sexual union! This is of course an analogy—but what a brilliant analogy—of the blissful union of Christ and his Bride: the Bride being that part of humanity who choose to join with him in love.

Some sections of Christianity have gotten off the track around this issue of joyful celebration. They seem to have forgotten a lot about Jesus' party stories. For instance, overlooking the fact that everyone is invited from all the highways and byways, they start considering merit and qualifications, as if you could only get in if you could afford the cost of 500 good works per plate. There is a lot about dinners and festive meals in the New Testament, and they seem to be not only "Come one, come all" parties, but "Come as you are" parties. You don't have to be respectable, or even good, to be included. You can be a "notorious sinner" and be more welcomed as a guest at the dinner party than the righteous-seeming host.

There is one notable and disturbing exception in the New Testament: the story of the wedding feast where one guest came without a wedding garment and was rejected. The question here is "What does the wedding garment signify?" The Puritan and juridical elements of Christianity would probably conclude that the wedding garment indicates good works and "clean living," not to mention temperance and severity of lifestyle, but everything else Jesus ever said or did would seem to me to speak against this interpretation. "John the Baptist has come eating no bread and drinking no wine, and you say, 'He has a demon'; the Son of Man has come eating and drinking and you say, 'Look, a glutton and a drunkard, a friend of tax collectors and sinners!' (Luke. 7:33). What if the wedding garment stood, rather, for a commitment to maturing in love, and a yearning to be with God—as C. S. Lewis describes his "Heaven creature"? What if the wedding garment in that context meant a growing capacity for joy?

It is not that good works are not important. The point is that, like any love-gift, they need to be given with no strings attached. A good tree produces good fruit. A full, mature human being, a "human being fully alive," will produce good works. And not out of a sense of grim duty, such as is indicated by the "Protestant Work Ethic." On the contrary, God loves a cheerful giver. When a gift, a good work, is given out of cheer, out of joy—out of one's very goodness of being—then it's a love-gift, and that kind of cheerfulness is also good practice for the heavenly celebration. A splendid example of this point is the story I told in Chapter One of Father Taylor's spontaneous gift of his attention and love to the older Sister.

Doug: We have talked a lot so far about trying to be good and faking it when we are bad and the stress that can cause. What about the word "sin." Could you describe your definition of sin?

ES: The Greek word most frequently translated as "sin" in the New Testament is *hamartia* which originally meant missing a mark or a target. When applied to moral things the idea is similar; it is missing the true end of life. Sin is a deliberate choice of the lesser good or the downright bad. Sin is a choice away from love and against one's conscience. One dictionary mentions "a deliberate violation of a religious or moral principle." There must be the element of deliberation or choice for it to be sin. I have heard it said, for instance, that when the hierarchy at Rome excommunicated Martin Luther, it did not convict him of *sin*. The Roman Church at the time could not contain Luther and his teachings within its communion because Luther's beliefs, actions and writings were too divergent from its norms. The Church could proclaim him a heretic, but not a sinner, because it could not establish that Luther had acted against his conscience.

I have asked myself: "What exactly does a deliberate or conscious choice mean? How conscious is conscious?" In pondering that question, I have come up with something that helps me, which I call "The Continuum of Inadvertence." By that I mean that there may be degrees of consciousness behind any sin, any particular choice for the lesser good.

Here's an example at the "inadvertent" end of the continuum. I was once out on mission to a parish Church, and was billeted at the house of one of the parishioners. Before we said goodnight, my hostess told me how to turn on the coffee machine in the morning if I awoke before she did, and where the milk was in the refrigerator. So the next morning in due course I opened the refrigerator, and saw this gorgeous baked ham ready to be heated up for Sunday dinner. And there was this little crispy delicious-looking bit sticking out on one end. Before I knew it—it was down my throat. Almost immediately I knew that I had done something wrong—something like gluttony, and maybe even stealing. (My hostess had invited me to help myself to milk—but not to Sunday dinner!) Did I make a conscious choice to swallow that tidbit? How conscious? Could my choice of action be called deliberate? It seemed to me that it was almost completely inadvertent.

On the other end of the spectrum is the kind of premeditated decision that runs something like this: "My supposed friend broke my confidence; I'm going to teach her a lesson, make her feel as bad as I do. As soon as I get a chance, I will." My experience is that the conscious intent of most of what we call sin is somewhere between the two extremes of the continuum. Only God knows exactly how deliberate each choice was, and how much instinct, negative programming and circumstances influenced it. All I can own and confess to is my willful consent, whatever part of the whole picture that may be. In addition I can resolve to continue to inform and follow my conscience.

You mention "faking it when we are bad." I suppose "faking" it has a social connotation. In the political arena the term may be "cover up." When it comes to sin, this impulse to negate badness, to sweep it under the rug, can have profound implications.

Both sins that we have committed and those that have been committed against us can be covered up so deeply that we are no longer aware of them at all; this is called *repression*. The next strata up towards consciousness we call *inhibition*: those bad things which we could remember, but we don't want to, or choose not to think about. Close to this is *self-deception* or *denial*—the bad thing is available to our consciousness, but we say "it shouldn't be" so convincingly to ourselves that "shouldn't be" becomes "can't be, is not." An example of this is my frantic denial on the 79th Street bus that I could possibly be a person who was late for a dinner engagement *twice!* Denial to oneself or others can be self-defense, or it can move to downright lying. The big trouble with lying is that it traps us in unreality. Only the truth will make us free.

We have talked a great deal about awareness and how essential it is for spiritual growth. In talking about badness and sin, it becomes clear how hard and often painful awareness can be. It isn't easy to empty ourselves of the will to repress, inhibit, deny, cover up and generally not acknowledge our faults, mistakes, and perhaps especially our sins—sins being those bad things to which we, at least to some degree, have consented.

You have mentioned Scott Peck's story about his "criminal" whom he keeps locked up but available for consultation. I also have met my own murderer. It was in a rather frightening dream. I don't need to recount here the specifics of the nightmare; there are two important points about it. The first is that I strongly felt the freedom to wake up before I actually encountered the representation of my own worst evil, and I, even asleep, *chose* to stay with my dream. And secondly, when I met my ugly killer-image, I knew I should not offer it violence in return. I simply looked, acknowledged it, and let myself wake up. That dream was one of the most freeing events of my life. As you mentioned in reference to the Joseph Campbell quotation, the evil was made conscious and lost its power to scare the wits out of me.

Doug: You have written previously about the seven classical sins of Pride, Greed, Envy, Lust, Gluttony, Sloth and Anger. If our basic premise is that acceptance and awareness of our humanness is a way to turn the bad news of our nature into good news, then could you discuss how such awareness does that for these different sins?

ES: Not many people in our culture talk about sin anymore. Maybe because a rather morbid attitude toward sin prevailed in parts of the Church in the last few centuries. Ignoring sin seemed to be a healthy corrective to a tendency to over-stress our sinful nature. However, it is undeniable that people do know themselves capable, and culpable, of choosing against the good. As you indicated in your question above, I have thought about the classical "Seven Deadly Sins" and speculated on what they might look like today. The point of this little exercise is once again to check into an aspect of our truth as human beings, so that truth can make us free.

I once drew up a table with four columns: 1) The name of the classical sin; 2) What the sin's behavior might look like today; 3) The false promise which tempts us to commit this sin; and 4) The right way to obtain what we need, the true or "narrow way" to the desired good.

Sin is trying to take a shortcut to joy. Sin tempts us to think it is a shortcut on the road *more* traveled. The trouble with this apparent shortcut is that it doesn't really get us where we most deeply want to go; on the contrary, it often lands us, like it did Bunyan's Pilgrim, in Vanity Fair or the Slough of Despond or some other deep trouble.

Pride—Let's first take a look at pride. Today the sin of pride might be seen as narcissism, ego-inflation, or self-aggrandizement. We are tempted to think it will win us self-esteem or "perfection."

There is, of course a good kind of pride, such as taking pride in our work, though I wish we had a different word for it. Pride, in the sense of healthy self-esteem, is identical with true humility. It is seeing ourselves as we really are. The pride which is sin, once had the name of "vainglory" which is quite appropriate: glory which is in vain, which is a lie. A poor self-image is the flip side of vainglory; both are the opposite of true humility. As we have said before, people tend to have "flip images" of themselves: a miserable image and an inflated image. Neither is accurate. They are both distorted like reflections in a fun house, where we move slightly and look much fatter or much thinner than we really are. True humility, which comes by way of careful self-knowledge, includes all the parts and images of ourselves, the bestial as well as the noble. One of the loveliest descriptions of humility is by Anthony Bloom in his book, *Beginning to Pray*.

> The word "humility" comes from the Latin word
> *humus* which means fertile ground. To me, humility
> is not what we often make of it: the sheepish way of
> trying to imagine that we are the worst of all and
> trying to convince others that our artificial ways of
> behaving show that we are aware of that. Humility
> is the situation of the earth. The earth is always
> there...somewhere we cast and pour out all the
> refuse, all we don't need. It's there, silent and
> accepting everything and in a miraculous way
> making out of all the refuse new richness in spite of
> corruption, transforming corruption itself into a
> power of life and a new possibility of creativeness.

The right way to get this "new possibility of creativeness" is by
the hard way of self-knowledge and self-acceptance.

Avarice—Perhaps the "besetting sin" of our society is greed, or what
used to be called avarice. A "besetting sin" describes the situation
when one pattern of "shortcutting" predominates. For instance, when
the pressure is on, do you tend to place yourself above such things
(that would be pride), go on a shopping binge (greed), gripe about
how other people have all the luck (envy), turn on the TV or
oversleep (sloth), find a sexual outlet (lust), go to the refrigerator
(gluttony), or chew someone out (anger) ?

It does seem, as we suggest in the chapter on the myth of
accumulation, that our culture's shortcut of choice may be greed.
Avarice does not know the meaning of gift. Its characteristics are
acquisition, exploitation and consumerism. The temptation is that by
accumulating more and more things we will find security,
invulnerability and ease. As we have seen, this is a myth or a lie.
The only way to come to true ease of mind and spirit is to empty
ourselves of the demand for security and sufficiency, and nurture the
capacities of trust and gift.

Envy—If greed or avarice is grabbing what we can get, envy is
hankering after what we can't get. (If the object of envy became
attainable, the sinful attitude toward it might shift to greed.) The lie
that envy is based on—its temptation—is that if we could only have
what we don't have, or be what we are not, we would be okay.

Remember the quip about the neurotic? "Wanting what we can't
have and not being able to bear what we've got." Part of the lie of
envy is that we *can* have it—we can get it, whatever we envy—and
then we will be happy and good.

One of the offspring of envy is judgmentalism. It is common to
condemn or "put down" what we envy in others in hopes that we can
feel better about our own impoverishment. Envy is an attempt to
shortcut the hard work of accepting ourselves as we are, with what
we have been given, and trusting our own okay-ness and indeed our
unique worth.

Lust—Lust is another of those words that we use to describe a
healthy condition as well as the sin. It is fine to have a "lusty
appetite" either for food or for sex. What the classical sin looks like
today is when we distort the natural instinct in order to serve the lie.
The lie is that having more and better sex will bring us happiness, or
at least "nepenthe"—the forgetting of all trouble; we will find
release, and/or affirmation, and fill our soul's hunger to be loved.

I knew a man once who had a Don Juan kind of sexual
addiction. It was a dreadful disease which robbed his life of
commitment and his spirit of peace. He could not enter into
conversation with one woman without casting an eye around the
room for the next. Consequently his lust was never satisfied: he
could never enjoy the woman he was with, because he was always on
the lookout for someone else. He was a very successful and attractive
man, but it was fearful to imagine his inner state. I was reminded of
Dante's image of damned souls driven by lust in the Second Circle of
Hell:

> Here, there, up, down, they whirl and, whirling strain,
> with never a hope of hope to comfort them,
> not of release, but even less of pain.
> —(John Ciardi translation, Canto V)

Being blown around by a dry hot wind is a fitting image for the
victim of sexual addiction and what has been called the "Playboy"
mentality of sex. The pursuit promises fulfillment, but the promise
is a lie. All is wind, all is vanity.

The true way to sexual fulfillment involves "ripening" in the
three levels of love we spoke of earlier, so that we see a sexual

partner as truly other, so that we can move from driven compulsion to mutual gift. As that happens, we are more able to risk our true selves and move to what Martin Buber calls a "Thou to Thou" relationship, a sharing of intimacy.

This maturing also makes commitment possible. I often hear people question the value of commitment. Once I was sitting in a restaurant with my niece and a young friend of hers. My niece pointed down the table to her parents who were celebrating three decades of married life. "Why?" she asked. "What's the point of that—hanging in there through all the crap for thirty years?"

An analogy came to me. I raised my wine glass and said something like this: "If you want a vintage wine, you have to begin with good grapes. But then you trample on them, put them together in a cask—a dark, still place—for a long time. In that confinement a lot of change takes place called fermentation and aging. Grapes are good, but if you want wine, you have to go through all that to get it. A committed relationship and the maturity that allows intimacy take time and caring attention. And 'hanging in.' Lust never gets beyond gobbling grapes."

Gluttony—Gluttony today may be recognized by the terms "eating disorders" and "alcoholism." The lie—the good that is promised—is much the same as that of lust: pursuit of this practice will deaden psychic pain, and/or fill the soul's desperate hunger and emptiness. I find myself sometimes using food and drink as a reward. In moderation, I don't think there is anything wrong with this. It may be, as we've said, practicing for the heavenly banquet. Food and drink are goods. Father Robert Capon, in his book *The Supper of the Lamb*, makes a fine point about the difference between fasting and dieting. The dieter tends to think all food is evil; the more calorific (which often means the more delectable), the more evil. Those who fast, abstain temporarily from food *so that* they may feast.

The thing to remember is that "food for thought," food for the spirit, is a different order of nourishment than food for the body. Perhaps the greatest help available today to get straight about how to be free of the immoderate and sinful use of food and drink is the Twelve-Step programs. They help people face their existential loneliness and be authentic. The truth is that nothing we ingest can fill the soul's hunger. Maybe that's what Jesus meant when he said, "I am the living water; I am the vine; I am the true bread."

Sloth—Sloth sounds like an old-fashioned sin, though in fact we may find it to be another besetting sin of our own times. In the Middle Ages it was called *acedia,* spiritual torpor. It is a peculiar quality of the sin of sloth, that persons or societies beset by it are both lethargic *and* restless. On the one hand they cannot find the energy to do anything worthwhile; on the other, they cannot truly be still and focused. They wander around aimlessly. In modern terms this sounds very much like what we might call a "work disorder." Often "workaholics" who run themselves ragged all week striving after impossible achievements become evening and weekend couch-potatoes. Whatever a person's work is, it is possible both to feel desperately bored and also over-burdened. There is not enough work to do; there is too much work to do. Both components of this attitude point to the lie that work will give meaning to our lives. It won't. It is our lives that give meaning to our work.

Sloth, which often resembles laziness, may not be so far from burnout—it may be the flip side of the coin. Burnout means there are no resources left, that a kind of functional bankruptcy is declared. The expectations that achievement will confer self-worth and that collapsing into stupor will bring heart's ease are both aspects of the same lie. The ancients fantasized a drug called "Nepenthe," which brought oblivion from all life's hardships and sorrows. Today, perhaps as "uppers" promote heightened activity, "downers" serve the same craving as Nepenthe did once for oblivion or lowering of consciousness.

But the cost of drug-induced escape or the "shut-down" of sloth is too high: it is the living of our real life. Neither burnout nor stupor is peace. The hard way to true peace is a balanced discipline and a commitment to responsible awareness.

Anger—We have already talked a good bit about anger. Again I wish we used another word for the sin because anger is a normal human feeling. It may be a divine "feeling" as well—in scripture we hear a good deal about "the wrath of God." Anger is a signal that one's territory is being invaded. It may be our physical, psychological or spiritual territory. An often-cited example of anger which is consonant with love is Jesus' overturning the tables of the money-changers in the Temple. His, and the Father's, territory was being invaded. As we grow in life experience and love, we are more able to choose when and how to express our anger effectively. If we

The Seven Deadly Sins
The behavior, the false promise and the truth about how to get what we need.

Name	Behavior	The False Promise	The Truth
1. Pride	*Narcissism *Ego Inflation	*Self-Esteem *Perfection	*Self-Knowledge *Humility
2. Avarice	*Accumulation *Exploitation	*Security *Ease	*Trust *Gift
3. Envy	*Wanting what one cannot have *Judgmentalism	*Self-Pity *Justification	*Self-Acceptance *Respect of self and others
4. Lust	*Sexual Addiction *Fragmentation of sexuality	*Fill soul's hunger to be loved	*Commitment *Intimacy
5. Gluttony	*Addictions *Eating Disorders *Alcoholism	*Affirmation *Reward *Fill the soul's hunger	*Acknowledge bodily sustenance is not spiritual sustenance.
6. Sloth	*Irresponsibility *Moral Bankruptcy *Drop-out, burnout	*Nepenthe or stupor masking as peace.	*Healthy discipline *Responsibility *Order
7. Anger	*Violence *Passive-aggression	*Power, Control *Certainty	*Surrender *Emptiness

express anger, for instance, whenever someone takes the cookie we had our eyes on, people will not pay attention to our signal when a major violation occurs. It is a sort of "Wolf! Wolf!" situation.

For the manifestation of anger that is sin, I would prefer to use "hostility." Hostility takes over when anger shifts into the desire to put down or harm the other. The extreme manifestations of this choice against the good are aggression and violence. One false promise underlying the temptation is that acts of hostility will confer control, power, and the certainty of "might is right." But might is not necessarily right. Even if it were, it is not enough to be right. It is more important to be loving than to be right. Hostility often stockpiles rectitude and facts in its arsenal, but true power is the power of love which, contrary to putting down and destroying, builds up and creates.

Doug: When we read things in the Bible like Jesus saying that even if you have lust in your heart for a woman other than your wife, you have committed adultery, aren't we to believe that even our thoughts constitute sin? And if that is true, how does it square with our premise of accepting the complete, authentic human?

ES: To understand the implications behind this question, it's necessary to say a bit more about what sin is and what it isn't. A word, then, about what sin is *not*.

First of all, sin is not what we have called above "negative programming." If I do not know that something is a sin, then for me it is not a sin. Here is a very mild example. When I was in graduate school, my roommate came home one evening and, flinging off her coat, cried, "What a terrible day!" In response I said, "You've had a terrible day? Wait till you hear about *my* day..." Before I finished getting the words out, I saw the hurt expression on her face and realized that if I continued I would be choosing against the good— sinning. I was able to stop and ask her to tell me about *her* day.

The point here is that in my environment, growing up, I had had a good deal of "negative programming" in this area. It was the done thing to top one another's stories, to carry on about how my operation was more serious than yours, my vacation was more interesting, my day was worse. Up until that moment I wasn't aware that such selfish non-attention to another was sinful, but after that I knew it could be *for me*. Not that I never had *my* turn to be listened to and commiserated with—my turn would come. But that evening with my roommate was not my turn, it was her turn, and in the future I would be a lot more aware of when it might be my turn to listen first. And if I chose to override that awareness with my own selfish agenda, that might be sin.

Sin is also not mistakes. Sometimes I go into agonies over stupid mistakes I make. Mistakes are things like *honestly* thinking an appointment was for the same day next week (unlike the cover-ups I was fantasizing on the 79th Street cross-town bus!). I feel more ashamed about some mistakes I make than I do about my sins. Father Langton once had to say to me: "If God can forgive us our sins, God can surely forgive us our mistakes!"

Sin is also not temptation. Some of the classic writers in Western spirituality have noted gradations in what is and what is not sin, which people today may think nit-picky to the point of laughter, but which may throw a bit of light on the question you ask about our thoughts and specifically "lust in your heart."

First, thoughts that spring to one's mind are not sin, they are just thoughts. Second, and most importantly, when some thoughts become temptations, they are just temptations. Temptation is not sin. Every human being is tempted. Jesus, being completely human, was "tempted in every way that we are" (Hebrews 4:15). Jesus teaches us to pray that we will not be led into temptation, because we *can* choose the lesser good, the evil. Resisting temptation is no fun, and we are wise to pray to be spared that test.

So how does an un-sinful thought become sinful? The spiritual writers identify a next stage called "delectation" from Latin "*delectatio,*" to delight. What this means is that when a thought becomes a temptation, we welcome it and start enjoying it, tasting it as if it were a hard candy we were rolling around on our tongue. Delectation also is not yet sin. However, this stage is dangerous to fool around with. If we entertain such thoughts (or as someone is reported to have said: "I don't entertain them, they entertain me!"), then we are liable to enter the next stage which is called "consent," which *is* sin. This is the point at which I might say to myself: "As soon as I get a chance I will do it." Just as it is not always easy for us to distinguish how conscious a choice to sin is, so it is also not always easy to know the exact point at which delectation becomes consent. Only God knows for sure.

Now, having taken a look at the range of what goes on in our minds from unbidden thoughts all the way to actual consent to sin, let's take a look at what outright sin has to do with "accepting the complete, authentic human." Take the story of David in the Bible. David "was a man after God's own heart" (Acts 13:22). Why? David was an adulterer and a murderer among other sinful things; his actions reeked of greed, lust, envy and violence. And he, too, like the rest of us, was tempted to deny and avoid conscious knowledge of this. He was lucky enough, however, to be confronted by a prophet named Nathan (2 Sam. 12). The thing is, when David was faced with the ugly truth about himself, he accepted it, repented, and got straight with God. It was not David's good works or sinless life that made him "a man after God's own heart." It was his courageous honesty in acknowledging his own sin and repenting of it.

Doug: In thinking about the conversations you have had with folks over the years, are people too self-judgmental? Do people make mountains out of molehills? If so, why is this a problem?

ES: Yes, I think many people I have talked with are, in general, too self-judgmental. And this is a problem for a number of reasons. The sources of self-judging go back to what we were discussing in the chapter on the Myth of Perfection. People measure themselves against ideals they have learned from parents, peers and the general culture, and inevitably find themselves wanting. They judge themselves against these unrealistic norms.

The problem manifests itself in various guises. My own self-judgment, for example, took the form of extreme anxiety. What did I have to do to be O.K.? From early childhood I had classical symptoms of anxiety neurosis and panic attacks. I felt myself responsible for my failings. I have known others for whom the judgment of their own shortcomings was a root cause of depression. And then there are the people who try to ease the pain of their self-judgment by blaming other people and external causes for their unhappiness. Some of us succumb to the temptation of putting down others in order to make ourselves look better and feel better. All of these manifestations of self-judgment are dangerous. They can be externalized in a range of behaviors from small, daily acts of abuse and unkindness, to extreme rage and, yes, may even lead to murder and holocaust. If we can only begin to accept ourselves, we can move to a healthy self-compassion, and only then to being truly understanding of and compassionate to others.

Doug: Are there ways we can move towards self-forgiveness?

ES: Some people may be born and grow up accepting themselves, but for most of us, self-acceptance isn't easy. Usually before self-acceptance, there has to be self-forgiveness. The more decades of self-judgment people inflict on themselves, the harder self-forgiveness can become.

I'd like to talk a little about forgiveness in general before I respond directly to your question about ways we can move towards forgiving ourselves. One of the ways of thinking about forgiveness, especially in some Christian circles, is that we should forgive immediately, "sight unseen." Not being able to do this has itself been for many a major cause of self-condemnation.

I was once in a therapy group and during one session we were all on the subject of hurts we felt we had received from our parents. The subject of forgiving arose. There was a lawyer in the group who at that point reminded us of the practice of the Governor's Pardon. She said that in this state the Governor could grant a pardon to a sentenced criminal. But before that happened, there had to be a prescribed series of events. First, there had to be a collection of evidence, then there had to be a trial, then a verdict, *and the verdict had to be 'guilty,'* and then a sentence. Then, and only then, could the pardon be granted. This lawyer had been brought up a Christian, and she said that the Christians she knew had a terrible time getting the sequence straight. They tried to collect evidence, have a trial and grant the pardon all at the same time, or in reverse order: they tried to grant pardon before the "guilty" verdict was pronounced!

Granted that the practice of law does not take into account the free grace of the Spirit—yet the analogy may be useful. In order to forgive, there must be clarity on what there is to forgive. It helps if the offending party asks for forgiveness, but if that is not in the cards, forgiveness is still possible if the evidence has been clearly ascertained, the trial well conducted and the verdict decisive.

Now, about ways we can move to self-forgiveness. Like forgiving our parents or anybody else, self-forgiveness cannot be an instantaneous thing. It may be a lengthy and painful process. This process was made clear to me when I was visiting with a dear long-time friend who was dying of AIDS. He was struggling to come to terms with a lifetime of rage, self-judgment and self-destructive behavior. It was one of the greatest privileges of my life to be with him in his passage to self-forgiveness. Working together, we found there are stages to go through in order to arrive at self-forgiveness and divine reconciliation. In a fanciful balance to the "Seven Deadly Sins," we called these "The Seven Lively Steps to Forgiveness."

First, there must be some realization that we are lovable and loved. For my friend, and many who have had painful and confusing childhood experiences of love, it is very difficult to trust the constant, nourishing love of God or of any human being. The first step may be to open ourselves to, and if we can, pray for, the ability to know ourselves capable of receiving unconditional love, that is, love "no matter what we have done."

Even if we have made only a bare beginning at this, we may go on to the second step, which is then to face up to the evil we recognize in ourselves—that which *is* unlovable, unacceptable. This will include both those things which stem from our "negative programming" *and* our willful choices against the good as we have known it. It will take all the discerning we have learned to sort this out as best we can.

The third step is to make the choice to accept (not condone, but acknowledge) the evil as part of our whole perception of ourselves, rather than to deny or try to exterminate it.

Then, as a fourth step, to realize that the milieu of this work is called truth. That "where" we go to enter this clearest dimension of our understanding is our own deepest reality.

The fifth step is to recognize that God is Truth, and that therefore God meets us precisely in this milieu of our own truth—not where we think we should be, or would like to be, or feel others need us to be, etc., but where we *are*. God is Truth, that which is. When Moses, standing before the burning bush, demanded to know who to say sent him, God said, "Tell them 'I Am' sent you." We are made in God's image—we are that which we are. My secret name also is not "I should be," but "I Am."

The sixth step is to realize, therefore, that the acceptance of one's own evil must become a part of one's truth, of one's relationship with God. A scriptural example of this is the story of David which we looked at earlier in this chapter.

The seventh step is perhaps especially difficult for those of us who have lived long decades with self-blame, guilt and shame. As we have bravely faced the evil in ourselves, we must now, with equal integrity acknowledge the good—the gifts and graces we have been given—by our nature, our nurture and by God. And not least, those good gifts and aspects of ourselves for which we can take at least part credit, because of our choosing what good we were able. (Even the rapist-murderer of whom I have spoken may have at other times been able to resist temptation.) As we try to empty ourselves of a focus on the evil in ourselves to concentrate on what real good we can find, we help prepare the soil for the seeds of self-compassion and reconciliation. After some practice this should feel like a shift from guilt to gratitude. The process may include some tears, first of compunction and repentance, then of relief and even joy.

As I said, this may be a lengthy and painful process; we make a start by believing that it's possible—this procedure of coming to a stance of compassion and joy towards ourselves, God, and others. Analytic psychotherapy is a great help for many people in identifying false guilt and negative programming, and in facilitating the movement to greater self-knowledge and acceptance. Carl Rogers said: "Therapy is the process of assimilating denied experience." Also, as in the case of King David, prophetic—that is, God-inspired—spiritual guidance can often facilitate much of the same work.

A final question may arise about all the negative matter we unearth in the process of awareness—and especially our sins. What do we do with it? The classical answer is "Give it to God." This may seem a strange, if not disturbing answer. Here's a story to illustrate it. It's about St. Jerome. From all accounts St. Jerome was not an easy person to get along with—an irascible, opinionated, though intensely dedicated man. One Advent, or pre-Christmas season, he decided to go into the wilderness for a retreat. As he said his prayers, it came to him to make some spiritual "birthday gift" to the Christ Child. The saint prayed and thought and then addressed God: "I will dedicate to you the fruit of my scholarship—my translation of the scriptures into the common tongue, the Vulgate." But there seemed to be a strange silence in the heavenly places as if in fact, his gift had not been accepted. So he thought and prayed a while longer. Then he said to God: "I understand, you don't want my great scholarship—you are more interested in my discipline and austerity of life. I dedicate that to you!" But again the heavenly silence. Back to his prayers. Then, "Aha!" he exclaimed. "You don't want my austerities, you want my devotions—the fervent love of my heart!" Incredibly, the heavens were still silent. Jerome was feeling peeved and at the point of giving up the whole idea. "Then what?" he cried to God in total frustration. "What can I give to you?"

And do you know what? Clear as clear in his mind the answer came: "Give me your sins, my son. Those are the only things I have not first given you." Why would God want our sins? I think, because sin and suffering are the raw material of glory. God can take all of reality and fashion it into glory—even to the horror and humiliation of the crucifixion.

As the seed must be broken open in order to sprout, as every baby is born out of pain, so creation groans and travails (Rom. 8:22) to bring the world into the kingdom. The sins as well as the creativity of humanity are part of the stuff of reality that is in the process of transfiguration. Because we are made in the image of God, we are called in love to be co-creators in this metamorphosis. We can choose to participate, each one according to the grace we have been given. We are called to emptying and integration, individually and in community. We are called into "maturity, to the measure of the full stature of Christ" (Eph. 4:13). And the way to do this is the process of forgiveness and reconciliation. The point of forgiveness, its heart and its end, is new life.

Section Two

Filling the Vessel:

Inviting the Spirit of Peace

— 8 —
Transition

Sometimes I feel that my life is a series of trapeze swings.
I'm either hanging on to a trapeze bar swinging along or
for a few moments in my life, I'm hurtling across space in
between trapeze bars. But once in a while, as I'm merrily
(or not-so-merrily) swinging along, I look out ahead of me
into the distance and what do I see? I see another trapeze
bar swinging toward me. It's empty, and I know that this
"new trapeze bar" has my name on it. Each time it
happens to me, I know that I must totally release my
grasp on my old bar and for some moment in time I must
hurtle across space before I can grab onto the new bar. It
is called "transition."
> —Danaan Parry

We have spent much of the book up until now describing some of
the cultural myths which create barriers to moving towards spiritual
freedom and wholeness. The purpose of describing the myths in such
detail is to become more aware of the forces which influence us in our
daily lives. But it is not enough just to become aware of these forces.
At any given moment, we have the option of emptying ourselves of
cultural myths and going for something which more closely resembles
our deepest desires and passions. One does not make such a change
all at once; it requires a transition.

In this chapter, we will discuss the challenges associated with
beginning the transition from being filled with cultural myths and the
agendas of others to moving towards embracing that which is unique
to each one of us. We will suggest that to settle for anything less than
embracing our deepest desires in communion with others is to ignore
the truth or what some call the will of God.

The Story of My Transition

Thus far, I have written about the many cultural beliefs which I
have internalized and continue to hang on to. To summarize the

transition I have been through; it has been moving from doing what others want me to do to following my own path. This transition began with the discovery at age 28 that I had been adopted at birth. This realization was *the* catalytic event which gave me permission to question the way I was living my life. It was initially an enormous shock to my system; in the end, it helped me to remove my social masks, question my system of beliefs and begin to discover my own deepest desires which had been hidden for so long.

I later learned that this is a typical part of the process of transition: we go along accepting many of the beliefs others impose upon us, doing what we are told, until a shocking event intervenes and dismantles our defense system. C. S. Lewis referred to this as nothing less than a wake-up call from God: "Pain is God's megaphone to rouse a deaf world." I was not doing what I was called to do but rather what everyone else was calling me to do. And because different people had different agendas for me, I spent a lot of time going in different directions.

Ram Dass has said that we humans are "slide projectors in search of screens." I would amend that to suggest that while some of us are slide projectors, more of us are the screen. I spent the first twenty-eight years of my life being the screen upon which other people's movies were played. The task of transition for me has been to become more "inner-directed" than "outer-directed," to start to write my own movie scripts rather than being a reflection of others. ES said earlier in the book that humans often ask God what to do and God responds by saying "Here is a blank canvas, paint me a picture." The artist is doing the work of God by projecting images from the deepest part of his or her psyche onto canvas. Even those of us who can't paint are called to do the same thing with our lives, but the noise of cultural beliefs and others' opinions block such authentic creativity. Transition is about unblocking the pathways to those deepest parts of who we are.

ES said that a spiritual director of hers once told her, "The will of God is identical with your own deepest desire." ES has previously written about this idea: "At the time, it seemed to mc the most enigmatic of statements. Until I realized that the 'catch' was in the word 'deepest.' Aha! Not always so easy to tune in to my own deepest desires; the ones on the surface are producing so much static." I would add that the desires of others also contribute to what amounts to a cacophony of noise which muffles even the strongest of one's own deep desires.

Many theologians and philosophers have described the transition as going from being "broken" to becoming whole or from having "fallen" to being redeemed. For me, the problem is being too full. I am full of what other people think and the transition is about moving from a state of fullness to emptiness; emptying out the images and beliefs of others to discover my own deepest desires.

I cannot grab the new trapeze bar which I see swinging towards me until I let go of the one I am holding. And this means taking a risk. The risk is that I will fall into the abyss of the unknown. Even though the known is painful and the social masks and manipulative behavior I have grown so accustomed to are no longer working, at least I know what to expect. It is predictable unpleasantness. But letting go? That creates the potential for the ultimate unpleasantness: I would be totally out of control! My fate would be up to some unknown force besides my own will! I would be a rudderless ship, left vulnerable to the fast current, storming waters and jagged rocks.

One recalls the famous scene in *The Empire Strikes Back* when Luke Skywalker has been cornered by the evil Darth Vader, whom he has learned is his father. In a dramatic scene, Vader has him edged up against the abyss of space and is giving him the choice to join the forces of evil or die. Our hero decides to jump off into the abyss rather than join the evil Vader's forces. As he is plummeting to near-certain death, Skywalker hears the voice of Yoda, his spiritual teacher: "Let the Force be with you." Miraculously, he is sucked into a tunnel just before perishing and is saved.

The symbolism is clear. Better to die following one's own deepest yearnings than to live as prisoner of another's. The "force" that will be with us and protect us is clearly a code word for "spirit." Let the spirit be with you. But why should anyone take such a risk? What if the choice isn't as clear as it was for Luke Skywalker? He faced selling out to the forces of darkness (which were clearly evil) versus leaping head-long into the unknown.

My choices aren't always that obvious. I have worked very hard to get to this point in my life. And sure, the persona I have created is really just an amalgamation of other people's beliefs, but it's taken my whole lifetime to build it, I say to myself. Am I going to throw it all away just because it's a little unpleasant? My life isn't a sell-out to the forces of darkness...is it? And another thing. I don't see anyone else in my world looking for the narrow road towards spiritual enlightenment. Everyone else seems to be content with working 50-60 hours a week, fighting rush-hour traffic and coming home to a hurried dinner, hassles with the kids, three hours of prime-time television and then going to bed. Are these people all following their deepest desire? Is the force with them? Or are they so filled with the rules and beliefs of others that their own yearnings have long since been drowned out?

The reason for taking the risk of letting go of the old trapeze bar, not knowing if we will fall into the abyss, is because it is the path to freedom and peace. Writers throughout the ages have described the journey in a variety of ways, but the pattern is roughly the same. We are born as divine creations of God, each given a unique identity and set of gifts. Then we move into the world and begin to fill ourselves up with the beliefs and "things" of the existential world and our unique gifts fade into the distance. At some point, we begin to feel hollow and restless and ask: Is this all there is? Often around mid-life a catalyzing event (depression, loss of job, divorce, health crisis, death of a loved one) cracks open the shell of armor we have built around ourselves and for the first time we begin to question our life. This becomes the most important moment in a person's life. The MacArthur Foundation's Center on the Study of Mid-Life calls these moments "psychological turning points."

When we reach this critical turning point, we can chose to convert (which literally means "to turn around") to a new way of living or we can try to just shake it off and decide that nothing has really changed (but thank God the crisis is over) and go back to living the way we had been living before. The person who chooses to change or make the transition from the old way of living to a new way is like the person who lets go of the old trapeze bar.

Finding a Guide for the Transition

In my case, the catalyzing event was the discovery of being adopted. I began evaluating my life by doing a lot of reading but also by finding a guide, someone who knew the territory and could help me along the way. Luckily for me, that person was ES. Through the simple process of meeting once every month or so and just talking over what was going on for me as I began to question everything about my "old" life, I was able to survive the process. It was not easy, not without pain, not without ridicule from family as I got divorced and from colleagues as I moved away from politics and into a church congregation. The transition is anything but easy, but having a guide was, for me, crucial.

I remember so many visits I had with ES where I innocently asked her about things going on and what she thought about them. And out of emptiness and grace, she was able to offer what seemed each time like the ideal insight. Many of those insights have already been discussed in this book and, taken out of context, some of them might seem rather ordinary. When it comes to the journey and spiritual direction, *context is everything*. The person must be ready to hear and it is the task of the director to discern what a person can and cannot hear at any given moment.

ES has a tremendous gift for this kind of work. I remember driving to dinner with her one night and she was commenting on my vanity license plate which reads PRETNDR. She said, "If I ever get a vanity license plate, it is going to say RESPNDR." This is because she is so clearly called to respond to the questions of others. One conversation I had with her stands out in particular. I had been struggling with the issue of making the transition from being a rugged individualist and a competitive, self-serving political type to becoming a reflective person of faith. I mentioned to ES that one of the hardest things about my transition and the events that went with it was that all of the people I knew thought I was crazy. I got comments like, "I don't understand what you are doing. You seemed to have it all together before."

ES thought for a moment and then said, "Do you know the story of the Ugly Duckling? Your assignment is to go read the story of the Ugly Duckling. But for now I will tell you my version of it." She went on to tell the ugly duckling story which we have already discussed in Chapter One. Suffice it to say that there is no way to describe how powerful that story was to me in the context of my life at that moment. I had gone for twenty-eight years thinking that, while I came from a successful family and had a good career going, there was always a gnawing sense that I was not like the people around me. I always wanted to talk about the deeper meaning of events and most everyone around me seemed content to skim along the surface. My being a contemplative, with the gifts of insight and reflection, was considered to be of little value and I was often ridiculed as being "too serious" or "moody." Nevertheless, I was able to conform to my environment and pretend to be a duck, so to speak (hence the license plate PRETNDR).

When my parents told me that I was adopted at birth, there was an almost instant realization: Of course! I searched for my birth parents, found them and also found two half-brothers and a half-sister who not only looked like me but had similar interests. I had found my family of swans. ES had given me a metaphor for my life and allowed me to realize that I would be okay.

As you have seen throughout this book, ES has many, many arrows in her quiver, seemingly a story for every occasion, but the mark of a truly gifted spiritual director is to pull out the one story that is just right at the moment. ES has said many times to me in the context of my own work with my Episcopal youth group, "Do not try to tell people what they cannot hear." She seemed to know what I could and could not hear.

There were many times when I thought about turning back and going on with my normal life: getting back into government service, going for a lot of fame and recognition, even running for political office to feed the ego, and giving up on all this "meaning crap" as some of my old friends called it. I realize in retrospect that what has kept me from doing that has been that I had a support system of a few very gifted people who themselves were on the path and who made themselves available to me at critical times to say, "It's okay, you are not the only one who views the world this way." Finding other swans has been the critical difference, like finding one's tribe.

It is critically important for anyone seeking to make this kind of transition to find a guide or a small group of people with whom to make the journey. Look for a few fellow swans to keep you headed where you need to go. I once did an exercise conceived by Barbara Sher in which one is supposed to ask a question of one's family, then imagine their response. The next step is to identify one's mentor or mentors and pose the same question of them and imagine the response. It was an exercise in distancing oneself from the programming one has received from their family system.

My question was "What is God's will for me?" I imagined my family's response to this to be "Get your head out of the clouds and get to work." I then imagined the response of two of my mentors: ES and Scott Peck; ES: "There is no more important question." Peck: "There is no more important question."

It is a tremendously freeing idea to chose one's own mentors. One of our colleagues on the FCE board of directors, Eve Berry, once described how she has her own personal board of directors: 12 people who have agreed to serve as her advisors, just like a board directs the affairs of an organization. They don't necessarily meet as a group but rather are available as consultants or confidants. In my case, I have not formally asked people to serve in this function officially, but I do have a list of folks whom I consider to be on my personal board of directors. It is an interesting mix of ducks, swans, wise people and friends. Who would you choose for such an assignment?

Seeking Guidance from the Wisdom Literature

It has also helped me in searching for my own deepest desires (God's will as opposed to the will of others) to have studied the wisdom literature. When one looks at the literature, it is filled with descriptions which help one continue.

One of my favorite images was provided by Joseph Campbell in his interviews with Michael Thoms of New Dimensions radio. He is quoting Frederick Neitzche on the stages of the human spirit:

> The first stage is the camel: The camel gets down on his knees and says, "Put a load on me." This is the condition of youth and learning. When the camel is well-loaded, he gets to his feet and runs out into the desert. This is the place where he is going to be alone to find himself and he is transformed into a lion. And the function of the lion is to kill a dragon and that dragon's name is "Thou Shalt." On every scale of the dragon, there are the words "Thou Shalt," which represent the rules and obligations of society. But the lion is strong and he kills the dragon and is thus transformed into a child. The child is then like "a wheel rolling out of its own center." The way to get in touch with that child rolling out of its own center is to respect the rules of society but to nevertheless go your own way.

This description of the four stages of the spirit rang true for me in a number of respects. The best way to talk about it is to treat each stage separately.

The Camel - *The camel gets down on his knees and says, "Put a load on me." This is the condition of youth and learning.*

I spent the first several decades of my life pretty much saying to everyone I knew, "Put a load on me." I will do whatever anyone else wants in order to gain their approval and the approval of society. It didn't matter what it was, I would unconditionally carry water for anyone who wanted me to. Many of us learn through socialization that the way you get along in life is to go along. This is one of the reasons we have had a section in each chapter up until now on the three main sources of such influence: family systems, peer groups and culture.

If I knew then what I know now, I would have reacted quite differently to all the advice and proscriptive input from others. I would have spent less time blindly adopting what others thought and did and spent more time listening to my own sense of what was right for me. This is not to say I would have chosen to become a narcissist, but rather one who honored both what others said and what the still small voice within was saying. It is only now at mid-life that I am listening for my own deepest yearnings and have to work hard to hear them over the din of the cultural noise I have internalized. The paradox is that the still small voice now is most often saying "serve others." More on that later.

The Desert - *When the camel is well-loaded, he gets to his feet and runs out into the desert. This is the place where he is going to be alone to find himself...*

The stage of the spirit where the camel runs out into the desert is the closest analogy to the beginning of the transition we have been describing. One must wander in utter loneliness and despair for a period of time before seeing the path. You begin by knowing that the load you are carrying, the path you are on, is somehow the wrong one, but you do not yet see the new path. It is the time when you have decided to let go of the old trapeze bar but the new one has not yet appeared.

St. John of the Cross refers to this as the Dark Night of the Senses. It is a time when one is truly lost. I personally found this to be the most lonely place I had ever been and, to make matters worse, it preceded the time when I had found a spiritual director who could help me along the way.

Jesus wandered for forty days and forty nights in the desert being tempted by the devil before discerning his authentic path. The way out of it, as Jesus' experience teaches us, is faith. He relied upon his faith in God to get him through the darkness of having not yet seen the new path. It is a time when one must accept true emptiness: I know not where the path leads, but I trust that God will show me the way. Or as Yoda would say, "Follow the Force."

The Lion -...*and he is transformed into a lion. And the function of the lion is to kill a dragon and that dragon's name is "Thou Shalt." On every scale of the dragon, there are the words "Thou Shalt," which represent the rules and obligations of society.*

This stage is about beginning to question the rules and obligations of society, the myths we have been discussing thus far. I got to the point where the load I was carrying, the "thou shalts," were massive and were simply not working for me. The image Nietzche uses here of the camel transforming into a lion is profound because it takes literally the strength of a lion to be able to stand up to and ultimately slay the dragon "Thou Shalt." I found in my own experience that once I had passed through the dark night of the senses, my desert experience, my power increased as if to become a lion. There was something about lurking in the abyss of the desert which eliminated fear. It was as if I had nothing left to lose, complete and utter emptiness, which made room for a kind of filling up of spiritual power.

I have always thought of the dragon here as a metaphor for those who have not chosen the path of authenticity or emptiness. The myths or cultural lies and the people who hold them become monsters which only the brave lion can slay.

In my case, I realized early on that I could not slay the dragon alone. I needed people who knew the territory, or you might say knew the "arena," in which the slaying would have to take place. ES told me many times that there would be people who would laugh at me behind my back, who would think I was nuts for doing what I was doing. In fact, I remember having a conversation with her about how Jesus was treated. He was certainly laughed at by the establishment, shunned by the Pharisees, misunderstood by his own family and ultimately murdered for following the narrow path of truth.

The Child - *But the lion is strong and he kills the dragon and is thus transformed into a child. The child is then like "a wheel rolling out of its own center."*

In order to become a child who is like a wheel rolling out of its own center, we must empty ourselves of the "thou shalts" which society imposes upon us. This is not to say that I will become a lawless rogue, disobeying all rules and raping and pillaging the land. There are rules and laws which are in place for the protection of the species, and our very survival depends upon compliance with them.

But there are many more rules and obligations, values and beliefs which we have internalized that are someone else's arbitrary view of reality (a slide show for which we have provided the screen). They must be examined. The image of the child here is a familiar one. Jesus evoked the image to describe the kingdom: "In order to enter the kingdom of heaven, one must become like a child." What is meant here is that one must go back to the time when we were empty of all the things that caused us to forget our divine origins. As Wordsworth says in his "Intimations of Immortality":

> Our birth is but a sleep and a forgetting:
> The Soul that rises with us, our life's star,
> Hath had elsewhere its setting,
>   And cometh from afar.
> Not in entire forgetfulness,
>   And not in utter nakedness,
> But trailing clouds of glory do we come
>   From God, who is our home:
> Heaven lies about us in our infancy!

The goal of the transition is to return to that sense of original innocence when we were filled with the spirit of boundless potential and energy, born from our proximity to the Divine Creator. From the heavily-burdened camel, to wandering in the desert darkness, to becoming the lion who slays the dragon "Thou Shalt," back to the innocence of childhood...such is the struggle and the glory of being human.

The Voyage Towards Spiritual Freedom

We can curse the path and resist it or we can accept it and say, as ES believes, "If so, then what?" Once one sees that the journey is about loading up and then emptying out cultural myths and lies, and involves the full range of human emotions, how are we to cope? Recognizing that the path is filled with both joy and pain, good and bad, makes it much easier to cope with the inevitable bumps along the way: the disapproving family members, the scowling neighbors, the judgment-filled coworkers.

All of the things that happen are part of the process of moving towards spiritual freedom and are necessary. In my own case, I could cope with the pain of transition because I had been counseled to understand that it was an essential part of the voyage towards spiritual maturity. I had come to trust the path of the spirit, the deepest desires within me. I was becoming a wheel rolling out of my own center and all of a sudden neither the precise direction I was headed nor the challenges I encountered were as important as what was propelling me: my authentic self.

For as long as I have known her, ES has reminded me of Jesus' saying, "The truth will make you free." The truth is that God calls us to authenticity, to honor our own thoughts and emotions and beliefs, not be possessed by those of others. This is God's deepest wish for us. To this end, the freedom comes in having a single source of direction rather than a hundred conflicting ones. It comes from the absolute belief that I am put on this earth for a purpose that is different from all others, which means only I can truly know my own path. It comes from the knowledge that those deepest beliefs really *are* God's will for me. Finally, freedom comes from the evidence I have seen since being on the path that trust and faith from within will never steer you wrong. There have been bumps along the road, but I treat them as an inevitable part of moving towards wholeness.

As Donald Nicoll has said in his book *Holiness*, "We cannot fail once we realize that everything that happens to us is designed to teach us holiness." Once one makes the transition to the spiritual path and becomes like a wheel rolling out of its own center, everything that happens, good and bad, joyful and painful, beautiful and ugly, *all of it*, is exactly what is needed to become a complete human being.

I drew a diagram which describes the voyage towards spiritual freedom, one that integrates a number of the concepts we have been

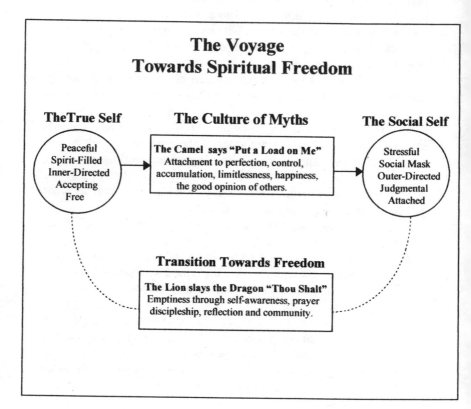

describing. This diagram represents the cycle of the typical human life: beginning with "The True Self" and then moving along the path towards the stage of Nietzche's "camel" where we begin to "load up" with many of the myths we have been discussing: perfection, control, accumulation, etc. The effect of such loading up is to create the "social self" which is burdened with not only the cultural lies we've mentioned but also the effects of having internalized them: stress, isolation, judgment.

The decision to go forward through the desert with the strength of a lion, systematically slaying the dragon "Thou Shalt," is a metaphor for emptying oneself of those beliefs which are getting in the way of authentically connecting with oneself, with others and with God. The process of self-emptying is an unavoidable stage for those wishing to move beyond the desert of the social self. It should be entered into with excitement and enthusiasm rather than with dread and fear. For the goal of such a journey is to reach the stage of the child or the True Self: a self free from addiction, open to new experience, connected to the source of creation, filled with the spirit of peace and accepting of oneself and others.

You may have noticed that the four stages of the spirit track fairly well with Spitzer's four levels of happiness which we discussed in Chapter Three. This is no accident. Philosophers, theologians and poets through the ages have used all kinds of different images, theories and stages to explain the human journey. And as we mentioned in the introduction, there are common threads that run through all of the various traditions. The journey towards spiritual freedom we have outlined here is not new, it is merely taking another run at an old question: What is the meaning of it all?

In order to begin to answer this for yourself, you might start by asking, "Where am I among the four stages of the spirit?" Am I still in that blissful stage of innocence where I feel free to be my true self or am I in the process of becoming the loaded-down camel, accepting the opinions and rules of others in order to go along. Or how about the desert? Am I fully loaded down and beginning to realize that such a load is no longer working and I feel like I am wandering through the desert in search of meaning?

Too many of us have not figured out how to make the turn, if you will, and begin the process of emptying the existential baggage we have accumulated over our lifetime. The reasons most of us never completely make the turn towards emptiness or the lion killing the dragon "Thou Shalt" are as varied as creation itself.

Our hope is that by gaining a clearer picture of the end, the payoff, which is peace and freedom, more of us will begin to take the risk. You may be saying, "So I go through all of this agonizing journey of loading down with the rules of society, wandering around in the desert, then turn and spend the rest of my life unloading all the beliefs and rules that have burdened me, only to end up exactly where I started? Is this some kind of cruel divine joke?

It is no joke, but it *is* the journey and far be it for us to speculate why it is this way. All we can do is learn as much as we can along the way and try to engage in life with a calmness at the center which never wavers. You will recall in the preface to Section One we defined the word "attachment" and talked about the Zen view of experiencing reality fully but then letting it go by. This may be a key to surviving the rougher water of the voyage:

> Life starts to look like watching the show. Happiness arises, you witness it; joy arises, you witness it; pain arises, you witness it; sorrow arises, you witness it. In all cases, you are the Witness, and not some passing surface wave of silly sound and fury. At the center of the cyclone, you are safe. A deep and inward peace begins to haunt you; you can no longer manufacture turmoil with quite the same conviction.
> —Ken Wilbur

Employing this kind of detached engagement can lead to a profound and divine transformation if we are willing to be patient and experience the pain, joy and ambiguity which arises along the way. It is what ES has called the second innocence, or the simplicity on the other side of complexity. And my bet is that while we may arrive in the same place, it will not look the same.

A Confession about Transition

I need to make a couple of disclosures about this period of transition as it relates to my own journey. The first is that I have had as much trouble as anyone at "making the turn" in order to move into Stages Three and Four. In my attempts to slay the dragon "Thou Shalt," I sometimes feel more like a house cat than a lion and I live in constant fear that the dragon will turn in violent opposition when I am not looking and fry me to a crisp with flaming tongue.

I continue to struggle with being attached to beliefs about power and control and perfection. I struggle every single day with spending too much money and still, even now, feel like a shiny new car might not give me eternal bliss, but it sure would be nice. I struggle with how other people view me. It is still very important that people see me as a competent, successful human being. I am frequently modeling behaviors for my son Nicholas which are going to make it difficult for him to follow the spiritual path. I am not a model of emptiness and my "vessel" is frequently more conflicted than peaceful.

I am, however, moving in the direction of emptiness, of being more at peace with myself. ES says the key is not how close to arriving one is, but the direction one is moving. Even if I am just making infinitesimally-small progress, molecule by molecule, in the direction of being less attached to the maelstrom of cultural lies I confront each day, that is progress. I find it hard to describe, but there are days when I really feel like I can be the great Witness and just engage in life, observe deeply and then walk away. Other times, I feel the stress of attachment looming over my shoulder and I fear I will go right back to loading up with more cultural lies. I hold on to the belief, however, that once one makes the intentional decision to walk the narrow road towards spiritual truth, it is possible to get sidetracked, but only temporarily. I for one can never go back to the stress-ridden, anxiety-driven life I was leading for so long. Will I give up temporal power and wealth and fame? Yes. Is it worth it to gain a little peace and to feel freer today than I did yesterday? Absolutely.

Dialogue on Transition

Doug: Is it necessary to go through the "put a load on me" stage of the camel, or can we somehow skip that stage and live a detached life without carrying the burdens of cultural lies?

ES: Aristotle said, "Man is by nature a political animal" (*Politics*). "Political," as used here, refers back to its Greek root in *polis*, a city, indicating that human beings naturally live in community. Saint Paul used the analogy of being individual members of one body. We are social and interactive creatures by nature; no one can exist in a totally detached way. The only way that human beings learn how to be human beings is from each other. So, yes, we do have to go through the "put a load on me" stage.

There are haunting stories of "feral children"—human infants who have been reared by animals or somehow survived *without* human nurture. Even if they are eventually found, it seems they can never be fully socialized, or become fully human. We have quoted Ram Dass before—we are all taught to be "somebodies." We "load on" not only genetic tendencies, but also some form of cultural, tribal and family myth.

One thing that is always passed down is the concept of "*ought.*" C. S. Lewis wrote: "These, then, are the two points I wanted to make. First, that human beings, all over the earth, have this curious idea that they ought to behave in a certain way, and cannot really get rid of it. Secondly, that they do not in fact behave in that way" (*Mere Christianity*).

This human capacity for choosing right and wrong, and knowing we often choose "wrong," is passed down generation after generation and may be thought of as "original sin." Along with the sense of sin, we inherit guilt. And we "take on the load" of ways to repress or minimize our wrong choices and consequent guilt.

Cultural lies offer ways to ignore our fallibility and to avoid making hard choices for the good. They are lies partly because they claim that perfection, control, limitlessness, goodness, etc. are, or should be, easily attainable, and that we can escape from guilt and powerlessness. Our myths advertise a wide gate and an easy road. But, as we have said before, the reality of the spiritual journey is not easy—"the gate is narrow and the road is hard that leads to life" (Matt. 7: 13-14).

Some people do find and choose the road to life. The good news is that, along with the lies that are loaded on us, the call to break out of them is also passed down. If there is original sin, there is, as Matthew Fox has written in a book of the same name, original blessing. There is a universal invitation to liberation and to holiness. From the fairy tales of The Ugly Duckling and The Emperor's New Clothes, to *Hamlet* and *King Lear,* literature is full of tales of the struggle to break out of the bondage of cultural expectations and find freedom in the truth no matter what the cost. Often, to be heard, the truth-speaker must be a child, a "madman" or, as in the case of *Lear,* a Fool.

Illustrations abound in our own time. One of my favorites is the film *On the Waterfront*. Marlon Brando leads the way for the dock workers to go back to the job—a victory that is paid for by his being horribly beaten—a fine example of a person defying the prevailing power structure and paying the cost. He does this in the cause of freedom for himself and for others. Most of the stories of Chaim Potok portray the human spirit breaking out of the confines of cultural baggage to find its true individuality. In history we celebrate the courage of women and men such as Saint Joan, Edith Stein, Sojourner Truth, Dietrich Bonhoeffer, Martin Luther King, Jr. and Desmond Tutu to name only a few of the saints, canonized and uncanonized, who have risked saying and living their truth.

Doug: What would you say is the most challenging thing about the transition?

ES: Three "challenging things" come to mind about the transition through emptiness to truth: fear of the unknown, fear of vulnerability and fear of commitment.

First, a word about the challenge of the unknown. In classical spiritual literature there is a stage, as we have noted, called "The Dark Night of the Senses." It is a stage where things of the senses— food, drink, gold, toys of all sorts—no longer satisfy the way they once did. The question arises: "Is this all there is?" Another way of viewing it is that Spitzer's lowest two stages, physical pleasure and ego satisfaction, no longer seem enough for happiness. But the soul has not yet become proficient in living according to spiritual values. Transition is the stage of the little tadpole who has grown the lungs of a frog and cannot return to live under water, but who is still struggling to breathe with lungs instead of gills. Being in between, being in the dark, is scary and disorienting. ("Disorienting" is the exact word—literally it means not knowing which way is East.)

Another analogy, as you have noted, is that transition is like the moment between trapezes. In this state it is easy to be afraid that one will let go of a possible way of being and not "catch onto" anything better, that one will fall and lose one's sense of self. If I am not a duck, what am I? Am I nothing? (Remember the image in Chapter Four of the schizophrenic young man who felt lost among worlds.) Am I crazy? Living in the unknown is new and fearful. As is so often the case, Shakespeare puts his finger on the temptation to give up the struggle: "...makes us rather bear those ills we have/Than fly to others that we know not of."

One of the scariest "ills" for me was the dread of what I would find out about myself if I plumbed those unknown depths for the real truth of my humanity. Actually it *was* pretty awful, but I not only survived, I exorcised the dread. I now know the worst—and if there is even worse to follow, I trust I can survive!

The second challenging thing follows closely: the fear of vulnerability or, literally, of being wound-able. People who are in the transition to truth or who have made the transition, are often identified as prime targets for popular censure. The wounds can range from ridicule—accusations of being weird—to actual damage, such as being fired from one's job or imprisoned for one's beliefs. In its most extreme form, breaking out of the cultural lies can be fatal—witness Socrates' being compelled to drink hemlock, or Jesus' crucifixion, or Martin Luther King's assassination. Jesus spoke to this: "Therefore I send you prophets, sages, and scribes, some of whom you will kill and crucify, and some you will flog in your synagogues and pursue from town to town..." (Matt. 23:34).

A curious dynamic asserts itself here. There is something in human nature that tends to exalt spiritual heroes before it brings them low. "The bigger they are, the harder they fall" mentality delights in setting up the truth-sayers before cutting them down. There are often Palm Sunday hosannas before Good Friday savagery.

Of course innumerable folk make the transition to spiritual truth and freedom without suffering major hostility from others. Mother Teresa of Calcutta is one illustrious case in point, though even she had to leave one community to start another. But a fear of what the cost *might* be is realistic. An adventure into the unknown is always scary. There is always the fear that the next trapeze will not reach us, or that we will not catch it. The good news, though, is that there is a safety net! One of my favorite assurances of this is in Deuteronomy (33:27, King James Version): "The eternal God is thy refuge, and underneath are the everlasting arms."

Finally, for some souls in transition there is the fear of commitment. There may be anxiety that if one responds to the call to the way of truth, more will be demanded than one is able to give. We get cold feet because we fear that the cost will be more than we are able to pay. The great cry at this point is, "Why me? I don't want to be a spiritual hero. Why can't I just stay a safe little duckling?"

Let me tell you the story of my encounter with this fear. I was afraid of committing myself to what I named "the interior way." I knew it had to do with hard truths. For years I had been avoiding the issue because I feared the possible cost. The time came, when I was about thirty, that a friend was going on a "retreat" to a convent (this was before I had any idea of a vocation to such a life), and my friend convinced me to go along to keep her company. It was the first time for both of us and we were a little scared. Once there, the silence was powerful. I walked out onto the grounds and into the little wood that bordered the property. It was autumn and the foliage was brilliant with color and sunlight. I began to feel an inner pressure, an invitation, to commit myself to something; gradually this something defined itself as the "inner way," the way of truth-seeking, no matter what the cost.

This was frightening—I couldn't know what the cost might involve. It was a crisis of trust. I deliberately put my commitment "on hold," and thought and tried to pray about other things for the remainder of my walk. When it was almost time for the community to say Vespers—evening prayers—I went into the Sisters' chapel. I knelt down in the guest section and the "invitation" came back with more force and a sort of gentle urgency. It seemed that the high walls were lined with invisible presences as if the very air were alive and waiting for my response. Give me a little more time, I said to myself and to any Being or Beings that might be waiting in the silence. The Sisters will be coming in any minute now for Vespers—I need more time.

After the prayer service the Sisters and other guests all filed out, and I was left there with myself and the unseen presences. After a time of holding off—of preparation, I suppose—I breathed deeply and said silently into the expectancy: "Yes! Yes! I will, I will go for the truth no matter what the cost. All right—YES!" And it was as if that assent and commitment were *received*, that they would now and henceforth be kept and honored in whatever space or dimension such promises are held.

The experience made very real to me both the profundity of the challenge, and the blessing of the invitation to venture into the mystery of reality.

Doug: How important is it to find one's own group of "swans" or one's tribe as part of making the transition? What if a person feels he has no tribe? Does everyone have a group that is like them which can be supportive during this process?

ES: Because we learn from one another, it is very important to find at least one "swan" if not a group or tribe, to understand and encourage us as we go through the transition.

To a great extent it seems to be true that "When the student is ready, the teacher will appear." Most often the teacher is a person who has accomplished his or her own transition, and has been living the "examined life." But sometimes the first intimation of being understood and encouraged can be found in a book, or even, as in my experience with Bach, in a piece of music. As one grows in the awareness, one may find more and more people who are of "the tribe," who have a talent for reality. "It takes one to know one."

When a person has *not* found an understanding supporter and feels alone in the dark, it can be tragic. For me, one of the most poignant scenes in Shakespeare is when Hamlet's school friends, Rosencrantz and Gildenstern, betray him. They choose to join Hamlet's mother and stepfather in the lies and cover-up around the murder of Hamlet's father. Ophelia is too young and emotionally fragile to understand and support. Polonius, whose age should be accompanied by wisdom, is less than no help. In his schoolmate, Horatio, Hamlet has a man whose friendship is solid as a rock, but it is not clear how understanding Horatio is of what his friend is going through. Horatio is a support, but not a mentor—perhaps not a "swan".

One of the most telling scenes in the film *Amadeus* is Salieri's admission to being the patron saint of the mediocre. One gets the message that Mozart has no tribe, no swans to understand his genius.

I once felt that there was no one there with me in the dark, the place between trapezes. In that time of seeming dereliction, divine compassion himself, Jesus, came to me as the one who understood and supported, until a human mentor became available in my life.

It must be said that no other human being or "tribe" of human beings can fully alleviate existential loneliness. As St. Augustine wrote: "O Lord, Thou hast made us for Thyself, and our hearts shall find no rest until they find their rest in Thee." However, the paradox is that we are called to encourage and support one another, in co-operation with grace, as we seek the truth of our humanity.

Doug: I have found that since moving towards honoring my own deepest desires and worrying less about the opinions of others, paradoxically, I feel more called than ever to serve others. Why do you suppose that is? Is it the "Love must act as light must shine and fire must burn" phenomenon again?

ES: In the first chapter I talked about how human beings develop or ripen from the natural narcissism of infancy to the mature capacity for self-gift. I think there is a parallel in spiritual development. We mature into the capacity to serve others. In my experience it is most often true that at the beginning of the spiritual search, after one has made the commitment to divine reality, there is a certain self-centeredness. This, like the other infancy, is not reproachable, but rather a natural stage in growth. When we are new-born in life, love or spirit, there is a period of self-absorption. In human love it is an absorption with each other; in divine love it is an absorption with God for one's own sake. Since God orders this ripening process, it is not surprising that it is in this beginning stage, this "honeymoon period," that spiritual gifts and consolations are showered on the soul like gifts from a lover.

Saint Bernard, a monk of the twelfth century, wrote a treatise, *On Loving God*. In it he describes four degrees of human love for God. First we love ourself for our own sake; then we love God for our own sake; thirdly we love God for God's sake; and finally we love ourself for God's sake. It is at this last, most mature stage that we have enough self-love in God to be filled and overflow. A corollary to "You can't give what you don't have," is perhaps "When you abound you are impelled to give." When a mother's breasts are full of milk for her child, it is painful not to give it.

Yes, love must act. Love is generative—it yearns to extend and perpetuate itself. If water does not run, if it is not "living water," it becomes stagnant. It is great good news that just as we human beings pass down cultural lies and the potential to choose against love, so also there is "positive programming"—the passing down of loving encouragement. This may be accomplished by good parenting and/or caring guidance. The reclamation of discipleship would go a long way towards alleviating the isolation of "rugged individualism."

Doug: Can we ever really make it back to the stage of divine innocence or is this just a romantic ideal?

ES: This is essentially the question Nicodemus asked Jesus. "How can anyone be born after growing old? Can one enter a second time into the mother's womb and be born?" Jesus' answer, as reported in the Gospel of John, is a bit oblique, but essentially he says, "Yes, indeed" (John 3:4).

We have talked about the two simplicities—one on this side and one on the other side of complexity; there are correspondingly two kinds of innocence. Perhaps it is not too fanciful to say that the first lies on this side of the law of the knowledge of good and evil. The second lies on the other side. It has nothing to do with ignorance, but rather with a wisdom in spirit which transcends the letter of the law.

There may be a relationship between this second innocence and what we have called emptiness. Both are represented as a kind of third stage. Both the first innocence and what in Community Building we call pseudo-community have aspects in common. Both have very little knowledge of differences and conflict and little experience of suffering. If a child has considerable conflict and suffering, we tend to say they have been robbed of their innocence. The first innocence, sooner or later, like the first simplicity, moves into complexity and the knowledge of good and evil.

There is a way to move beyond complexity and the reliance upon knowledge, which entails the acceptance of paradox and finally of mystery; we can never figure it all out. The new physicists have come to a kind of Socratic declaration: "I only know that I do not know." In much the same way, a Community Building group is called to the realization that it must give up control and trying to fix. Both complexity and chaos are stages of growth out of first stage simplicities. They are transitional stages. They in turn may be transcended by an emptiness and second simplicity which make space to receive the spirit of divine reality and new life. This freedom and ripening is always in process. It is not somewhere to get to or be complacent in.

I have never met anyone who would say, "Now I am totally empty," or "Now I am divinely innocent." The point of being empty is to invite the spirit of community; the point of being innocent is to invite the spirit of holy wisdom. The closest I've read about such a declaration is Saint Paul's saying: "It is no longer I who live, but it is

Christ who lives in me" (Gal. 2:20). Even there it is obvious that Paul's personality is still very much in process. Paul has become simplified and emptied to the extent that Christ's spirit of love and truth are able to be held and perceived, though still "in a glass, darkly."

As long as we have freedom to choose, we are free to go in and out of or deeper into this innocence. I imagine this would also be true of what the Eastern spiritualities call "Illumination." There is a certain sense in which one does not go back again into the *same* complexity or the *same* chaos. There is a sense that one is no longer "going" anywhere. But neither is the mystery of inner wisdom or divine innocence a static thing. Anyone can regress or relapse. Everyone can go deeper into oneness.

The quality of divine innocence is not "romantic" but rather it is real in the most profound sense. It recognizes and assimilates memory of past experience and vision of future potential, to focus them simply in the now-moment. It knows that the present is held in eternity, which is glory. This second innocence discerns the difference between license and the true liberty of the children of God. The peace of this second innocence is beyond understanding. Its joy is radiant with the spontaneity of love. It is the pearl of great price, which is worth any cost. The Sufi mystic, Rumi, might be called the poet of divine innocence. Near the end of his life, he wrote:

I have died, time and time again,
and Your breath has always revived me.
If I die in You a thousand times more,
I will die in the same way.
I was scattered like dust, and then you gathered me;
And how can I die scattered before Your gatheredness?
Like the child that dies at its mother's breast,
I will die at the breast
Of the mercy and the bounty of the All-merciful.
What am I saying? How could the Lover ever die?
—Rumi, *Light Upon Light: Inspirations from Rumi*

—— 9 ——
Inviting the Spirit

**In the silence of the heart, God speaks. If you
face God in prayer and silence, God will speak
to you. Then you will know that you are nothing.
It is only when you realize your nothingness,
your emptiness, that God can fill you with
Himself.**

—Mother Teresa

The transition from seeking acceptance by conforming to
cultural myth, through a time of emptiness, to becoming a wheel
rolling out of its own center is a difficult one. And if one tries to do
it on one's own, it is nearly impossible. This is why it is so important
to find a guide and to learn as much as one can about the transition
before embarking on it. In addition, it is important to emphasize that
the point of emptying oneself of cultural myth is not to reject the
world around us and retreat to some secluded cabin in the woods.
Rather, the point is to become free to more fully connect with the
world by making room for and inviting the life-force we call
"Spirit."

In this chapter, we will discuss some of the barriers to
connecting with Spirit and provide some very concrete steps you can
take to invite the Spirit into your life on a daily basis. In so doing, we
hope to show how to better connect with oneself, with others and
with the rest of Creation; how to become a wheel rolling out of its
own center.

Barriers to Connecting with Spirit

I have a relative, Aunt Hazel, who believes in a power greater
than humans, but has significant doubts about who or what that
power is and what role such a force has in our lives.

Every holiday season, when the family has gathered to celebrate
Thanksgiving or Christmas, there is always a long stretch of
afternoon where the men and some of the women sit around

watching football. Aunt Hazel invariably will come into the living room at some point during the game and say a version of the following: "When the football players from both teams get down on their knees to pray before the game begins, how does God know which one's prayer to answer?"

I have heard this question through the years and have never known what to say. Of course, Aunt Hazel wasn't looking for an answer; it was really a subtle poke at those who pray, disguised in the form of a rhetorical question. More recently though, I have thought seriously about this question because it addresses the core issue of a significant debate: Is there such a thing as a personal God who will individually look out for us and answer our particular questions, wishes and dreams?

As so many people ask, "If there is a personal God, then why did my sister have to die?" If there is a personal God who looks out for me, then "Why does my wife, who has faithfully gone to church every day of her life, have degenerative Multiple Sclerosis?" If there is a personal God, "Why does most of the world's population suffer from abject poverty and disease while only a handful of us enjoy wealth and prosperity?" And if there is a personal God, then "Why does it seem that many of my prayers go unanswered?"

It may be Rabbi Harold Kushner's refrain of "why bad things happen to good people." Kushner, who wrote a book by this title after his young son died from a rare illness, likened it to the case of Job. In thinking about the issue of justice, the existence of a personal God and why innocent people like Job were forced to suffer, he lists three declarative sentences, not all of which can be simultaneously true:

A. God is all-powerful and causes everything that happens in the world. Nothing happens without his willing it.
B. God is just and fair, and stands for people getting what they deserve, so that the good prosper and the wicked are punished.
C. Job is a good person.

One could insert oneself in the place of Job under "C. Job is a good person" as a way of thinking about this. If I have done nothing wrong (Job is good) and God is compassionate and loving, and I suffer some horrible misfortune, then God must not be all powerful.

Thinking about the nature of God and of prayer is vital to our discussion here of filling the vessel. Because if we are not at all certain how or if the process of filling up with Spirit works, then why empty? One potential barrier to inviting the Spirit is the difficulty of finding evidence that emptying and inviting the Spirit is worth the risk.

One person we interviewed for this book said: "I am not a church-goer, but I pray every single night. I have to admit though that there have been times when my prayers have not been answered. Once a friend's father was sick and I prayed for him to live. When he died, I was scared to death. If God won't answer a prayer as important as saving someone's life, then maybe we really are on our own here."

In addition to the skepticism generated by prayers going unanswered, there are many people in this age of reason and science who are generally skeptical of anything that cannot be proven scientifically or which does not generate profit. Billionaire Bill Gates, when asked by a reporter if he attended church, said, "I have never found it to be time-efficient." That seems to summarize the view for many of us who are racing as fast as we can go down the information superhighway and simply don't see the payoff to spending time in prayer.

And at some point skepticism can turn to cynicism. Cynicism can arise when we hear story after story of public figures who experience a religious conversion or profound humility only after getting caught in a major crime such as adultery or murder or fraud. There is a real cynicism in our culture about the use of religion and conversion as a way out of past sins.

To make matters worse, the Western culture of rugged individualism has made it problematic to rely on Spirit. It is too often viewed as some indefinable, silent force, popular primarily among those who are either naive or who have screwed up and are looking for a way out.

Nevertheless, we do find ourselves in the midst of a major resurgence of interest in things spiritual and holy. There are many potential explanations for this resurgence but the most important one is probably the aging of America. For it is as one arrives at middle age and beyond that questions of meaning and the importance of one's significance to the cosmos typically arise. Many of us aging baby boomers are confronting our own mortality and that of loved ones for the first time: aging parents are sick or passing away, peers are experiencing loss. Even our own sense that we will never get old is challenged by new pains or an irregular blood sample that requires more testing. At middle age, we wake up to the fact that we will not live forever, which generates hard, self-reflective questions like "Just what is the point of it all?"

The Reluctance to Join Mainstream Institutions

Mainstream religious institutions have historically been the primary source of answers to such questions. Interestingly, the two fastest-growing kinds of institutions are on polar extremes in terms of their philosophies. On one end, there are the ultra-conservative institutions that are narrowly proscriptive in their approach and attract people who want certainty in a rapidly-changing society where there is a perception that morals and traditional values are in decline. Conservative churches provide certainty in an uncertain world and many of them are experiencing record growth rates.

On the other end of the continuum, there are the rapidly-growing institutions that express themselves as ecumenical or inter-denominational. They are congregations that honor the individual nature of each congregant and believe that the glory of God's creation lies in honoring the absolute uniqueness of each and every individual. These institutions minimize specific proscriptions about the way a truly "Godly" person should act and emphasize that the point is to worship regularly, in whatever form that worship might take.

Despite the resurgence of interest in things spiritual, there is still a major disconnection between those interested in spirituality and the number of people attending church regularly. A *Washington Post*/Harvard University survey found that 42 percent of Americans report attending church once per week; 50 percent of women report attending once per week, while just over 33 percent of men report likewise (*Washington Post* 11/13/98). But this is a far cry from the nearly 90% of all Americans who report they believe in a higher power. Why the discrepancy between those who believe and those who worship on a regular basis? Part of the reason for many individuals' resistance to joining mainstream religious institutions is that so many people have been damaged by them. A common joke among psychiatrists is that if it weren't for religious institutions and the patients they generated, their practices would have gone under a long time ago!

My own early experience with religion clearly scared me away from participation for almost twenty years. I recall attending a weekend retreat in 1980 sponsored by a mainstream religious institution that gave me a sense of the problem. The weekend was designed to help couples learn to communicate better by writing "love letters" to each other and practicing the art of "dialogue." I had been married only a short time and my wife and I had not really experienced any of the issues a number of couples there had experienced.

Many of the couples had gone into the weekend with tough relationship issues to deal with and many of them left having made real progress. This was especially true of John and Debra, a couple who had convinced us to go with them to this marriage weekend. They had been married for almost twenty years and, as happens to many couples, they had grown apart and were on the verge of separating. But they had adopted two beautiful children and they decided to attend the weekend in an attempt to do whatever they had to do to turn things around. Needless to say, their expectations for the weekend were high.

As long-standing members of the sponsoring church, they were hoping to find the magic bullet that would revive their passion and save their marriage. They thought that by inviting the power of the Holy Spirit, they could escape what seemed like an inevitable slide into divorce.

Looking back on it now, John and Debra's marriage kind of reminded me of my own marriage. They were, by all outward appearances, highly-competent, highly-successful members of society. Like my marriage would become, however, this outward appearance only masked deep layers of unaddressed and unresolved conflict that dwelt beneath the surface.

As the weekend progressed, we would periodically bump into John and Debra. They both appeared to be bubbly and almost euphoric, saying, "Isn't this the most amazing thing that's ever happened to you?" John, who was a self-professed workaholic obsessed with productivity, said, "I haven't even looked at the watch the whole time I have been here. Isn't that amazing?"

We were instructed to practice communicating authentically with our spouse, ever mindful and seeking the invitation of the Holy

Spirit to help us rediscover the sacred bond to which we had each committed ourselves. While we could see the virtue of such an exercise and were willing to participate in it, neither my wife nor I experienced what we considered to be an even-remotely profound experience.

At the end of the weekend, all the couples came together and the facilitators asked people to stand up and testify about how they had done and what the weekend had meant to them. John and Debra were among the first to stand up and, trembling with emotion, describe how, coming into the weekend, they weren't sure if they were going to last even another week together. Now, because of this church weekend, they had found that they were more in love and together than ever before. After John and Debra sat down, another couple stood up and gave a similar testimonial. This went on for some time, with couple after couple standing up and describing the transformation which seemed to have occurred for them.

Finally, the organizers came up to the front and said, "You can see how profoundly people's lives have been changed by this one weekend. Now we have said we don't require that any of you pay for this weekend. It is part of the church's mission to do this work. But we would like to show you how some people have responded to this work." They then held up a check for $10,000 which one couple donated to the church after their successful weekend, then a $2,000 check from another, $500 from another. Then they read testimonial letters from each of these happy couples whose lives the church had turned around and continued: "Now we do have a recommendation for those of you who would like to support this work. The actual cost per couple of one of these weekends is $150. We would like to suggest that those of you who feel called make a donation of $300 to allow someone else to experience this life-changing weekend."

At the time this happened, I was just starting out my career as a consumer advocate and, admittedly, I was not a believer. But even now, as a baptized Christian and a member of the vestry of my own church, I am appalled by the tactics that were employed at the close of that weekend. You guide people over a long, intense weekend to the point where they are at the peak of their emotional vulnerability and then you pitch them for $300 using tactics we now see on the home shopping channel or on high-pressure infomercials.

I don't know how much John and Debra paid that day. What I do know is that they were chosen as the "couple of the week" by the church for having made the most remarkable progress during the weekend and they were invited to attend a subsequent weekend as a model couple.

They never made it to the second weekend three months later because by then they had separated and entered into a very nasty custody divorce case.

There is always a temptation to make too much of such stories and throw the baby out with the bath water. As Bill Grace, Executive Director of the Center for Ethical Leadership, has written: "If a religious institution has failed someone, it does not mean that a person's spirituality is unimportant. That would be like refusing to engage in physical exercise because you had a bad experience at a gym."

John and Debra were trying to save their marriage and turning to the church was a reflection of their upbringing and faith. "When the chips are down, ask for God's help" and that meant the church.

When they got to the weekend, they reverted to what had always worked for them in the past: they put on the social mask of "everything is fine" and pretended to have been transformed into the perfect couple again. In reality, too much damage had been done in their marriage and it was never realistic that one weekend would fix their deep-rooted issues.

The church was trying to make the weekends financially viable so future groups could experience them. But because of the emotional manipulation, my wife and I left feeling further away from wanting to join in the religious life.

There are countless other examples of the sins of religious institutions and the people in them manipulating the power bestowed. One need only recall the case of Jimmy Bakker, the televangelist who, after building up a multi-million dollar ministry through television, was convicted of swindling hundreds of his followers through crooked investments.

The entertainment business has captured some of these abuses on film, reflecting the widespread and growing cynicism of institutional religion. One film, *Leap of Faith*, starring Steve Martin, chronicles a crooked traveling faith-healer/evangelist named Jonas Nightingale whose truck breaks down in the rural town of Rustwater, Kansas. His traveling "ministry" reveals a clever scam whereby, as the faithful walk into the tent, his "disciples" learn facts about them and then transmit those facts to another disciple, a computer whiz named "Janie" who logs the personal data into a computer program based on where the unsuspecting congregant is seated. She then has a transmitter which she uses to whisper these facts to Jonas on stage.

Jonas calls out the names of these people one by one and recites facts which "only a man of God" could have known about them. Later in the movie, Jonas is discussing the upcoming performance with Janie and she is worried that the local law enforcement people will be there and that they may get caught unless they really heal people. To which Jonas says, "That's okay. Remember our insurance policy: God can only heal you if your faith is strong enough." The implication is that if anyone questioned his faith-healing effectiveness, he would just say, "Well, I guess your faith isn't strong enough to be healed."

At the end of this movie, a young boy who was crippled in a car crash is inexplicably healed when Jonas gets him on stage, lays on hands (which Jonas admits is just an act), and for the first time he is able to walk on his own. We are left with a mixed message: even though the preacher is a deeply cynical scam artist, the people in the small town nevertheless believed him and believed in a loving God, which may have facilitated the miraculous healing of the boy.

So what are we to do with all of the skepticism and cynicism that these kinds of human manipulations of religion and faith have left us with? How can we get past the fact that many of the institutions of religion are run by human beings who themselves have flaws? Does prayer work when some believe and others are merely faking it? And what strategies can we employ to seek contact with the forces beyond ourselves that ES and I are calling spirit? I asked ES to go into some detail on the subject of inviting the spirit.

Dialogue on Inviting the Spirit

Doug: What happens when I pray and what I prayed for doesn't occur? Should I assume I did something wrong or that God wasn't listening? A related question is how do I know when God is listening or involved in my life? Are there markers or indicators I can look for or listen for?

ES: When I pray and when what I pray for doesn't happen, I sometimes can just go along with it. Other times I may take a good look at why it didn't happen as I prayed it would. What can I learn from this different outcome? As we've noted before, it may be necessary to go through anger at God, or the opposite, a despairing kind of giving up. But eventually I find it fruitful to come once again to the "If so, what now?" position. I try to wait till I come to a place where I *can* see what's going on. I find if I keep hanging in with my truth and putting one foot in front of the other, I do finally come to where I can see and rejoice in how God is "involved in my life," even at the times when it feels least likely.

I learned a wonderful lesson about the times when I don't see any "markers or indicators" of God's attention or action in my life. It was years ago when I made a pilgrimage of sorts to Assisi, in Italy. I was traveling by myself, and it was a spiritual venture. One of the things I wanted most to do was to climb nearby Mount Subasio and visit the Eremo delle Carceri—the caves where Francis and his brothers went to retreat and pray. I was told it was a three-mile hike up from the town, so I bought myself a pair of walking shoes and started off.

The road was fairly steep, consisting of a dry mustard-colored dirt that made the shrubbery at its sides dusty and drab. There was no view. After I had plodded upward for what seemed a long way, I stopped at a small turn-out by the roadside to rest. From there between the foliage I could catch a glimpse of the bottom of the hill where I had begun the climb. It was reassuring.

But after a few minutes I realized I wouldn't get anywhere sitting there, so I rose and started back up the winding track. After another considerable distance, I was tired and found another turn-out with a large rock on it. I climbed to the top of this rock and was presented with an incredible view!

The whole valley around Assisi was spread beneath me. There were olive orchards, a field being plowed by white oxen, the gate of the city through which I had come to start up this road, in the distance the great basilica of Santa Maria delle Angeli, and a vista of hills and sky. I could even look upward and catch a glimpse of the courtyard of the Eremo—my intended destination. It was thrilling! I sat in the sun and a light breeze, marveling at it all. But then, I realized that it was all very well to sit and enjoy all this, but I wasn't getting anywhere. In order to get where I wanted to go, I would have to forsake the splendid view and get back on that dusty, obscuring track of a road.

I was back on the climb—one tired foot after the other—when I realized what a great analogy this was for the venture of prayer. When I was seeing where I'd been, and even had a glimpse of where I was headed, I wasn't moving; the real movement came when I was slogging along seeing nothing much but dust!

Remembering that experience helps me wait for the larger perspective and be patient about receiving any "markers or indicators" of God's involvement in my life. It helps me to remember that, when there are no indications at all, that may in fact be just the time when real ground is being covered.

Often when I am in the lonely stretches of dusty road and my level of trust in God's involvement in my life is very low, I remind myself of the prayer that is called "St. Teresa's Bookmark," because it was found in her breviary at the time of her death in 1582:

> Nada te turbe,
> Nada te espante,
> Todo se pasa
> Dios no se muda,
> La paciencia
> Todo lo alcanza;
> Qien a Dios tiene
> Nada le falta;
> Solo Dios basta.

Which roughly translated is: "Let nothing disturb you, nothing frighten you: all things pass, only God remains. Patience gains everything, whoever has God needs nothing else; God alone is enough."

Doug: What about the question my Aunt Hazel asked? Is there such a thing as a personal God and if so, how do we explain it when bad things happen to us?

ES: First, a word about the idea of a *personal* God. When I first consciously entered into relationship with God, I thought God was my personal God the way a computer is one's personal computer. During the time when I was a Franciscan, I was saying my prayers on St. Clare's day, August 11th. In my mind's eye I saw Jesus—my personal friend—with his arm around St. Clare, and they both seemed to be regarding me with compassionate love.

My first response was jealousy! I didn't want St. Clare in the picture. To put it mildly, I wasn't interested in how God was personal to *anyone else*. And then, mercifully, God helped me empty myself of that immaturity, and I came to delight in the image of being embraced by both of them and becoming a sort of spiritual threesome. A community. I began to see how eventually it would be most delightful to include *everyone*.

If there is a creator God who created us "in God's image" as persons, then God must be at least as personal as we are. As we have said, God's divinity is as much beyond our comprehension as Shakespeare's humanity is beyond Hamlet's comprehension. However, we can know God, and have a "personal relationship," not in the dimension of reason, but in love. I wrote a poem about it:

PARABLE

Great King Cophetua loved a beggar maid.
It was years ago when I first heard the story—
I can't remember where—but it has stayed
against all odds in my mind's inventory.

I know I have seen the Burne-Jones, at the Tate—
the beggar throned, king suppliant at her knee;
and wondered briefly, could their love translate
God's passion for my poor humanity?

Just recently a friend tracked down the source:
Percy's Reliques, Falstaff's drunken cries;—
I see more clearly now the story's force:
the capacity of love to equalize.

Daily Cophetua governed on his throne,
enacting laws, receiving potentates;
crowded by suitors, he was as alone
as his loved maiden, begging at his gates.

But with the coming of the jeweled dark
when all the traffic of the day was done,

tangled in perfumed silk, their passion stark
as space between breath and breath, they met as one.
Incredible that I am called to be
no longer servant, but beloved friend!
Pledged not till death, but to eternity,
beggar forever and giver without end.

Now, having said I believe in a personal God who somehow can be personal to me and calls me to a love-relationship, which we call prayer, let's look at the second part of your question. How do we explain when bad things happen to us? We have already talked about much that can contribute to some understanding of that problem, especially in Chapters Six and Seven when we were dealing with happiness and goodness, and consequently also with suffering and badness. The "five not-so-easy lessons from suffering to glory" with which we ended Chapter Six is one stab at understanding the purpose in bad things happening.

Another help to me is remembering my brother Paul and his skill at poker. A bad hand is a bad hand—there's no call to be a Pollyanna—but if everyone got a Royal straight flush every time, there would be no game. If there had been no crucifixion, there would be no resurrection. The only thing I might add here is that I always try to learn more about what I am considering "bad" at each particular instance of diminishment.

Doug: Can you give me some simple steps I could take to begin to pray?

ES: Prayer is a life-long affair and in some sense there are no "simple steps." For me it would be like talking about simple steps to begin a human love affair. In both cases, human and divine, I would try to make myself as attractive and wholesome as possible and think of what I have that I could give to my lover.

Beyond that, there are several areas in which to seek and meet God. For me there have been five approaches or "doorways" to prayer. There may be as many more as there are persons who seek a more real and loving relationship with God.

Even if a person began praying a long time ago, there is a need to begin again, the way we have to start each new day with waking.

St. Francis is reported to have said at the end of his life, "Brothers, let us begin again, for up to now we have done nothing."
My first approach or "doorway," then, is nature. I think it was St. Thomas Aquinas who said, "Grace builds on nature." Nature in this sense refers not only to fields of daffodils and sunsets, but to the complex reality in which we live. Morris Berman wrote a book called *The Re-enchantment of the World* in which he contends that, before Isaac Newton, the world was thought to be enchanted, full of wonder. Newtonian physics created the mind-set that, given time, humanity could measure and comprehend the entire natural world. Thus wonder and mystery gave way to knowledge.

This knowledge would give us more and more power to utilize and control the planet's resources; also, unfortunately, to exploit and diminish them. It is primarily the new sciences, particularly quantum physics, which have re-opened the world to enchantment. We can no longer be certain that some day we will know it all, measure it all, control it all. Heisenberg, for instance, asserts that we will never be certain of both the speed and the position of a given sub-atomic particle. When we admit uncertainty, we open the door to wonder, awe, and a reality greater than we can imagine.

This awareness is not, however, without antecedent. There were pioneers. Rudolf Otto published a book in 1917 called *Das Heilige*, translated as *The Idea of the Holy*, in which he used the word "numinous" to describe nature. In the 1940's and '50's the French Jesuit, Teilhard de Chardin, taught that all matter has a "within," thus confuting the popular polarization of the material and the spiritual. Today there are many people writing from this new, more integrated perspective. Some classics in this field are Gary Zukov's *The Dancing Wu Li Masters*, K. C. Cole's *Sympathetic Vibrations*, Larry Dossey's *Time, Space and Medicine*, Thomas Berry's *The Dream of the Earth*, and Margaret Wheatley's *Leadership and the New Science*, to name only a few.

The point is that we are now being invited to see ourselves in a re-enchanted world, where nature is a doorway into mystery—into the divine *mysterium tremendum*. Rosemary Haughton wrote in an article entitled "Liberating the Divine Energy" (in *Living with Apocalypse: Spiritual Resources for Social Compassion*):

Many people who are not particularly religious
have become aware (sometimes with mixed
feelings), that scientists have begun to talk a
language verging on the mystical...all this is
giving us a different theological language, one of
dynamic relations, one in which it is no longer
ridiculous or "unscientific" to consider the power
of compassion as a key factor in economics or
medicine and in which the ultimate material of the
universe is perceived to be love. The earth herself
struggles to bring to birth a new humanity. The
image is Paul's, but it is also the model that most
accurately expresses the scientists' awareness of an
inherently and dynamically related universe, a
universe of love.

There are two things to watch out for as we approach God
through nature. The first is to be aware of the difference between
icon and idol. An icon is an image which invites participation in a
reality beyond itself; an idol retains the meaning in itself. If we use
nature as an idol we will never get beyond the sunset or the science,
to God. If we make ourselves or another person an idol, we will
never see God in ourselves or in them. Hubert Northcott, an
Anglican monk, wrote:

> The sight and smell of a rose will come to one as a
> breath of heaven, drawing him [her] straight to
> worship. Another will be unable to get beyond its
> sensuous beauty and to that person it will be a
> hindrance (*The Venture of Prayer*).

The other thing to watch out for is the distinction between
magic and miracle. *Magic* is always in some way an attempt to
control or manipulate the physical and/or metaphysical world.
Miracle is gift. The important question is not whether magic is
intended for malevolent or benevolent effects, nor is it really whether
magic "works" or not. It may "work." The borderland between the
natural and supernatural orders is no doubt quite permeable, and, as
in the story I told about my experience with Tarot cards in Chapter

Two, we perhaps can sometimes or in some way predict or influence the way things happen.

But such attempts at control are at the opposite pole from the "dance" of spirit and Spirit. Again, the one is exploitation, the other gift. Think of an orange. The rind is edible, and if you were starving, it might provide some nourishment. In the same way it may be possible to nibble around the edges of the supernatural. But why bother? We are invited beyond the rind, beyond human attempts at control, into the juicy sweetness, the mystery of divine love!

My second doorway into prayer is through scripture. Unfortunately the Bible, also, can be made into an idol, and it's important to go beyond the written word to the Spirit of Truth who inspired the writers. Here's an analogy: think of the person who is dearest to you. Now suppose that person goes away—on a business trip, to school, or on a vacation. After a while you receive a letter or e-mail from them, and what a wonderful message! Your person has written you about how much you mean to them, recalls special times you've shared, tells about some ways you have been especially helpful to them—all things that they have wanted to share with you, but that they've never said when they were with you. Well, you carry this letter or print-out with you all day, and whenever you get a chance, you take it out of your pocket to be sure you've remembered exactly how they described their love and gratitude for you and your relationship. When your day's work is done, you go to your favorite chair, put your feet up and take out your letter for a good, unhurried re-read. Just then the door opens—and surprise! Your person has unexpectedly returned! What do you do with your letter? If you're anything like me you drop the piece of paper and go hug your dear one.

The Benedictine monks have a way of reading scripture which is very similar to this. It's called *Lectio Divina*. To practice this kind of scripture reading, you read a passage only until you feel yourself in the presence of the Living God, and then you put down your Bible and rejoice in the presence of the Beloved.

The third doorway or approach to God is in the depth of our being—or the height, or the ground—all dimensional descriptions for this meeting place are poetic. We might also call it the space in our being that has been emptied to receive the spirit. Though this "space" does not really have a "where" to it, I sometimes like to think that below our conscious, subconscious, unconscious, there is a little trap door where, when it is opened, our individual spirit meets Holy Spirit. They meet, but *they do not merge*. For me, St. Bernard best describes this meeting:

> The union of God and man is brought about, not by confusion of natures, but by agreement of wills. Man and God, because they are not of one substance or nature cannot be called "one thing," *unum* (like the father and the son); but they are in strict truth called "one spirit," if they adhere to one another by the glue of love (*Sermon lxxi, On the Song of Songs*).

If we *believe* this is true, we know God by faith, and that is what is important. If at rare moments we *experience* this meeting with God, that is what is called a mystical experience. It does not have to be like St. Teresa in ecstasy. Have you ever had the experience of fretting over a problem for some time, and then waking up the next morning with the answer in your head, clear as clear, and you don't know where it came from? That is an experience of the Holy Spirit of wisdom and truth communicating with your human spirit.

The fourth doorway or way to see God is in other people. If God as Spirit is in me, then God is in you in the same way. This may sound easier to recognize than it is. Actually to see the compassion of God shine out of a pair of human eyes is quite rare—at least it has been so for me. Many times all I can see is fear, defensiveness, protective mask, or ignorance; not compassion, but human frailty.

The people of India have a story which helps me in this matter. At one time in India people made lamps out of camel stomachs. When cured, these membranes had the consistency of parchment and the shape of globes. They were decorated with painted designs and then a candle was inserted at the bottom so that the globe served as a lampshade. Now the point is that the candle flame was the same in every lamp. But the shade varied greatly. Some camel stomachs were very thick and heavily decorated; some were paper-thin and translucent. So with us human vessels. Even though the light is the same—for Christians, it is called the light of Christ—some shades, or personalities, are so thick and covered over, that it is almost impossible to *see* the light. Hitler may have been one such. Each of us has people in our lives with relatively thick shades—I know I do!

Equally, you can probably think of someone who for you seems to have a very thin shade, through whom you can see a good deal of light. This way of trying to know the truth of people I meet is for me a wonderful way to approach God.

None of these ways, however, is a "simple step." Maybe, as I said, there *are* no simple steps; there is no Owner's Manual, because love cannot own, and love-objects cannot be owned. God knows we cannot find God easily in nature, in scripture, in the convolutions of our own hearts nor in those of others. So Jesus, quite simply, gives us his humanity and divinity in the consecrated bread and wine of the Eucharist. Granted, God is still hidden: "Truly you are a God who hides himself, O God of Israel, the Savior" (Is. 45:15). Hidden, yet in spirit met, and in love, known.

Doug: When we pray, is it okay to ask for things, like "Please God let me win the lottery"? (Putting aside the question of whether it is good for you to win the lottery.)

ES: It is always okay to ask. It is particularly okay for good friends or lovers to ask things of each other—even winning the lottery, as long as we understand that only one can win and many may be asking. As I've said, it's *demanding* that gets us into trouble, or, if we don't get what we think we want, picking up our marbles and quitting the game in a huff. Demanding and pouting are not modes of mature love or friendship, but asking is.

It is important to remember that prayer, like every other aspect of human life, is developmental. Many people seem to see prayer only as petitionary, "asking" prayer. That is: we ask, and God gives or doesn't give. That is only the beginning. It is natural for a baby, or any of us finding ourselves at a "Level One Love" point in our lives, to get into the "gimme, gimme" mode. But as we mature spiritually, so our spiritual relationship—prayer—becomes more mutual, and more like the dance analogy we introduced in Chapter Two.

Here's another little parable. One day I met a friend whom I had not seen for a couple of months. When we met, *my* side of the dialogue ran roughly like this: "Hi! You look great! I like your hair that way. Listen, before we go have a cup of coffee, I need to say something. I know I promised to send you the ISBN number of that book we were talking about, but I totally forgot about it until this morning on the plane. I'm really sorry! What makes me feel worse, is that *you* remembered to send me that article you wrote. It was very helpful to the research I was doing—thanks. Before I forget—I know you care a lot about Sister Elizabeth. She's having a really rough time right now, more tests next week and the prognosis is not good. She's in my thoughts and prayers a lot; could you add your prayers? While we're on the subject—could you say a prayer for me too? I'm a little scared about going on that mission half way round the world and working in such an unfamiliar culture. And could I borrow again your set of adapter plugs?"

It was because *her* side of the dialogue, which I have not recorded, was so responsive, that I felt free at the end to ask for a specific little thing that I needed. Shortly after that conversation, I realized that I had paralleled the five classical modes of prayer: adoration, contrition, thanksgiving, intercession and petition! The thing that struck me forcibly about our interaction, was that everything I said flowed naturally out of the condition of our friendship. In the same way, my relationship to God is the ground and source of all the modes of my prayer. It may not be true for everybody, but for me it's really hard to ask something from a person from whom I feel distanced. On the other hand, if I feel close to somebody I feel free to ask just about anything. I trust the other to say "no," if they need to for any reason, and that a "no" or "maybe later" will not in any way damage our relationship. Why shouldn't it be that way with God?

Doug: What is the relationship between prayer and emptiness? You have implied elsewhere that spirit and/or grace cannot be present unless there is "room at the inn" so to speak. Is part of inviting the spirit conditioned on our ability to empty?

ES: I think there is a relationship between prayer and emptiness. I am reminded of the way people who practice Zen meditation speak of acquiring "empty-mind." Also, Father Thomas Keating uses an analogy of temptations and distractions in prayer being like little boats on a stream; the point is not to climb into them and get carried away, but just recognize them and let them float by. Almost all of us need some sort of discipline to help us wake up, pay attention, and get beyond "busy-mind." The point is to make room for that welcoming "space" where our spirit meets with Holy Spirit. God's giving of God's self to us is an emptying of Godhead into humanity.

In a similar way, giving ourselves to God requires a self-emptying. As we've said, the thing about mature love is that it respects and makes room for the reality of the other as well as the reality of oneself. In our love-relationship with God this is called prayer, and it requires a similar emptying of all the defenses and immature behaviors that might stand in the way of mutual self-gift.

Doug: How often should one pray? And should we separate our prayer life from the rest of our activities? How can I make my whole life a prayer or is this unrealistic?

ES: Let me talk about all these questions in the same context. They have to do with the discipline or practice of prayer, and with the transcendence of the discipline.

A friend of mine, Brother Bede Thomas, O.H.C., used to say to his novices: "You think you have a prayer life? You don't have a prayer life, you just have life." That's one side of the paradox. The other side is that we *can* talk about a certain aspect of our lives, such as prayer. Prayer is a discipline, and is also beyond discipline.

A great deal of practice is needed in order to dance in a ballet or perform gymnastics so that these arts look effortless. Part of this training involves a routine—that is, a regular schedule of when and in what circumstances and how often to work at the skill. It's the same with prayer. The point is not the training; the point is the freedom and grace that the training eventually confers. When the discipline of prayer is transcended, when skill becomes art, *then* it begins to pervade one's whole life.

But before our "whole life is a prayer" we need to do some Olympic-class training. The practice of prayer almost always requires a consistency of time and place to begin with. Zen Buddhists know this well. If you ask a Zen teacher how to meditate you will be told something like this: "Put your zafu (special pillow) on your zabuton (mat), sit in one of the classic (e.g. lotus or half-lotus) positions, straighten your spine, place your active hand under the other, thumbs touching lightly, rest your tongue lightly on the roof of your mouth, and focus your eyes on the ground about four feet in front of you. Now, count your breaths up to ten. When you can count up to ten without your mind wandering, practice watching your thoughts. Come back in a week." Alas! Christians don't have such a nicely-ordered discipline, though many followers of Jesus adopt aspects of Zen practice for their own prayer.

At first we have to learn how to pay attention. Then we need to practice. One of the most helpful Christian disciplines of prayer I have heard of, I learned several decades ago from the Very Reverend Alan Jones, who is now Dean of Grace Cathedral in San Francisco. As I remember it, he told me that he divided the time set aside for his meditation into three parts. That is, if he had half an hour, he divided it into three sections of ten minutes each; if he only had ten minutes total, then the divisions were roughly three periods of three minutes each. During the first section he would pay attention to whatever was clamoring for his attention—no matter how un-edifying it was. He just let the distraction or fantasy have its day. Then in the second part of his time he would invite God into the picture, to look alongside him at what he was so caught up in, and try to see it with God's "eyes" or perspective. (This of course isn't helpful if one's God is a judgmental God but only if God is an ally who can bring compassion, and possibly humor to the situation.) Then in the third period of time, having paid attention and due respect to whatever was going on for him, there was the possibility of simply being still and present with God.

This isn't so far from the Buddhist practice of "watching your thoughts." The point is that forcibly suppressing distractions won't work, but if you let them play themselves out in a fairly ordered time-frame they may eventually run themselves down. At that point you can in effect say to them, "Okay, we've run this scenario through a number of times—your turn may come again, but for now, why don't you go sit on the shelf for a while and let me be quiet?"

Again, a discipline of prayer usually needs to start with a routine, a sameness of time and place. Perhaps a place which already is, or we have made, sacred space by keeping silence there and some icon of God's love. Eventually special times and places of prayer will "spread out" into our lives, so that in a sense "one's whole life is a prayer." However, it is still as important to have "quality time" with the divine lover as it is with human lovers. It may be true that my human significant other is "with me" in all my daily activities, a part of my very being; but we need a certain amount of time to be present to one another without distraction that can only come when we close the door and are intimate. So also with the relationship of human spirit/Holy Spirit.

Doug: How do we "dance" with spirit?

ES: I can't think of much else to say about how we "dance" with spirit. It is a question of attention, practice, and joyful giving of oneself to the partner and the "music." This is as difficult a question to answer specifically as "How do we *love*, exactly?" I will only add here that if, say, I am loving a human being with a "Level One Love," the chances are that my love will be immature and narcissistic. To stretch the "dance" metaphor, I will be trying to pull my partner around and even if I force us to go in the direction I want to go some of the time, the main outcome will be frustration and stepping on each other's feet. The analogy holds fairly true with Levels Two and Three. We need to ripen in prayer, just as we do physically and psychologically. Growth in each dimension informs the others.

Sometimes our maturing in prayer happens imperceptibly, but once in a while it is noticeable. One of those "quantum leaps" happened to me at a time decades ago when I was handling two jobs, either of which alone would have challenged me. Under this pressure I felt myself at times regressing back to my self-image of the needy orphan waif. One evening I was in my office after a long day of being pressed for time and picked at and projected on by the people with whom I lived and worked. I was frazzled. I realized that in the office next to mine my Superior was also working late. She was a woman of great wisdom and compassion. It occurred to the orphan waif in me to run to her, unload my neediness, and ask for sympathy and affirmation. Then another voice within me posed the question: What would it be like *not* to do that? She, too, has had a long day and is surely trying to wind up her affairs so she can get to bed. What if you spared her and took all this directly to God? And so I went into the chapel. I was just at the point of unloading all my neediness onto God, when a question once more posed itself within me—What if you didn't dump it all on God either?

It seemed a very clear invitation. I found in that instant that I could accept—that I could choose not to throw myself helplessly on the other—even God. That I could contain my spirit and simply be there. What followed was indescribable, but I'll attempt a few words anyway. It was a moment of the most unbelievable intimacy between my spirit and Holy Spirit—of a free exchange, of myself simply present to God and God to me. My "Level One" neediness, instead of being ministered to, was elevated to a "Level Three" mutual gift. I understood in a new way Jesus' saying: "I do not call you servants any longer, but I have called you friends" (John 15: 15).

I'm aware that one person's story is not always applicable to another's experience, and that this may well be such a story, but I include it as an example of a specific instance of how human spirit and God's Spirit may move closer in the "dance."

Doug: What is the most common mistake people make when they pray?

ES: I think the most common mistake that people make when they pray has to do with expectations. People tend, knowingly or unknowingly, to come to their prayer time or retreat time with certain preconceptions about what they should or could feel during prayer. It may be helpful to name these possible feelings, and then try to empty ourselves of expecting any or all of them. There are six things I have expected to happen at one time or another—and you can try to identify others of your own.

First, I have had a dread of "the pits." There have been times when I have feared that if I stopped *doing* and was quiet, I might become aware of things better left un-thought. Memories might escape from my unconscious that I had shoved down there because they were too awful. I might find out how angry I was or how sad, or remember some horrible thing I had done to someone or that had been done to me. Or I might discover that I really didn't believe there was any meaning to life, or any God, or that anyone cared that I was on earth or not. It took me a long time to realize that dread of "the pits" was a good thing to recognize so that I might empty myself of expecting it. I used to have a teaching of St. Paul's that was sort of my talisman for such times and was a real comfort to cling to:

> For I am convinced that neither death, nor life, nor angels, nor rulers, nor things present, nor things to come, nor powers, nor height, nor depth, nor anything else in all creation, will be able to separate us from the love of God in Christ Jesus our Lord (Romans 8:38-9).

So then I would tell my dread to go sit on the shelf for a while.

The second expectation I've had is that prayer will be, even if not horrendous, still repulsive. I won't like sitting there. Why should I put myself through this frustration?

The third expectation is that even if it isn't distasteful, it will be simply boring—a waste of time, when I have so many more productive things to do.

The fourth expectation is that it will be at least relaxing. I will just be quiet, and all my worries and tiredness will drop away.

The fifth expectation is that prayer will be a time of illumination. All sorts of things will become clear to me—and the spirit will inspire me with brilliant truths and beautiful thoughts.

The sixth expectation is that my prayer should be union with God—a sense of God's presence and a kind of basking in it.

Now the mistake in hanging on to the expectations is that any one of them or all of them or something entirely different might happen. Or might not. Have you ever been looking forward to seeing a friend (or an adversary) and find yourself imagining a conversation with them? I have, and I find that it hardly ever turns out the way I expected it would. If I empty myself of expectations, a conversation with my friend may take surprisingly delightful turns, and one with my adversary might be blessed with a step towards reconciliation. As Woody Allen is quoted as saying: "Eighty-five percent of life is showing up." So too, in our conversation with God. Just show up, and anything can happen. It's all part of the relationship.

I'd like to say a bit more about the expectation I called "illumination." Sometimes people make a mistake in thinking an illumination, or "light bulb" thought, comes from God when it really doesn't. If there's any doubt where a special idea or vision came from, that's a good time to go to someone who has been saying their prayers a long time and whom you trust, or who is recommended to you as a trustworthy person in spiritual matters. It's easy to make the mistake that a thought came from the Holy Spirit of truth, when, in fact, it came from another spirit entirely.

Saint Teresa of Avila has some solid teaching about this discernment. Roughly, she says that a thought or vision is from the spirit of truth if it 1) brings with it peace and harmony, and not unease, and leaves you refreshed and not exhausted, 2) if it cannot easily be forgotten, and 3) if there is an intuitive sense that you did not "compose" the experience yourself. When the thought or vision comes from the spirit of lies, or one's own spirit alone, it may 1) be disturbing and disquieting, and there may be agitation during the time that it lasts, 2) it may produce darkness and affliction in the soul, and 3) it may leave you with dryness and disinclination towards prayer and good works.

Basically, I would add that if after any such illumination, you feel cheered, renewed and peacefully energetic, and if you feel yourself grateful for a gift that has brought you closer to God, then you *have* received such a gift. They used to be called "consolations." Very often they are "honeymoon" gifts, and so, as the spiritual relationship matures, they may fall away. Not to worry. Remember the quote from St. Paul's letter to the Romans: nothing can separate us from the love of God. If, on the other hand, you feel more anxious, compelled to act in a certain direction, or distraught, then it may be not an illumination from the Holy Spirit, but a smoke screen from the spirit of untruth. Best, then, to check it out.

And just a word about telling people about your consolations in prayer. Checking them out with a wise person like a spiritual director is one thing, and a very good thing. But telling all and sundry is questionable. Before you do, ask yourself what you're doing it for. I use the analogy of speaking of the intimacies of a human love. Often it doesn't really edify the one to whom it is told, but either bores them or makes them jealous!

Another mistake people often make around expectations in prayer is not in the area of feelings but of results. I try to empty myself of the expectation of seeing any results at all—even of "growing" or getting somewhere in my prayer-life. That's really the point of the story I told about climbing Mount Subasio. I just try to show up, choose reality, and keep going.

Doug: How do you respond to the person who is a believer but who has had negative experiences with the institutions of religion? Should they just pray by themselves?

ES.   A lot of people who come to talk to me have had negative experiences with institutional religion. I have known a few who were so severely damaged at a vulnerable age that they may never be able to be healed of evil they were subjected to in the name of God. At the other end of the spectrum, I have known quite a few disenchanted people whose experience of church was not negative enough even to call "bad"—perhaps it was just "blah," just not positive enough. And of course there are many people whose early church experience was at various places between the extremes of horrifying and tepid. Some of these folk call themselves "believers," perhaps more speak of themselves as "lapsed" or "former" believers. Most, I think, would accept the term "searchers." That's why they come to talk.

Scott Peck, in *The Different Drum,* outlines four stages of spiritual growth: Stage I: Chaotic, Antisocial; Stage II: Formal, Institutional; Stage III: Skeptic, Individual; and Stage IV: Mystic, Communal. Those searchers who come to talk are generally in "Skeptic, Individual" or Peck's Stage III of spiritual growth. Their seeking for truth and meaning has led us into dialogues similar to the ones recorded so far in this book. People who have left Peck's "Formal, Institutional" Stage II, tend to equate that stage with the experience of formal religion which they have left behind. And yet many such people who have talked to me come to the point of asking, "So does all this have anything to do with the institutional church?" Or, more simply, "Why go to church?"

I wish I had a short, simple response, but I don't. In order to respond at all I need to go beyond logic and enter the dimensions of mystery, symbol, and analogy. I'd like to begin with our vessel analogy. The point of having a sailing vessel is to carry you across water. When my brother gets ready for our fishing trips, he starts by going into the garage and emptying out of the boat all the extraneous stuff that has accumulated there over the winter. Then he puts in our fishing gear, and when we're ready to start he hitches the boat-trailer to the car and puts in the ice-chest with the food and drinks for the trip. It's stretching the metaphor, but you might say that the church is the ice-chest that carries our food for the voyage.

The beginning of church for Christians is what happened on the Thursday night before the Friday Jesus was arrested and killed. That night, he first gave us this food for the journey at a fellowship meal with his friends. We call it Maundy Thursday because *maunde* (from Latin *mandare*) was Middle English for "commandment." Jesus didn't give a lot of commandments; mostly he told stories. But that Thursday night he did give us two commandments. He commanded us to love one another, and he also enjoined us to, "Do this in remembrance of me." There is one basic reason for the institutional church, and that is that Jesus instituted it when he said, "Do this."

Do what? Break bread and eat it, pour wine and drink it, all of us, in fellowship. So we do it. The friends and followers of Jesus have been doing this, as the Good News spread around the world, ever since that last supper. Saying the prayers, breaking the bread, remembering Jesus and telling the good news.

That Thursday night Jesus knew he was not going to be with his friends in the same familiar, human way much longer. He knew Judas was negotiating with the authorities who were out to get him, and that his earthly life was coming to an end. He was aware of our human needs, and he well understood the truth behind the story told in Chapter Three about the lonely child who wanted a God "with skin on." Jesus offers a way that he can continue to be with us and strengthen us, to remain our Lord.

By the way, English-speaking people have a great blessing in the use of the word "Lord" for Jesus. The Romance languages use derivations of the Latin *dominus,* from which we get words like "dominate." But "lord" comes from the Anglo-Saxon *hlafweard* which means "bread keeper" (from *hlaf* we get "loaf" and from *weard* we get words like "warden" and "guardian"). So in our language, Lord Jesus is not a figure of domination, but the keeper and giver of bread. And we are his companions. Switching from Old English to Latin, we note that "companion" comes from roots meaning "with" and "bread." We share with the one who called himself the "living bread that came down from heaven" and promised "...the bread that I will give for the life of the world is my flesh" (John 6:51).

So why do we need church today? In a profound way, that gift and that sustaining power provide a centering force in our lives. We live in a culture of specialization; fragmentation is not too strong a word. We have spoken a great deal already about many people's feelings of isolation and disconnection.

> Turning and turning in the widening gyre
> The falcon cannot hear the falconer.
> Things fall apart; the centre cannot hold;
> Mere anarchy is loosed upon the world.
> The blood-dimmed tide is loosed, and everywhere
> The ceremony of innocence is drowned.

William Butler Yeats wrote those lines in 1920, but they have power to haunt us today. Our Western culture wants a center that will hold. We hear distressing phrases like "coming unglued" and "falling apart." It is no wonder that people in this culture often feel splintered and fragmented. We are offered too many choices—not only of breakfast cereals, but of world-views. Like the falcon in Yeats's poem, individuals can find themselves flying in widening circles which have spiraled away from any direction-giving voice.

Furthermore, we humans are prone to polarize things like body and spirit, mind and matter, which cannot *actually* be separated, and so we need a way to focus and center all the dimensions of our life experience. Mircea Eliade wrote:

> A universe comes to birth from its center; it spreads out from a central point that is, as it were, its navel...the center is precisely where...space becomes sacred, hence pre-eminently *real*.

For an embryo the center of the world is the navel—the point at which the umbilical cord brings nourishment from the mother's body. The ancient Greeks universalized this truth in the belief that Delphi, with its oracle, was the center (the navel or *omphalos*) of the world. For the ancient Jews, the temple at Jerusalem was the sacred center of the world. These places were not merely geographical centers; they were central to, and were symbols of, the meeting of the physical and spiritual dimensions of human experience.

For Christians, especially for those who celebrate liturgically, Jesus provides such a center in the sacrament of bread and wine. In order to see how this is so, we need to take a closer look at the words "sacrament" and "symbol." The Latin root *sacer* means "holy";-*ment* is a noun suffix denoting a means or resulting state. So a sacrament is a means to holiness. Now a look at the word "symbol." In ordinary usage a symbol stands for something that isn't there. In a more radical (root) sense, a sense in which some Greek Orthodox writers use it, a symbol is the very visibility of the invisible, the presence of the absent. Jesus's great gift of the sacrament of his body and blood, in the form of bread and wine, is the great symbol at the heart of the church.

A symbol in this high sense is a particular kind of emptying. At least one scholar has implied that the mystery of the incarnation

itself, the Word made flesh, is an emptying, a kenotic event (from
Greek *kenoo*, to empty); that in Christ, God, without being depleted
of divinity, "poured out" divinity into humanity:

> I do not think it is stretching the theological
> meaning of *kenosis* to say that a symbol is a
> *kenotic* event, an "emptying" of the sacred through
> its manifestations in perceptible form, a limitation
> of illimitable reality. (H. Patrick Sullivan, "Ritual:
> Attending to the World", in *Anglican Theological
> Review*, Supplementary Series, #5, June, 1975.)

As St. Paul wrote in his letter to the Colossians, "He is the image
of the invisible God" (Col. 1:15). In that sense we may call Jesus the
symbol of God. And as Jesus "empties" himself into bread and wine,
they become symbols of *Christ* in this special sense: being absent
from us he is also present with us.

The word "symbol" comes from two Greek roots: *sym-* = with,
together (as in symphony, to sound together) and *ballein* = to throw
(as in ballistics). Christ's symbolic act of self-giving throws together
the material and spiritual dimensions of our experience. (It is not
coincidental that the word "diabolic" comes from Greek roots
meaning to cast apart, fragment.)

Jesus is both symbol and center. There are two kinds of
movement around a center. The first is called "centripetal." That's
the kind of center a whirlpool has—a center which draws everything
into itself. The second is called "centrifugal"—the center of an
action which is like an electric mixer—which sends everything
outward, sometimes spraying cake batter all over the counter! These
two movements, drawing in and sending out, are central to human
life. They are, first of all, the action of the heart—systole and
diastole; they are the action of our breath—breathing in and
breathing out. We used this analogy also in speaking of
contemplation and action in Chapter Four. Many things which may
seem to be polarities may more truly be complementary.

I have known communities and churches that have put all their
energy into one or the other of these movements, calling the drawing
inward "liturgy" or "spirituality" and the sending outward "mission"
or "apostolate." There can be real dissension about which to
emphasize and put resources into. But as "love must act," so there

cannot be systole without diastole, or breathing in without breathing out—or we are dead. In our human bodies the heart draws in the blood and pumps it through the lungs to purify and renew it *so that* it may carry new life outward to the ends of our toes, and then it reverses the process. In the same way the life-renewing heart of God draws us into communion and nourishes us *so that* we may in turn go out into our communities—to the ends of the world—and give of what we have been given.

This gathering in and opening out is, in fact, the shape of the liturgy that we call Eucharist. It is the heart of the church. It is the reason for church. Many people think of the Eucharist, or Holy Communion, or the Mass, or the Lord's Supper, as it is variously called, as a service of words in a book. Historically, however, it is rather a series of actions: four actions, in fact—**take, bless, break, give.** "Then [Jesus] took a loaf of bread, and when he had given thanks, he broke it and gave it to them, saying, 'This is my body which is given for you. Do this in remembrance of me.' And he did the same with the cup after supper, saying, 'This cup that is poured out for you is the new covenant in my blood'" (Luke 22:19-20).

This is the action of the Eucharist, and it consists first of a centripetal movement and then of a centrifugal. We draw together, we take or bring to the assembled company ourselves, our souls and bodies, time and talents, our gifts of bread, wine, and the money which symbolizes our work; we bring our hopes, fears, and—as St. Jerome learned—our sins. We offer all these things, blessing and giving thanks to God. So far it is an inward and upward movement. Jesus said, "I, when I am lifted up from the earth, will draw all people to myself" (John 12:32). Then comes the breaking of the bread. In that breaking, all the brokenness of humanity is accepted and received into God, and through Jesus's broken body, transfigured with him. We are not only broken, but we are broken open, as a seed is broken open by the spring rains to send forth new life. With this opening the outward movement begins. Having taken, blessed and broken, Jesus gave. We are given to, nourished, so that we in turn may give to others. Jesus said, "Go into all the world and proclaim the good news to the whole creation" (Mark 16:15). St. Paul wrote to the church in Corinth, "Now you are the body of Christ and individually members of it" (1 Cor. 12:27). We are the body; we are the church. The rhythm of giving and receiving is not only the rhythm of the heart, the rhythm of breathing, it is the rhythm of love.

You asked if we should just pray by ourselves. Praying by ourselves is a very important thing to do, if we mean by that, finding a quiet place apart in which to center ourselves and invite the Spirit. But it will be clear by what we've said already—especially in refutation of the Myth of Rugged Individualism—that in some dimension of reality, no person "is an island," and there is no such thing as totally individual prayer. Also, what we call private prayer, though it is good and proper, does not take the place of communal prayer—rather, it complements it.

Doug: In the case of Jonas Nightingale and the boy whose own faith, bolstered by others, may have healed him, is it a question of "not everyone has to be sincere as long as a critical mass of people believe"?

ES: My response to this question may be as short as my response to the one above was long. Briefly, I don't know. I'm fairly sure that healing in any circumstance is not a question of quantity or critical mass. God is love and love gives freely, as it wills. With God, it is never a "tit-for-tat" affair; we cannot bargain as we would in "Level Two Love." God's healing and mercy are not cause and effect events. A love-gift, such as a healing, cannot be predicted nor rationally analyzed. Only asked for, and then thanked for.

It is truly scandalous that we find, in the name of the institutional church, the kind of manipulation and scams of which you have cited such graphic examples. When I hear of them, a couple of things come to mind. First: "If these are supposed to be my friends, give me my enemies," and then St. Augustine's wonderful saying: "Just because wolves wear sheep's clothing is no reason that sheep should not wear their own!"

Doug: Why do you and the sisters pray five times each day whether you need it or not?

ES: Well, the facetious answer is that we're creatures of habit! On a closer look, however, that may be a bad pun but there is some truth to it. The five times a day in chapel give a habitual shape to our life. The prayers we say at those times are in praise of God and they are focused around portions of the Psalter, or Psalms of David. Praying this way has traditionally been called the *Opus Dei*, the Work of God. People of the Covenants have been chanting these songs of praise since the days of the first great Temple in Jerusalem. The tones to which they were chanted in the Temple were the ones St. Gregory the Great collected and standardized, and in the chapels of our convents we use an updated version of the Gregorian chant. From the times of the Desert Fathers and Mothers, the monastic life in the Christian tradition has always incorporated the saying of the psalms in a rotating cycle. I suppose one reason that chanting or reciting the psalms is so important to Christians is that they were, in a sense, Jesus' prayer-book; we hear in scripture that he quoted from them.

In addition to the daily Eucharist, we gather for the monastic "office" or round of prayer. These times in chapel provide us with a rhythm of praise: first thing in the morning, noontime, the end of the working day, and before bedtime. Somebody once called them the "escalator" of prayer. There I am, fretting a bit about letters to write, phone calls to make, travel plans to organize, meals to be served, people to talk to or problems to be solved, and the bell rings for Vespers, the prayers at the end of the day's work. I drop everything else. The psalms, scripture readings and hymns carry me up from the ground floor of my anxieties to a level of peace and praise. There is a good deal of silence before, during and after these prayer times and the silence is as meaningful as the words. When I travel to do teaching or Community Building I sometimes miss that structure, but it is comforting to know that at home my Sisters are keeping it for me. When they are away on their various ministries and I am home, I likewise know I am singing God's praises for them.

Doug: Is the goal to become, in effect, a spiritual vessel for God? Do you consider yourself a vessel for God? Mother Teresa has written, "I am God's pencil. A tiny bit of pencil he can use to write whatever he wants." Is this the sense you get from your own relationship with God?

ES: Yes and no. On the "yes" side, your quote from St. Francis at the beginning of the Epilogue says it all. I do pray to be an instrument of peace, pardon, faith, hope, light and joy, etc. If that's what Mother Teresa means by being God's pencil, yes. In the 12th century, Hildegard of Bingen wrote somewhat similarly of being "a feather on the breath of God."

On the "well, maybe not" side, I would like to restate the call to be friends and co-creators with God. Pencils and feathers have no choice and no will of their own. They don't get to contribute much to the message or have a say in which direction to go. I have a story to illustrate this point.

Twenty-five years ago I made my Life Profession. The preacher was Fr. David Hemming, of the Anglican Society of St. John the Evangelist. I don't have a copy of that sermon, but the central image is fixed in my memory. David Hemming said that as a child, he had been taught that our obedience to God's will was to dispose ourselves to be like clear panes of glass through which the Holy Spirit might shine into the world. But then he went to sing in the choir of Kings College, Cambridge, and spent many hours marveling at the splendor of the stained glass windows in the chapel. It came to him then that we are not, in fact, meant to be clear panes of glass, but richly varied, magnificently colored and absolutely unique stained glass windows. The light is indeed God's, but its beauty in this world is most gloriously manifested through the particularity of "a human being fully [and uniquely] alive."

Doug: Is the kingdom of God within us, as it says in Luke 17:21? Can prayer release God within us?

ES: The way I can best understand the presence of the kingdom of God within us is once again by faith and analogy. I have never run across a logical proof. I think of Edward Leen's teaching that the soul is the capacity for infinite reality to be held finitely. There is St. Bernard's description of human spirit meeting Holy Spirit. There is also St. Paul's, "Do you not know that you are God's temple and that God's spirit dwells in you?" (1 Cor. 3:16). And I am reminded of Teilhard's contention that there is no dichotomy of matter and spirit—that all matter has a "within." God's Spirit *is* within us, greets our spirit, and releases in us an abundance of divine energy. I guess the first and last thing I have to say about God in us and us in God is that, being a love relationship, it is as inexplicable as the existence of love itself.

We are called to grow in love, choose the truth, and risk all for joy, that we "may become participants of the divine nature" (2 Peter 1:4). This came to me as the call of the Divine Lover:

Where have you peace?
Thoughts will not cease;
dreams give you no release

Sense is a snare;
all things a care—
time but a comet's flare.

Put not your trust
in things of dust;
fame's but a mumbled crust.

I am the bread;
take me instead—
all without me is dead.

Would you be free?
Love, look at me—
I am eternity.

Epilogue
Becoming a Vessel of Peace

> Lord, make me an instrument of your peace.
> Where there is hatred, let me sow love;
> Where there is injury, pardon;
> Where there is doubt, faith;
> Where there is despair, hope;
> Where there is darkness, light;
> And where there is sadness, joy.
> O Divine Master, grant that I may not so much seek
> To be consoled, as to console;
> To be understood, as to understand;
> To be loved, as to love.
> For it is in giving that we receive;
> It is in pardoning that we are pardoned;
> And it is in dying that we are born to eternal life.
> —St. Francis of Assisi

As we approached the end of our dialoguing, I shared with ES my feeling of being both grateful and overwhelmed by the sheer volume of wisdom that had been communicated during our talks. It felt as though we needed to conclude with a discussion of the essence of the teachings we have been exploring. What are the core messages which we can take with us as we attempt to move towards becoming vessels for peace?

Among the many ideas we have discussed, four themes emerge as foundational:

Move Towards Unconditional Acceptance. We are unconditionally loved and the goal of spiritual growth is to move towards living and loving unconditionally.

Practice Emptiness Every Day. In order to fill up with unconditional love, we need to be vigilant in emptying ourselves of all that which is not unconditional love.

Choose the Good. Since we have been given free will and the power to choose both good and evil, living as a vessel of peace means choosing that which is good, that which fosters love and acceptance.

Become a Wheel Rolling Out of One's Own Center. This is the notion that God's will for us is identical to our deepest desire. Therefore, we must constantly look for and stay aligned with that deepest desire.

Move Towards Unconditional Acceptance

Perhaps the most important foundational idea of our discussions is that we are unconditionally loved and accepted as creatures of God. It is truly remarkable how many people we have encountered during the course of writing this book who seem to live their lives in constant negotiation with what they see as a judgmental God.

There is tremendous power in the idea that irrespective of what we do, we are unconditionally accepted exactly the way we are. The reason so many of us have trouble believing this idea is because we fail to see the difference between divine *unconditional* acceptance and human *conditional* acceptance. And even those of us who see this distinction spend so much more of our time in the realm of the human, with its rigid conditions and judgment, that divine unconditionality has little or no chance to take hold.

Many of the myths which we have explored are purely human constructions, beliefs that have emerged through millennia between and among human beings. The hope for humanity lies in more of us emptying ourselves of the pathology of these myths in order to drink in the unconditional acceptance available in the space between myths, in emptiness. Too often, we become filled with human non-acceptance to the exclusion of divine acceptance. To the extent that I become attached to these human judgments and worry about my place in the human world, it is easy to forget God's fundamental acceptance of me.

The realization of divine unconditional acceptance has fundamentally changed the way I am in the world. How have I become convinced that I am unconditionally accepted by God, even if not by my fellow humans? It has been from listening to the wisdom of ES and others but also from my own reflections, logical reasoning and study of the wisdom literature, not the least of which is the Bible itself:

> He said to his disciples, "Therefore I tell you,
> do not worry about your life, what you will eat,
> or about your body, what you will wear.
> For life is more than food, and the body more than clothing.
> Consider the ravens: they neither sow nor reap,
> they have neither storehouse nor barn,
> and yet God feeds them.
>
> Of how much more value are you than the birds!
> And can any of you by worrying add a single hour
> to your span of life?
>
> If then you are not able to do so small a thing as that,
> why do you worry about the rest? Consider the lilies,
> how they grow: they neither toil nor spin;
> yet I tell you even Solomon in all his glory
> was not clothed like one of these (Luke 12:22-27).

The very first question I asked ES in Chapter One was about whether or not we are unconditionally accepted by God. Not only are we unconditionally loved and accepted by God, but God IS love. To the extent that we embody love and acceptance for ourselves and for others, we are the embodiment of God and/or spirit. We are, in short, vessels for love.

"There is no fear in love, but perfect love casts out fear" (1 John 4:18). ES has quoted this, I have heard it in church, I have read it in a dozen books about spirituality. But it wasn't until I was counseling my own son recently that it sunk in for me. One simple line that came out of me created a kind of metanoia or instant enlightenment for my own understanding of the relationship between love and fear. I was trying to make the point that we should face our fears head on and work through them. In this context I said "Besides, if God unconditionally loves us, then what is there to be afraid of?"

In my own life, my fears were based on not understanding the scope of the gift we have been given. I had no understanding of divine love, because, ironically, I was so busy doing things to gain human love or approval. But the lilies of the field do not worry what the trees in the adjacent forest think of them. Indeed one branch of the tree doesn't worry what another branch thinks of it. Perhaps I should stop worrying what others think of me.

Whenever I seem to be drifting away from the sense of divine unconditional love, I try to focus on Jesus' image of the lilies blowing in the fields, soaking in the sunshine, free from fear, free from the human stresses we experience.

A great eastern sage, Sri Nisargadatta, when asked if only saints had unconditional love, said that everyone has unconditional love; the difference is most of us have other things that get in the way. A saint is nothing but unconditional love. Perhaps the challenge of embodying spirit and becoming a vessel for peace is to become more and more filled with unconditional love and less filled with judgment and hatred. As recently as five years ago, if someone had asked me what percentage of my personality I thought was unconditional love, I would have said about two percent - on a good day. Today, I still struggle with judgment, but I believe that on a good day, I am over 50 percent unconditional love. I don't think I will ever get to the point where there is nothing but unconditional love in me (I hold no illusions about the chances for sainthood) but it is incremental movement *in the direction of* unconditionality that I strive for.

Practice Emptiness Every Day

The concept of emptiness is an essential teaching of this book. We are constantly exposed to messages that have the effect of filling up our vessels. The task is to continually seek ways to empty oneself of the cultural noise that gets in the way of spiritual growth. If we do not make intentional efforts to empty, there will be no room for the spirit of peace to enter. Robert Morneau likens it to having no room at the Inn:

> On their travels, tourists seeking accommodations watch for the "Vacancy" sign outside motels. Dismay sets in when, one after the other, all they see is the cruel "No Vacancy" message which happy proprietors switch on when every room is filled. This image reflects when life is cluttered with excessive activity, glutted with material possession...It can well happen that the consumption of time and energy is so great that the mystery of God is

shelved, if not forgotten. There is simply no inner space and the divine Guest remains at the door, facing the blinking "No Vacancy" sign. Matters of the spirit are thus ignored or neglected.

It is vital that we consistently take steps to empty out such barriers to the divine spirit. ES has mentioned various strategies for prayer which can help. Also, establishing regular times for contemplation and meditation is useful to regain a sense of perspective on one's purpose and role in this fast-moving society. The key to emptying is self-awareness. One cannot empty that which one is not aware of. A model that can help increase self-awareness is the Community Building Workshop (CBW). The CBW is a way to be intentional about increasing one's self-awareness by spending a concerted amount of time and energy focused on releasing anything that gets in the way of finding peace. At the back of this book, we have provided the address and phone number for the Foundation for Community Encouragement (FCE) which sponsors community building workshops.

Self-awareness is beginning to enter the mainstream of intellectual thought as even corporations begin to understand the importance to their success of finding and keeping employees who have high levels of what Daniel Goleman has called "emotional intelligence" (E.Q.). This term refers to the ability to manage one's own emotional states, and to understand those of others. The Community Building process of sitting in a circle and reflecting on those things which one needs to empty out in order to make room for spirit is like an "emotional management" training camp. Only by looking inward at the forces which fill us up and stress us out, can we begin to learn how to manage those forces and move towards peace.

Choose the Good

A third major idea that we have described in this book builds on the first two. We hear the Biblical promise, "The truth will make you free." I would submit that the primary "truth" is that we are unconditionally accepted and consequently are free to do whatever we choose to do. What this means is that how and what we choose becomes of paramount importance. Because whereas we may be guaranteed freedom, we are not guaranteed wholeness or fulfillment. Recall ES saying, "We will get *old* just by breathing, but we may not necessarily get *ripe*."

Becoming ripe and whole is a byproduct of choosing that which is good *over the long term* and this requires hard work, reflection and intentionality. We were given a most precious gift, the gift of free will. But with such a gift comes tremendous responsibility.

In religious circles, much is made of the process called "discernment." This is really just a fancy word for thinking about a decision before making it. The two areas to think about are "how" to choose and "what" to choose.

With regard to the "how," one of the most powerful strategies I have ever been exposed to that can improve our choice-making ability is to think about the empty space or gap between stimulus and response. When I experience a "stimulus" during the day, a particularly stressful interaction with my boss or a negative comment from a coworker or a car cutting me off on the freeway, I use these events as signals to stop and reflect on the events, rather than just reacting impulsively. I think about my emotional state right after the event, I think about all of the things that led up to the person reacting the way they did. Then, before taking action, I ask myself the "what" question: "What can I choose that will foster good news in the long run?" You will recall ES saying, "Joy is a manifestation of choosing the good." I would add that in my experience, peace is also a manifestation of choosing the good.

The longer and more consistently one can live in the gap or emptiness, the easier it becomes to really evaluate the full range of options before acting. I think of these moments as "God moments" because they are opportunities for us to incorporate God's unconditional love into our daily lives. It is in this gap or empty space between stimulus and response that one can tap into unconditional love and find compassion. Deepak Chopra calls this gap the "field of pure potentiality." The mystics call it the dwelling place of God. The longer I evaluate a situation, living in the gap, the more compassion I find building up inside me. It is almost like pulling off the road and stopping to fill up with gas. You stop to fill up with compassion. But if you go too long without stopping, you'll run out. And as ES says "you cannot give what you do not have."

I hope to evolve to the point where I can regularly step into the gap and fill up my tank with compassion in order to become, as St. Francis says, an instrument of God's peace.

Become a Wheel Rolling Out of One's Own Center

The key to spiritual growth is to move away from following the "thou shalts" which society thrusts upon us in our youth and to become a wheel rolling out of its own center. To get to this point, one must fully embrace the other key learnings we have described thus far. For in order to muster the strength to follow one's own path, one must be convinced that it is the will of God for us to do so.

And while the call is to follow our deepest desires, there is scant evidence of this truth in our culture. Everywhere we turn, we are encouraged not to follow our own deepest desires but rather to follow the deepest desires of those others in the marketplace who want us to buy something from them and, in effect, follow their lead.

It is in many ways the ultimate act of courage to follow one's own deepest yearnings and, in Nietzche's image, it requires the strength of a lion to do so. There are strategies one can employ to make the transition easier, such as finding a guide, joining a group of others who are trying to make a similar transition, and inviting the spirit to join you along the way. ES has provided some excellent tips on how to be intentional in inviting the spirit to join in a kind of dance or co-creation along the path.

The goal for me is to move from being a stressed out workaholic who is always scrambling to please others, to a more inner-directed, intentional person who seeks his own deepest desires and follows them in concert with the Spirit. In short, it is about finding peace, and the best way to promote peace on earth is to start with oneself.

The Rev. Dr. Barbara King beautifully described this sentiment of starting with oneself in a recent sermon:

> Let there be peace on earth
> and let it begin with me.
> Let there be peace on earth
> and let it begin with me.
> Let there be peace on earth
> and let it begin with me.
> Peace in our food,

> Peace in our bodies,
> Peace in our home,
> Peace in our world,
> Thanks, God,
> Amen.

Peace must begin with me. By emptying my "vessel" of the surface chatter of cultural myths and judgment, most of which are merely artificial human constructs, I make room for the flow of eternal love and peace which, like the ancient rivers, flows freely and naturally. To become a spiritual vessel is to flow with that river of love, gently gliding around the human barriers placed in the river bed, navigating in partnership with the benevolent-life force which, like a lover, softly asks, "What shall we do today, honey?"

Dialogue on Becoming a Vessel of Peace

Doug: Even though we have covered a lot of ground in this book, from your point of view, what is the essence of the teaching we have been discussing?

ES: You've done such a great job of summing up that I don't feel the need to add anything. However, true to our process, even though I don't feel the *need*, I do recognize the *invitation*—and who am I to refuse the invitation to one last dance?

If I had to put in one word what I see as the essence of the teaching in this book, that word would be "consciousness." The glory, and the challenge, of our nature as *Homo sapiens* is to become more and more aware. When God asked the young Solomon what he desired above all things, Solomon chose wisdom, or a "wise and discerning mind" (1 Kings 3: 5-12).

Consciousness develops, or ripens, along with the other aspects of our lives. I can see four aspects of this development. Each aspect seems to me to come as an invitation or call; as with any call, each can be responded to, ignored, or actively resisted.

First there is the call to **wake up**. This is the point at which a person sees *what is*, not what one expects to see, or has been taught to see. It is the point at which the Ugly Duckling sees that it is not a duck, the moment when one realizes one's mask is a mask, the day when one asks, "Is this all there is?"

Secondly, after the wakening there is the call to **choose the truth,** to make a commitment to reality. Often this is a very difficult thing to do, and it reminds me of the passage in Genesis (32:24-30) where Jacob wrestles all night with the angel of God. Though he is wounded, he prevails at dawn, and receives a blessing and a new name. Finding my truth in God's reality often comes only after a long time in the dark and a hard wrestling match, but the prize for "hanging in" and maybe suffering some pain is a new sense of being.

Thirdly, there is the call to what I sometimes think of as **the larger picture** or a more comprehensive perspective. Once when I was in a museum I came into a gallery and on the far wall was a landscape by Van Gogh. I was struck with the power and beauty of the overall design. At that distance it was by far the most arresting picture in the room. Slowly I moved closer, until I was right up within a foot of the canvas. I saw, now, not the whole structure but the unique contribution of each marvelous brushstroke. I realized that I could not see both the whole design and each brushstroke at the same time, but that the problem was with the limitation of my vision and not with the painting. So also with my comprehension of reality. Even though I cannot see the whole picture while I am conscious of a moment's "brushstroke," there is the call mentally and spiritually to "stand back," to try to place the awareness of the particular moment in the context of eternity.

And finally there is the call to **grow in love.** The point here is to try to remember what we are growing in awareness *of.* Cosmic, divine reality—God—is Love. It is not enough merely to become aware. Machiavelli seems to have been a fairly aware person, but what he grew more and more aware of was how to aggrandize himself and manipulate others. The anonymous author of *The Cloud of Unknowing* wrote: "For I tell thee truly, that the devil hath his contemplatives as God hath His." We have often in these pages discussed "acceptance." Growing in love toward ourselves is becoming aware that at any given moment our best is good enough—in fact it is wonderful—so long as we grow in conscious discernment of how to choose the best. It is the same with others. Their best is their best. How can we relate to them in a way that nurtures their growth in awareness of the good? And there is always the call to grow in consciousness and trust of God's love.

One of the holiest of puns is the one on "wind" and "spirit" made by Jesus in the Gospel of John. "The wind (*pneuma*) blows where it chooses, and you hear the sound of it, but you do not know where it comes from or where it goes. So is it with everyone who is born of the Spirit (*pneuma*)" (John 3:8). We can gleefully extend the metaphor. Growing in consciousness of God, we hoist the empty sails of our vessel so that the wind/Spirit of love and truth may fill them and empower us in our voyage into the sunrise.

About the Authors

Doug Shadel is the co-author of three previous books: *Schemes and Scams* with John T. (Foreword by Walter Cronkite), *Outsmart Crime* with Al Ward (Foreword by Ken Eikenberry) and *The Power of Acceptance* with Bill Thatcher (Foreword by M. Scott Peck, M.D.). Shadel has appeared on ABC's 20/20, CNN, National Public Radio, Dateline NBC and Good Morning America. He currently serves as the Consumer Affairs Representative for AARP. Shadel has a doctorate in education and lives in Seattle with his wife Renee and his son Nicholas.

Ellen Stephen, O.S.H. (ES) is an Anglican nun. She serves on the Leadership Council of the Order of St. Helena and lives in the Convent of the Order in New York. She is also a facilitator and past Director for the Foundation for Community Encouragement. One of her principle ministries during the past 20 years has been as a guide for spiritual seekers, providing spiritual direction to hundreds of individuals, including some of the major writers and thinkers of our time. ES has a master's degree in creative writing from Stanford University and has written several books of poetry.

To contact Doug Shadel or Ellen Stephen or to order more copies of *Vessel of Peace*, please write to them in care of:

Three Tree Press
126 SW 148ᵗʰ St. C100-282
Seattle WA 98166-1984
206.243.0577
Email: threetreepress@aol.com

For more information about how to participate in a community building workshop, please contact:

The Foundation For Community Encouragement (FCE)
P. O. Box 17210
Seattle, Washington 98107-0910
206 784-9077
E-Mail:inquire@fce-community.org
http://www.fce-community.org